P9-DNB-354

But Which
Mutual
Funds?

But *Which* Mutual Funds?

How to Pick
The Right Ones
to Achieve
Your Financial Dreams

NEW HANOVER COUNTY
PUBLIC LIBRARY
201 CHESTNUT STREET
WILMINGTON, N C 28401

BY STEVEN T. GOLDBERG

Kiplinger Books, Washington, D.C.

KIPLINGER
BOOKS

Published by
The Kiplinger Washington Editors, Inc.
1729 H Street, N.W.
Washington, D.C. 20006

Library of Congress Cataloging-in-Publication Data

Goldberg, Steven T., 1949–
　　But which mutual funds? : how to pick the right
ones to achieve your financial dreams / Steven T.
Goldberg.
　　　　　p.　　cm.
　　Includes index.
　　ISBN 0–938721–53–4 (hardcover)
　　1. Mutual funds.　　I. Title.
HG4530.G65　　1998
332.63'27—dc21　　　　　　　　　　　　98–12425
　　　　　　　　　　　　　　　　　　　　　CIP

© 1998 by the Kiplinger Washington Editors, Inc. All rights reserved.
No part of this book may be produced or transmitted in any form or by
any means, electronic or mechanical, including photocopying, record-
ing or by an information storage and retrieval system, without the written permission of the Publisher, except where permitted by law.

This publication is intended to provide guidance in regard to the subject matter covered. It is sold with the understanding that the author
and publisher are not herein engaged in rendering legal, accounting,
tax or other professional services. If such services are required, professional assistance should be sought.

9 8 7 6 5 4 3 2 1

First edition. Printed in the United States of America.

Book cover designed by Mary Pat Doherty

ACKNOWLEDGMENTS

SOMETIMES I HAVE GLANCED OVER THE ACKNOWLEDG-ments at the start of a nonfiction book and thought derisively, "Sure, I just bet all those people helped with that book." I never realized how much an author must rely on others' expertise.

I wish to thank colleagues at Kiplinger Books and coworkers at *Kiplinger's Personal Finance Magazine*. This book would not have been possible without Pat Mertz Esswein's always-supportive editing, and Fred W. Frailey's editing and advice. Manuel Schiffres carefully read over the manuscript for errors. Robert Frick read an early draft and offered numerous helpful suggestions. Rosemary Beales Neff smoothed rough spots with her copy editing of the book, while Brian Knestout and Margaret Ringer painstakingly checked facts. The magazine's art department lent their design expertise. Dianne Olsufka proofed the finished pages. David Harrison guided the book from inception. I also want to thank Theodore J. Miller, Kevin McCormally, Janet Bodnar, Kristin W. Davis, and Kenneth R. Sheets. All of them made invaluable contributions.

Karen Kratzer assisted with retirement and tax matters, as well as the tables. She also read over the manuscript for errors. Steve Norwitz and Judy Ward at T. Rowe Price produced tables and answered endless questions. Brian Mattes and Gus Sauter at Vanguard explained the fine points of tax-managed investing.

Finally, I wish to thank Laura Nelson Baernstein and Pearlethea Hugee for moral support.

Table of Contents

ing for periods of one year, five years, or ten years or more • Average after-inflation returns of stocks since 1802 are strikingly similar to those since 1926 • Two bad bear markets

Introduction

S THE WRITER OF THE MUTUAL FUND DEPARTMENT OF *Kiplinger's Personal Finance Magazine,* I receive queries every day about funds from readers, friends, relatives and even coworkers. While they use different words, many of these people essentially ask the same thing: "With thousands of funds for sale, which ones are right for me?" The question usually comes from people who know little about funds or who are overwhelmed by the flood tide of fund information available, or both.

If I'm getting hundreds of letters and e-mails like this every year, there must be hundreds of thousands, if not millions of other people with the same question. These people know investing is important, but they aren't sure how to go about it. Moreover, they don't want to spend any more time on investing than they absolutely must. They've turned to mutual funds partly because they've heard or believe that funds are the simplest way to invest.

From that seed, this book began to germinate. While dozens of mutual fund books are for sale, virtually none of them answer the question that bedevils so many investors and prospective investors. Why not write a book that offers investors solid portfolios of funds that are suited to their individual needs? And who better to edit and publish such a book than Kiplinger's, which has such a widespread reputation as a reliable, canny and objective source of information about funds? For 50-plus years the most trusted name in individual investing, the magazine has more than one million subscribers because of its down-to-earth guidance and lack of fluff.

To show that investing in mutual funds isn't nearly as hard as it's made out to be, I decided to work with a family who knew nothing about mutual funds. You'll follow their progress throughout the book.

Since each investor's situation is different, no one fund or group of funds is appropriate for everyone. Instead, this book provides 12 solid groups of funds that are suited to specific needs—whether you are a parent saving for college for your young children, a middle-aged person saving for retirement, a retiree living off your income or a couple saving for the down payment on your first home.

But Which Mutual Funds? offers good funds and more. It uses simple language and a straightforward approach so you can determine how much you need to invest each month to accomplish your life's financial goals—whether they are far in the future or just around the corner. After you take a self-scoring test that measures your tolerance for stock-market declines, you'll know how much of your money should be invested in stock funds, bond funds and money-market funds—the most important decision any investor makes. Finally, you'll find specific groups of funds that can fulfill your goals.

The book also gives you the nuts and bolts of how and where to buy funds, covers all the details of mutual fund taxes (and describe some shortcuts), and tells you how to avoid common investment pitfalls. Most important: All this information is contained in Parts One and Two, the first 142 pages of the book. If you're a beginning investor, you need only read these pages to assemble a top-notch financial plan.

Investment neophytes such as the DiBenedettos may choose to invest in the fund portfolios that are provided. But there's nothing magic about these fund portfolios. None of them contain your only choices—nor will they necessarily be the top performers. Each portfolio is a solid group of funds designed to work together—delivering healthy returns, while limiting overall fluctuations.

Let me make a confession. I like mutual funds. They are, in addition to my work, a hobby. I enjoy learning about obscure funds, and about arcane terms of art such as Sharpe ratios, alpha and r-squared. That's why I work at Kiplinger's.

For investors who want to understand more about mutual

funds, the rest of the book is for you. Parts Three, Four and Five tell you how to pick winning funds yourself and how to combine them into well-diversified portfolios. They also help you better understand how the fund portfolios recommended in the earlier chapters were selected.

Just as some folks take pleasure in tinkering with cars, or in lawn care or in home improvements—rather than treating them merely as chores that have to be done as quickly and painlessly as possible—other people enjoy tracking mutual funds, or feel they haven't done a thorough job until they understand the "whys" of their investment choices. And just as people who cut their own grass tend to have greener lawns, so mutual fund do-it-yourselfers often end up earning higher returns on their investments.

Understanding more about how funds work is likely to make you a better investor if only because you're more apt to stick with an investment plan when you fully understand it. If you already know a fair amount about funds, these sections of the book can help you where you're weak. Even fund aficionados will find things they didn't know.

But these last three parts of the book are strictly optional. This book was written primarily with the beginning investor in mind—the investor who wants to put together a good investment plan as quickly and painlessly as possible, and then get on to other things.

Whatever path you choose, I wish you many happy returns.

Steven T. Goldberg

PART ONE

The First
(and Most Important)
Steps

This section explains why investing in mutual funds is such a good way to achieve your financial dreams. You'll establish your investment goals and learn your tolerance for risk—that is, prolonged market declines. Finally, you'll determine what percentage of your money to put into stock funds, bond funds and money-market funds—the most important decision any investor makes. You'll also meet Paul and Nancy DiBenedetto, neophyte investors who are learning alongside you.

Getting Started

How this book will help you with mutual funds

AUL AND NANCY DIBENEDETTO ARE INTELLIGENT, well-educated people. But when it comes to investing, they're all thumbs. They've never taken the time to learn about it. "We're illiterate in this area," Paul says ruefully. "We know we need to do something, but we never seem to get around to it." Adds Nancy, "What's held us back is the time I've spent at work, and with our 2½-year old son, Paul Jr. But we know we need to start saving for his college."

The trim, athletic couple are like millions of Americans who know they need to learn something about investing but have yet to start—or, if they have started, lack an overall investment plan. With the government and employers picking up an ever-smaller proportion of the retirement tab, the DiBenedettos know they need to become proficient investors. They've skimmed financial articles in the newspaper and even picked up a magazine or two. But the sheer number of investment choices overwhelms them.

If you see a little bit of yourself in Nancy and Paul DiBenedetto, you're reading the right book. It will take you, quickly and easily, through the process of determining:
- **your financial goals,**
- **how much you need to invest** to meet them, and
- **how to invest in top-performing mutual funds** that work together so that you can attain those goals.

If you don't want to learn all the ins and outs of mutual fund investing, but simply want to assemble a good mix of funds, all you need to read are Parts One and Two—the first 142 pages of the book. You can read the rest of the book when you are ready to learn the fine points of investing. If you're a more experienced investor, however, you'll find plenty in this book to

Funds bring the skills of first-rate money managers to any investor who can come up with the $2,000 or so it takes to open a fund account.

improve your investing skills, particularly in Parts Three, Four and Five. Don't be fooled by the easy-to-understand language. I'll discuss the topics that top financial advisers address. The only difference is that I'll leave out useless jargon so that any investor—beginner or veteran—can use advanced concepts to increase his or her wealth. Like so many other subjects, mutual funds have a language all their own. While some of the arcane language is necessary, much of it seems designed mainly to make the simple appear complex. One of the more vexing things about mutual funds—and investing in general—is that disagreements crop up over what the terminology means. It's enough to make you want to stick your money under the mattress and forget about it. But, rest easy. You can skip most of the jargon and still become a first-class investor.

In the course of reading this book, you'll meet the DiBenedettos several times. I enlisted them because many of the questions they have are likely to be ones that other beginning investors have, too. Paul, who was 39 when this book was written, teaches third grade; Nancy, 31, is a hospital recreation therapist. They live in Fairfax, Va.

What Are Mutual Funds?

THE DIBENEDETTOS ARE REFRESHINGLY CANDID ABOUT THEIR lack of knowledge about investing and mutual funds. "What is a mutual fund?" is Nancy's first question. "Aren't there other ways to invest?" Sure. Plenty of people invest in real estate or individual stocks and bonds. But these take much more time to master, and they usually won't yield better results than funds will. Mutual funds remain the best investment choice for those who want to spend as little time as possible monitoring their investments. They're also often the best investment medium for stock-market aficionados because they give you access to top investment managers.

To answer Nancy's first question: Funds simply pool money from investors like you to buy stocks and bonds (and sometimes other investments). The investors own the fund and share in its profits (or losses) and the expenses of running it. Funds employ

How Funds Pay You

FUNDS EARN YOU money in the four ways listed below:

Dividends /

The stocks or bonds a fund owns pay dividends or interest. The fund distributes this money to you as dividends. You pay taxes on that income at your ordinary income-tax rate.

Increase in net asset value

The stocks or bonds a fund buys increase in value, and the fund's manager holds on to them. When this happens, the fund's *net asset value* (the price at which you can sell a share of the fund) increases. You don't pay any taxes on your gains in this instance until you sell the fund.

Distribution of capital gains

A fund manager buys stocks or bonds and sells them at a higher price. The fund distributes your share of the gains to you at least annually as capital gains. Under the tax code:

Short-term capital gains (gains made on stocks or bonds the fund held one year or less) are taxed at your ordinary income-tax rate.

Long-term capital gains (gains made on stocks or bonds the fund held for more than 12 months) are almost always taxed at a 20% rate. The exception: If you are in the 15% tax bracket, long-term capital gains are taxed at only 10%.

Note: Mid-term capital gains no longer exist. That category for gains on stocks or bonds the fund owned for more than a year but not more than 18 months (and almost always taxed at 28%) was created by Congress in 1997 and abolished in 1998.

When you sell fund shares

What if you buy a fund for a low price and sell it for a higher price? You pay taxes in exactly the same way as in the example immediately above. For instance, if you held the shares 12 months or less, your gain would be taxed as ordinary income, while if you held shares of the fund more than 12 months, your gain is taxed at a 20% rate.

---

highly paid professional managers who decide what stocks and bonds to buy and sell. The funds' boards of directors are charged with looking out for shareholders' interests. The shareholders elect the directors. Sometimes directors seem to worry more about increasing the profits of the company that sponsors the fund than they do about maximizing shareholders' gains. However, scandals involving mutual funds have been rare.

THE PLUSES OF FUNDS

What's so great about mutual funds? Funds bring the skills of first-rate money managers to any investor who can come up with the $2,000 or so it takes to open a fund account. Most of these managers were formerly available only to the wealthy. Moreover, funds provide one of the lowest-cost ways of investing. Odds are, you'll pay much less in fees to a well-run mutual fund than you would to a broker to pick stocks for you. And it's a lot easier to select good funds than it is to find a good broker, because funds have public track records that anyone can examine. Another advantage: Funds offer instant diversification among a variety of stocks or bonds—almost all funds contain at least 20 securities, and most contain 50 or more. That's enough to keep your nest egg from being wiped out if one company's stock thuds to earth. And, if you're dissatisfied with a fund or if you need your money, you can simply pick up the phone and have your money transferred to another fund—or mailed to you. These pluses explain why Americans have invested more than $5 trillion in funds—more than the total in the nation's savings and loans.

Americans have invested more than $5 trillion in funds—more than the total in savings and loans.

LOADS AND NO-LOADS

Here's a rule of thumb you can *forget* when it comes to mutual funds: *You get what you pay for.* What you pay to buy a fund is called a "load." A load is a sales commission paid to someone who helps you pick a fund. Load stock funds typically charge 5% of what you invest in the fund. So if you're investing $1,000, you'll pay $50 to the salesperson and only $950 will go to work for you. Here's the key thing about loads: Whether a fund is a load fund or a no-load fund has everything to do with how it is sold and nothing to do with how it performs. Study after study has shown

So What If the Sky Is Falling?

HERE ARE SOME of the things you can stop worrying about if you invest in funds: the direction of the economy, the rise or fall of interest rates, the rate of inflation, and the daily ebb and flow of the stock and bond markets. Just tune out this "noise" from the daily news, and leave the driving to the professionals who manage your funds. After all, when you buy shares in mutual funds, you're hiring other people to do the worrying for you. Make them earn their money. That's not to say you should overlook changes in your personal situation or your funds' performance. But you don't need to worry over the news from Wall Street. You can also ignore anything you hear about more esoteric investments, such as options, index futures, commodities, and the like. Never heard of any of these? Good, you don't ever need to learn about them.

Sound Familiar?

HERE ARE SOME common reasons that people delay investing:
- "I don't have enough money."
- "I don't have enough time to learn about funds."
- "I want to stick to something safe, like a bank certificate of deposit."
- "It's hard to choose among all the different funds."
- "I'm afraid. I don't want to make mistakes and lose my money."
- "I just never seem to get around to it."

that sales charges don't make funds perform better. On average, funds that levy sales charges underperform funds without them—by approximately the amount of the sales charge.

No-load funds usually sell directly to investors. Investors call toll-free numbers to get applications, and send them back with their initial investment. No-load funds aren't free, of course. All funds charge annual expenses—say, 1.5% of the money invested in the fund, or $15 of every $1,000 that you invest in it.

Load funds are sold through brokers, financial planners, insurance agents and banks. They come in an extraordinary variety. Some charge sales commissions when you buy shares of a fund. Some charge commissions when you sell your shares. Others assess commissions *every year* you own the fund. And still others impose combinations of these different sales charges. Since you're reading this book and learning to invest on your own, you'll never want to buy a load fund—unless there is a truly exceptional fund for which there is no comparable no-load fund. Besides saving you money up front, sticking with no-loads will also make life simpler—you can automatically eliminate about half of all funds from consideration.

> **Drawbacks? The biggest one, ironically, is that there are so many funds— close to 7,000 mutual funds now.**

THE DOWNSIDE

The biggest drawback of funds, ironically, is that there are so many—close to 7,000 mutual funds now—almost two times the number of stocks listed on the New York Stock Exchange. No wonder the DiBenedettos don't know where to start. "If there are so many of them, how do we choose?" Nancy asks. "There are so many commercials for mutual funds, they just confuse me."

The number of choices is paralyzing to the DiBenedettos—and to many other investors. One article talks about how great one fund is, and the next article criticizes the first and recommends a second. It's not that there's not enough information on funds; it's that there's too much, and most of it fails to address the question the DiBenedettos—and you—need answered: "Which mutual funds are right for me?"

The Advantage of Starting Early

THE TABLE ON THESE pages illustrates the power of compounding. When you earn money from investments, you can reinvest it. What you earn in subsequent years on that reinvested money is compounded wealth. For instance, suppose you invest $100 in stocks annually. The first year you earn 11%—the long-term average for stocks. You then have $111. The next year you earn 11% again. At the end of the second year, you have $223.21, rather than $222 ($111 plus $111), because your money has compounded in value. Over just a few

Account Value of IRA Investor Who:

| | STARTS EARLY | | STARTS LATE | |
AGE	AMOUNT INVESTED	END OF YEAR BALANCE	AMOUNT INVESTED	END OF YEAR BALANCE
30	$2,000	$2,214		
31	2,000	4,665		
32	2,000	7,378		
33	2,000	10,382		
34	2,000	13,706		
35	2,000	17,387		
36	2,000	21,461		
37	2,000	25,972		
38	2,000	30,965		
39	2,000	36,492		
40		40,397	$2,000	$2,214
41		44,719	2,000	4,665
42		49,504	2,000	7,378
43		54,801	2,000	10,382
44		60,664	2,000	13,706
45		67,156	2,000	17,387
46		74,341	2,000	21,461
47		82,296	2,000	25,972

Why You Should Start Now

MANY PEOPLE HAVE ANOTHER REASON THEY DON'T START investing: Something always crops up to spend money on. No matter how much you earn, it still can be hard to get ahead of the monthly bills and focus on your long-term goals. The best way to save for the future is to "pay yourself first"—that is, decide how much you will save each month, and

years, compounding doesn't do much to add to your returns. But over the long haul, it makes an enormous difference.

The table shows how two investors will do—one who starts early and has plenty of time for his or her investment money to compound, and one who starts late.

As you can see, investing just $2,000 annually from age 30 to age 39 will leave you in a better position at age 65 than investing $2,000 from age 40 to age 65. The investor who begins early invests just $20,000 altogether, while the late-comer invests a total of $52,000.

	STARTS EARLY		STARTS LATE	
AGE	AMOUNT INVESTED	END OF YEAR BALANCE	AMOUNT INVESTED	END OF YEAR BALANCE
48		$ 91,101	$2,000	$ 30,965
49		100,849	2,000	36,492
50		111,640	2,000	42,611
51		123,585	2,000	49,384
52		136,809	2,000	56,882
53		151,448	2,000	65,182
54		167,652	2,000	74,371
55		185,591	2,000	84,542
56		205,450	2,000	95,802
57		227,433	2,000	108,267
58		251,768	2,000	122,066
59		278,707	2,000	137,341
60		308,529	2,000	154,250
61		341,541	2,000	172,969
62		378,086	2,000	193,691
63		418,541	2,000	216,630
64		463,325	2,000	242,023
65		512,901	2,000	270,134

SOURCE: T. ROWE PRICE ASSOCIATES INC.

then invest that money *before* you pay your other bills. The
DiBenedettos already do this. In the last year or two, as they have
finished paying off student loans and watched their salaries rise
to a combined total of $80,000, they've saved more. When they
stopped making the $347 monthly payment on Paul's car, they
began stashing that money in a credit union savings account. A
little later, when they paid off Nancy's car, they began putting
that $237 monthly into the credit union. Now, they need to set
their goals for the future and begin investing to meet them.

Like the DiBenedettos, you may have put off getting start-

What You Need to Save Per Month

HERE'S HOW TO FIGURE how much
you need to save each month to
accumulate $10,000 by your dead-
line for any goal. Say that you have
15 years to retirement. In the table
below, find where 11% (the average

YEARS	RATE OF RETURN				
	3%	4%	5%	6%	7%
1	$820	$815	$811	$807	$802
2	404	400	395	391	387
3	265	261	257	253	249
4	196	192	188	184	180
5	154	150	146	143	139
6	127	123	119	115	112
7	107	103	99	96	92
8	92	88	85	81	78
9	81	77	73	70	66
10	71	68	64	61	57
11	64	60	57	53	50
12	58	54	51	47	44
13	52	49	45	42	39
14	48	44	41	38	35
15	44	41	37	34	31
16	41	37	34	31	28
17	38	34	31	28	25
18	35	32	29	26	23
19	33	29	26	24	21
20	30	27	24	22	19
21	29	25	22	20	17

ed in investing. But if you finish just the first two parts of this book, your reasons for procrastinating will evaporate. Here's the most important reason to get started now: The sooner you begin investing, the less money you'll need to invest to reach your goals, and the more money you can spend on things you want now. How can that be? Through the financial miracle known as compounding. Compounding means simply that you will earn money on the money you have already earned. The impact of this simple phenomenon is enormous. Consider this example of two investors:

historical rate of return for stocks) and 15 years intersect. The result, $22, is about how much you need to save monthly. To save $100,000 would require ten times as much—in this case, $220.

RATE OF RETURN				
8%	9%	10%	11%	12%
$798	$794	$789	$785	$781
383	379	375	371	367
245	241	237	234	230
176	173	169	165	162
135	132	128	125	121
108	104	101	98	95
89	85	82	79	76
74	71	68	65	62
63	60	57	54	51
54	51	48	46	43
47	44	42	39	36
41	39	36	33	31
36	34	31	29	27
32	30	27	25	23
29	26	24	22	20
26	23	21	19	17
23	21	19	17	15
21	19	17	15	13
19	17	15	13	11
17	15	13	12	10
15	13	12	10	8

One is a youngster who puts $2,000 into an individual retirement account (IRA) every year from age 16 to age 25, and then stops investing. Assuming stocks continue to earn 11% annually, as they have on average since 1926, he or she will have more than $2 million ($2,173,890, to be exact) by age 65. This example needn't be hypothetical. If your children earn money from baby-sitting or lawn mowing, you can open an IRA for them. And the money that goes into their IRAs doesn't have to be the same money they earn, so, if you like, you can invest an equivalent amount in IRAs for them and let them spend what they earn. (I'll discuss IRAs in more detail in Chapter 5.)

The other investor starts putting $2,000 annually into an IRA at age 40. He or she can contribute $2,000 *every year* through age 65 and still wind up with roughly half of what the early

The Magic of Compounding

COMPOUNDING IS A powerful force in building wealth. This table shows you, rounded to the nearest $10, how fast $100 a month will grow at different rates of return, assuming you invest at the beginning of each month. If you save more than $100 a month, say, $500 a month, sim-

How $100 a Month Will Grow

YEAR	RATE OF RETURN				
	3%	4%	5%	6%	7%
1	$1,220	$1,230	$1,230	$1,240	$1,250
2	2,480	2,500	2,530	2,560	2,580
3	3,770	3,830	3,890	3,950	4,020
4	5,110	5,210	5,320	5,440	5,550
5	6,480	6,650	6,830	7,010	7,200
6	7,900	8,150	8,410	8,680	8,970
7	9,360	9,710	10,080	10,460	10,860
8	10,860	11,330	11,820	12,340	12,890
9	12,410	13,020	13,660	14,350	15,070
10	14,010	14,770	15,590	16,470	17,410
15	22,750	24,690	26,840	29,230	31,880
20	32,910	36,800	41,280	46,440	52,400
25	44,710	51,580	59,800	69,650	81,480
30	58,420	69,640	83,570	100,950	122,710

investor has. (See the table on pages 8–9.)

So even if you have just a bit of money—say, $50 a month—
now is the time to start investing. As you begin investing and
watch your nest egg grow, you'll find it will become easier to save
even more for your goals.

COMPOUNDING FOR YOURSELF

Want to compute the effects of compounding for yourself? It's
simple, thanks to the "rule of 72." To find out how many years it
will take your money to double, just take the annual percentage
gain you expect to make on an investment, expressed as a whole
number, and divide the result into 72. For instance, if you're
making 7% annually on an investment, it will take you 10.3 years
to double your money (72 ÷ 7 = 10.3). If you're earning 9%

ply divide the amount you invest monthly by $100—and multiply it by the appropriate number in the table to get your total return. In this instance, $500 divided by $100 equals 5. Assuming you're earning an 8% return and are investing for eight years, you'll have 5 times $13,480 or $67,400 at the end of those years.

RATE OF RETURN				
8%	9%	10%	11%	12%
$1,250	$1,260	$1,270	$1,270	$1,280
2,610	2,640	2,670	2,700	2,720
4,080	4,150	4,210	4,280	4,350
5,670	5,800	5,920	6,050	6,180
7,400	7,600	7,810	8,020	8,250
9,260	9,570	9,890	10,230	10,580
11,290	11,730	12,200	12,680	13,200
13,480	14,090	14,740	15,430	16,150
15,850	16,670	17,550	18,490	19,480
18,420	19,500	20,660	21,900	23,230
34,830	38,120	41,790	45,890	50,460
59,290	67,290	76,570	87,360	99,910
95,740	112,950	133,790	159,060	189,760
150,030	184,450	227,930	283,020	352,990

annually, it will take you eight years to double your money (72 ÷ 9 = 8).

An easy way to think about stock-market investments, which historically have earned more than 10% annually, is that they should, *on average*, double every seven years. Contrast this with bank rates of return, say 5%, which would take almost 15 years to double. Of course, a bank account is federally insured, and you can't *lose* money. Another way to look at how fast your money grows is to consult the table on pages 10–11, which shows how much you need to save each month at varying rates of return to earn $10,000 by the time you need it. A second table, on pages 12–13, shows how a $100 monthly investment will grow at different rates of return.

Building a Solid Portfolio

THERE ARE A FEW GREAT FUNDS, A FEW AWFUL FUNDS AND A LOT of so-so funds. This book will steer you away from the mediocre funds and toward the best ones, and it will teach you how to size up funds yourself.

But this book goes beyond simply picking funds. Imagine bringing your car into your mechanic and, before telling him what's wrong, asking him, "Mike, what's the best part you have? Well, whatever it is, install it on my car." No one would say that. You might end up with a new transmission when you need brake shoes. But many beginning investors want to know: "What's the best mutual fund?" The answer, just as with your car, depends on what you need it for.

Even then, it usually isn't enough to pick one good fund, or even two or three good funds. Much of the advice about mutual funds badly fails investors because it doesn't get around to what's most important: how to put together a good portfolio of funds that suits their needs. *A portfolio is a group of funds that work in sync in all kinds of investing environments.* In different investment climates, one fund may do badly while another soars. The important thing is that your overall holdings don't get decimated. Only by building a portfolio of funds will you reduce risk and increase your odds of earning big profits. In the first half of this book, you'll learn how to use top-flight funds to build bulletproof portfolios for different goals. The DiBenedettos, for instance, will need very different funds to invest for retirement some 30 years from now than they will to buy their dream house in a year or so.

Before choosing funds, you need to establish your goals. After determining how long you plan let your money grow and how much tolerance you have for gut-wrenching market declines, you can construct an entire investment plan of first-class mutual funds from the portfolios in Part Two. If you plan to use one of these ready-made sets of funds, you can skip Parts Three, Four and Five, which I've written for investors who want to go beyond the basics. (Later, if you want to learn more, you can return to those chapters.) Or, you can complete the entire book and be prepared to confidently and knowledgeably assemble your own portfolio.

Introducing Your Guide

ONE LAST QUESTION: WHO AM I TO TELL YOU HOW TO invest? I'm in my late forties and have been a journalist, as well as an investor, for more than 20 years. What's more important, I have the resources of *Kiplinger's Personal Finance Magazine*, my employer for the past five years, behind me. *Kiplinger's* invented the personal-finance genre; it's been publishing the magazine since 1947. It has become the most trusted name in investing because it provides straightforward, no-nonsense information, and because it doesn't pretend to predict the unpredictable—such as what will happen to the stock market over the short term.

Key Points
- *Even if you know little about funds, this book will help you become a savvy investor.*
- *Mutual funds are the easiest and best way for most people to reach their investment goals.*
- *The time to start investing is now.*
- *Picking good funds is just part of the job; assembling them into good portfolios is equally important.*

What Are Your Goals?

And a look at the returns of different investments

IKE MOST PEOPLE, PAUL AND NANCY DiBENEDETTO have more than one dream. Sitting in a crowded living room amid Christmas decorations one winter afternoon, Nancy says: "This is absolutely the last year I'm living in this two-bedroom condo." Paul, keeping a watchful eye on Paul Jr., nods in agreement. The couple have taped a photograph of their dream house from a magazine to the refrigerator. It's a four-bedroom colonial—Paul and Nancy plan to have another child or two—with a wraparound porch, garage, finished basement, family room, living room and "big, big kitchen, because everybody lives in their kitchen," Paul says.

"What other goals do you have?" I ask Paul. "To be a millionaire by age 40," he says, laughing. "No, a billionaire. To win the Publishers' Clearinghouse sweepstakes." Assuming they don't win, the DiBenedettos want to save enough to pay for roughly half, if not all, of their children's college educations. Although the DiBenedettos both went to state universities, they'd like to give their children the option of attending more expensive private colleges.

Then there's retirement. That's three decades away, and Paul and Nancy haven't given it a great deal of thought. But they are both outdoors people. They like skiing, tennis, hiking and camping. Nancy also Rollerblades, while Paul runs regularly. Besides continuing those activities, the DiBenedettos would like to travel in retirement—visit Europe, the Bahamas, perhaps Hawaii. "Taking vacations in retirement would be more important than having an 18-room house," says Paul. While a new house is important, they've decided that saving for college is their number-one priority right now, and retirement is number two.

You'll need to conduct a similar personal inventory before you can create an investment plan. Why? Because it won't do you much good to set a dollar goal—that is, an amount to shoot for—without first knowing what you want to spend it on. And knowing what you're aiming for and how long you have to achieve the goal largely determines the risks you should take and, therefore, the investments you should make. This is a crucial step, and one you need to give yourself plenty of time to ponder. Like the DiBenedettos, do you value traveling in retirement more than having a big house? Or do you want both? No matter; everyone will have different goals. Many people will find that their goals change over time. That's fine. Most times, you can easily readjust your savings and investment plans to meet your changing goals.

How Much?

NEXT, YOU NEED TO HAVE SOME IDEA OF HOW MUCH TO SAVE for each goal. While I'll provide worksheets on how much to put aside for retirement and college in Part Two, it's important to make a start now, with whatever amount you can afford.

The DiBenedettos already have amassed $14,000 in savings accounts, as well as $20,000 in Nancy's pension plan at work (which is funded entirely by her employer) and $27,000 in Paul's 403(b) tax-deferred retirement plan at school. The couple is saving more than $1,450 monthly, including $400 in Paul's 403(b). (403(b) plans are similar to the 401(k) plans in private industry, but they are offered to employees of educational and other non-profit organizations.)

Nancy and Paul have set the following goals for putting their money to work:

$269 a month toward Paul Jr.'s college

The average private college currently costs about $21,500 a year (that figure includes tuition, room and board, books and personal expenses) and costs are expected to rise about 5% annually. That means four years of college for Paul Jr. starting in 2013 is likely to cost a staggering $192,659. Figure half that money will come from financial aid, loans, and jobs Paul Jr. works to help foot the bills. To amass the other roughly $96,000, the DiBenedettos need to save roughly $3,200 per year—assuming they earn 9.5% annually on their money before taxes. (I'll get into more detail in Chapter 6 on how much you need to save for college.)

$700 a month toward their retirement

The DiBenedettos are currently saving that much in their retirement accounts because they figure their investments will have to generate $409,398 more than they have now to afford the things they want in retirement. This number doesn't include their pen-

---

Your Goals

USE THIS WORKSHEET to map out your goals. Don't worry if you have to guess now at how much you need to save for some of these goals. You'll be able to refine your projections in Part Two. Use only those rows that apply to you.

Like the DiBenedettos, you need to assign priorities to these goals. These will vary from family to family, but most people will make their first priority an emergency fund—unless they already have one. Retirement and college are typically the next most important goals, respectively, and savings for other goals usually comes after that.

You may wish to consult the tables in Chapter 1 to figure your monthly investment amount for each goal.

Goal	TARGET AMOUNT	MONTHLY INVESTMENT	YEARS UNTIL YOU'LL SPEND THE MONEY
Emergency fund	$ _____	$ _____	_____
Retirement	_____	_____	_____
College fund #1	_____	_____	_____
College fund #2	_____	_____	_____
College fund #3	_____	_____	_____
Home down payment	_____	_____	_____
Vacation home	_____	_____	_____
Other	_____	_____	_____
TOTAL	$ _____	$ _____	_____

But Which

sions and estimated Social Security payments. To see how reached this number, see the discussion and workshe Chapter 5. That chapter will help you figure out how to inve retirement, including how much you'll need to save each m____.

$500 a month toward their new house
They are planning to spend roughly $225,000 on a new house, and expect merely to break even on the sale of their condo. For a 10% down payment, they'll need $22,500. So far, they've saved $14,000, so they are on their way. (I'll talk more about saving for a house and other shorter-term goals in Chapter 7.)

Altogether, the DiBenedettos are saving $1,469 per month—$17,628 per year. If their savings program seems too ambitious for you, start with whatever you feel you can put aside.

How to Invest Your Money

NOW THAT YOU HAVE ESTABLISHED YOUR GOALS AND PRIORIties, and set at least tentative dollar amounts that you need to put aside to meet them, it's time to begin looking at investing. With so many choices available among mutual funds, it's easy to miss the forest for the trees. Studies have shown that the most important decision you make is not which funds you invest in, but rather how you allocate your money—what percentage of your total investment goes into stocks, bonds and

---

First Things First

BEFORE YOU START investing, make sure you've paid off all your credit cards and any other high-interest debt. (This does not include your home mortgage, because the interest is tax-deductible and probably a relatively low 6.5% to 8%. Over the long haul, you can expect to earn a higher return in the stock market, 10% or more, than you would by paying down your mortgage.) The dollar amount you pay in interest on credit cards may not seem like much each month, but paying off a debt

bearing a 12% interest rate gives you an instant 12% return on your investment. So your wisest first investment is to pay off your balance every month. Also, make sure you have enough life and disability insurance, and three to six months' living expenses in a bank account, money-market fund or short-term bond fund. If you don't mind assuming more risk, you can live without that emergency fund, so long as you have an adequate home-equity line of credit.

Stocks, Bonds and Cash

A STOCK IS an ownership share in a company. If the company's profits increase, over the long haul the value of your stock in the enterprise should also increase. If the company's profits fail to grow, however, your stock will likely decline in value. **A bond** is an IOU. You, the bondholder, lend money to a corporation, a state, local or foreign government, or a government agency. You get your money paid back with interest—but you don't share in the growth of the company (or government, for that matter).

Some mutual funds own stocks and others own bonds; some own both. **Cash** is shorthand for very-short-term bonds, which usually pay your money back within six months or a year. Cash can be:

• money in a bank checking or savings account
• a short-term Treasury bill
• a *bank* money-market fund or a *mutual fund* money-market fund. A mutual fund money-market is much like a bank money-market, but bank money-markets are insured against loss by the federal government while mutual fund money-markets are not. Mutual fund money-market funds usually pay slightly higher interest rates than bank money-market funds.
• a short-term bank certificate of deposit, or
• an ultra-short-term bond fund.

Most investors put their cash into mutual fund money-market funds because they're simple, convenient and pay relatively high interest rates.

"cash." This section explains the relative risks and rewards of each type of investment (see the accompanying box for definitions). You'll get different rates of return from each type, and the higher the return, the greater the risk. Stocks usually return more than bonds, which usually return more than cash. By the same token, stocks are more volatile than bonds, which are more volatile than cash. By "more volatile," I mean that their returns fluctuate more from month to month and year to year, so that there is more risk of short-term loss.

Because deciding how to allocate your money is so crucial to your investing success, a lot of high-priced professionals—such as financial planners, stock brokers and the like—try to make people believe that determining the amount you should invest in each asset type is as hard as calculus. They use complex computer programs, long workbooks

Bear and Bull Markets

A bear market is generally defined as a drop in stock prices of 20% from their previous high.
A correction refers to a decline of more than 10%, but less than 20%.
A new bull market is declared when the market recovers from a bear market and goes on to make new highs.

and interviews to generate precise percentages for investors in particular circumstances. But the truth is that deciding how much to put into these different types of investments really isn't a science and needn't be all that difficult. It requires knowing only two things:

Your time horizon. How long will it be before you'll spend your money? The longer you have, the higher percentage you should put into high-returning stocks.

Your tolerance for risk. How much of a drop in the value of your portfolio can you handle without selling your investments in a panic or staying up at night worrying? The more you can tolerate the ups and downs of the stock market, the more you should invest in stocks.

By the time you've finished the next chapter, you'll know what percentages of your money to invest in stocks, bonds and cash. But first, here's an idea of what you can expect to earn from different types of investments. On average, since 1926 stocks have returned 11% annually, while five-year government bonds have returned 5.4% annually and cash has returned 3.7% annually. Meanwhile, inflation has averaged 3.1%. Over rolling five-year periods, stocks have outperformed bonds and cash more than three-quarters of the time. (By rolling five-year periods, I mean the first period started in January 1926 and ended in December 1930, the next period started in 1927 and ended in 1931, and so on.) And, after inflation, stocks actually have been *less likely* to lose

Understanding Bond Basics

BONDS CAN BE a little tricky to follow. To keep them straight, remember: When the interest rates on bonds fall, bond prices rise, and, conversely, when interest rates rise, prices fall. If a newscast says that bonds rose yesterday, that means their prices increased, while their yields (or interest rates) decreased.

That may seem counterintuitive. After all, when yields rise, you might expect your bonds to become more desirable and the price to rise, as well. Why are bonds so seemingly perverse?

Imagine you buy a bond that yields 6%. A year later other, similar bonds are being sold that yield 7%. Your bond is worth less than the 7% bonds for the simple reason that it doesn't pay as much interest, so it declines in value.

money over rolling five-year periods than either bonds or cash.

But before you put all your money into stocks, bear in mind the following:

Stocks are far more volatile than bonds, meaning their returns bounce around more month to month and year to year. Cash is the least volatile investment.

In their worst year (1931), stocks plunged 43%, while five-year government bonds lost only 5.1% in their poorest year (1969), and the worst return on cash was a loss of 0.02% (in 1938).

Stocks have fallen by at least 20% about once every five years since 1926. On average, it has taken two years and five months for an investor who put money into stocks just before a 20% or greater decline to break even. After the 1929 crash (when stocks lost 86% of their value over three years), though, it took until 1944 to break even. And after the brutal 1973–74 bear market (when stocks fell 48%), it took more than three years to break even—and ten years to break even after inflation.

For a more detailed look at what you can expect to earn from stocks, bonds and cash, turn to Chapter 12, "A Look at the Long Term." But you get the idea: Stocks are great long-term investments; bonds and cash make more sense for shorter time periods. Think of stocks as a roller coaster, bonds as the bumper cars and cash as a carousel.

Key Points

- *Start by determining your investment goals.*
- *Pay off credit cards and other high-interest debt before investing.*
- *The most important investment decision you make is what percentage of your money to put into stocks, bonds and cash.*
- *While stocks offer a bumpy ride, they are the best long-term investment.*

Do You Like Fast Cars?

How much of your money to put into stock funds, bond funds and money-market funds

I

T'S EASY TO LOOK AT THE NUMBERS AND CONCLUDE THAT you should put all your long-term money into stocks. And many investors do just that. But before you join them, you'll want to determine your tolerance for risk—that is, your ability to mentally withstand market crashes as well as long, dispiriting bear markets. After all, humans aren't machines; we aren't entirely rational. "What do you mean I'm not rational?" huffs Paul DiBenedetto. "Once you give me the information, I can make a rational decision." I asked Paul and his wife, Nancy, to take a simple, two-question test. Before you learn how they did, take it yourself:

1. Winning money
Which would you prefer?
a. You win $80,000.
b. You have an 80% chance of winning $100,000—and a 20% chance of winning nothing.

2. Losing money
Which would you prefer?
a. You lose $80,000.
b. You have an 80% chance of losing $100,000 (or a 20% chance of losing nothing).

Paul and Nancy answered "A" to question one and "B" to question two. Harold Evensky, a financial adviser in Coral Gables, Fla., who devised the test, says almost everyone chooses the same answers, even though there is no statistical advantage to A or B in either question. With A, you have a 100% chance of making or losing $80,000, and with B, a 20% chance of making or losing nothing. But you and I are not like *Star Trek*'s Mr. Spock, who makes decisions solely based on logic.

Paul now agrees that his decision making isn't totally rational. Offered a sure $80,000, most of us are unwilling to gamble it all for a chance to win just $20,000 more. Yet faced with the possibility of losing $80,000, most of us will grasp at even a fairly small chance of getting off scot-free. Evensky and psychologists say the test shows that most of us are less risk-averse than we are loss-averse; in other words, it's a lot harder for us to stomach losing money than to give up the opportunity to make more money. The test helps explain why some investors tend to sell stocks too soon after they rise in price, and to hold on to stocks that have fallen in price almost indefinitely, hoping to break even. More to the point, it demonstrates that there's an emotional side to investing. Ignoring its existence can be perilous to your financial health. (Those who want to learn more about how to sidestep emotional and other obstacles to successful investing should be sure to read Chapter 10, "13 Investment Pitfalls and How to Avoid Them.")

Declines That Make Your Teeth Grind

WATCHING YOUR MUTUAL FUNDS FALL IN VALUE IS NO FUN. But investing in stock funds guarantees that you'll watch them fall a good deal of the time. When your net worth starts shrinking, keeping your wits about you isn't easy. Evensky says: "We know that most of our clients have real time horizons of 20-plus years, but their psychological time horizons are often about ten seconds." Evensky isn't trying to insult investors' intelligence; he's speaking from long experience. He's learned that investors sometimes sell in panic when the stock market either plunges sharply or falls gradually in a protracted bear market. Many people find it tougher to hang on than they thought they would until they have experienced such a market. It's all too easy to throw in the towel and sell—often at just the wrong time. Peter Lynch, onetime manager of Fidelity Magellan fund, puts it this way: "The key organ for investing isn't the brain—it's the stomach. When things start to decline, will you have the stomach for market volatility and the broad-based pessimism that comes with it?"

People who lived through the 1973–74 bear market, when the average stock lost nearly half its value and many stocks lost much more, know how hard it can be to hold tight. "It was two years of nothing but down," recalls Gerald Perritt, a Chicago money manager. "Things looked like a good deal, and you'd buy them, and they'd go down more." Inflation ate up much of what stocks were able to eke out in the remainder of the decade. In 1979, *Business Week* ran a famous cover story: "The Death of Equities." The story argued that the stock markets were never again going to offer the kind of appreciation they had in the past.

When stocks have fallen for a long period, it feels to many investors as though they will keep going down. Not long after the *Business Week* prediction, however, came the start of the biggest and longest bull market of the century. The question for you to ponder is this: Would you be able to hold on to your stock-fund investments after the market had pummeled them for losses of 20%, 30% or even more? An old Wall Street adage notes: "The stock market is an expensive place to find out who you are."

Keep in mind, too, that the news media relish stories about stock-market declines. The inevitable crashes and bear markets in stocks often become front-page stories and breathless reports on television and radio—while a steadily rising stock market typically garners scant media attention. When the market goes down, reporters flock to interview those experts who have been bearish for years. These "perma-bears" often issue dire warnings: They may predict that stocks are doomed to have a bad couple of years—or a bad decade—and confide that "the smart money" has already been buying raw land, or German bonds, or gold, or some other investment that is equally inappropriate for most people.

Dollar-Cost Averaging

PROCRASTINATION IS THE ENEMY OF INVESTORS. YOU KNOW all the excuses: Either you don't have enough money, or you'd rather spend it on something else, or the market seems too risky just now, or you're already so far behind that starting would be pointless. "There's always a real solid reason to delay investing," says Jon Bull of Santa Barbara Capital Management. "It's natural to weigh both sides and put off plunging into uncertainty, which is what investing in the stock market is all about."

You'll feel better about making a move if instead of plunging you take a tentative step or two. The easiest way to accomplish this is *dollar-cost averaging*. That's just a fancy way of saying: invest the same amount regularly, whether the market goes up, down or sideways. Say you inherit a large sum that you don't plan to draw on for decades, and you put a small portion of it in stock funds each month until you've invested the full amount. Alas, big lump sums don't come around often for most of us. An equally valid application of dollar-cost averaging is to invest a modest but fixed amount from your salary in shares of stock funds every month. Funds typically allow a monthly (or quarterly) minimum of $50 or $100.

An almost mindlessly simple strategy, dollar-cost averaging nevertheless forces you to buy more shares when stocks are cheap and fewer shares when stocks are dear. Suppose your fund is selling for $10 a share. A $1,000 investment that month buys 100 shares. Then say the fund doubles in value to $20 a share the following month. Your $1,000 investment that month buys just 50 shares. So, you end up buying half as many shares when the price is higher. Dollar-cost averaging is a no-sweat way to implement the first half of Wall Street's most hallowed—but fiendishly hard to implement—strategy: "Buy low, sell high." It forces you to keep investing even when stocks are falling.

If you want to adorn this simple strategy, make your usual periodic purchase when the market rises and then step up your buying when the market declines—talk about going against the grain! You can set your own rules here. You could decide, for example, to invest $200 a month in stock funds, but to increase your monthly investment to $300 any time the market declines by at least 1% from the previous month.

Academic research has shown dollar-cost averaging isn't *statistically* the best way to invest a lump sum. Because the stock market has gone up more often then it has gone down, these studies show, you're usually better off just dumping the entire amount into stocks as soon as you can. The trouble with this approach is that it ignores human nature: It's extremely difficult to take a big sum and invest it all at once in stocks, particularly if prices are in decline. More often than not, people who plan to invest their money all at once end up delaying for months or even years while they wait in vain for the market to get cheaper or to seem "safer." Even worse, investors may invest a lump sum at a peak and then sell in a panic when the market dives. The beauty of dollar-cost averaging is that it is emotionally easy for people to implement.

Removing Temptation

INVESTING IS "LIKE ANYTHING ELSE THAT'S GOOD FOR YOU, LIKE your exercise program or your diet," says Kenneth Doyle, a financial psychologist who teaches at the University of Minnesota. "You're not going to convince me it's fun to sit down and think about my financial future." So have someone else swallow the medicine for you. If you're eligible for a 401(k) or 403(b) tax-deferred retirement plan at work, your employer will automatically deduct your contribution from your salary. And lots of mutual funds are more than willing to debit your checking account automatically for that $50 you've decided to invest each month. The DiBenedettos do all their investing this way. "After a while, you don't even think about it," says Paul. Funneling money into the market this way—in bull markets or bear—imposes a discipline that most investors need.

By automating your investing, you don't have to reconsider the decision to invest every month, and you thereby dodge a lot of emotional turmoil. Furthermore, you remove the temptation to spend earmarked money for a night on the town, new clothes, toys for your children—or any of a dozen other things that crop up every month and can sabotage the best-laid investment plan. You never see the money, so you never spend it, and you'll be pleased by how fast it grows.

Taking the Test

MOST PEOPLE SHOULDN'T PUT ALL THEIR INVESTMENT money in stocks—whether via dollar-cost averaging or all at once. The key to deciding what percentage of

How Much Risk Should You Take?

WHAT FOLLOWS IS A SIMPLE test designed to gauge your tolerance for risk. You can use it to determine how much of your money you should invest in stock funds versus less risky funds. There are no correct answers. As you become a more experienced and knowledgeable investor, you may want to retake the test. You'll probably then find you can comfortably invest a larger percentage of your assets in stocks. The test also accounts for the fact that people without a decent financial cushion may want to invest a little less aggressively. That's because a crash or a prolonged bear market could conceivably wipe out most of your savings if you don't have the wherewithal (either in savings or income) to avoid selling at the bottom.

1) The Dow Jones industrial average plunged 500 points today. Your reaction is to:
    a) consider selling some stock funds.
    b) be concerned, but sit tight because you figure the market is likely to go up over long time periods.
    c) consider investing more, because stock funds are cheaper now.

2) The news media is filled with stories quoting experts who predict stocks will lose money in the coming decade. Many suggest investing in real estate. You would:
    a) consider selling some stocks funds and buying real estate.
    b) be concerned, but stick to your long-term goals.
    c) dismiss the articles as a sign of unwarranted pessimism over stocks.

3) Which of the following statements best describes you:
    a) I often change my mind and have trouble sticking to a plan.
    b) I can stay with a strategy as long as it seems to be doing well.
    c) Once I make up my mind to do something, I tend to follow through with it regardless of the obstacles.

4) If you won $100,000 in the lottery, you would:
    a) pay off or pay down your mortgage.
    b) invest it safely in bank certificates of deposit and bond funds.
    c) invest much of it in stock funds.

5) How much experience do you have investing in stocks or stock funds?
    a) none.
    b) a little.
    c) a comfortable amount.

6) How would you react if your stock funds fell by 30% in one year?
    a) I would sell some or all of them.
    b) I would stop investing more money until the market came back.
    c) I would invest more in stock funds.

7) At work, I am:
    a) not covered by a retirement plan.
    b) covered by a plan but tend to change jobs frequently.
    c) covered by a generous plan and expect to stay with the company until I retire.

8) Equity in my home and probable inheritances will provide:
    a) very little help financing retirement.
    b) a decent amount, but not enough to fund a large part of my retirement.
    c) a substantial amount of money.

9) If you can't sleep at night, you:
    a) lie in bed worrying.
    b) have both pleasant and unpleasant thoughts.
    c) look forward to the next day.

10) If you had a financial reversal, you would:
    a) take a long time to recover and be more cautious.

b) take some time to recover, but mostly get over it.

c) bounce back quickly.

(SOURCES: VALIC, JAMES GOTTFURCHT, OTHERS)

Scoring: For each *a*, give yourself 6 points; for each *b*, 7.5 points; and for each *c*, 10 points. If you score 60 to 70 points, you're a low-risk investor. A score between 71 and 85 points makes you a moderate-risk investor. And if you score 86 or more points, you're an aggressive investor.

How Much Money, Where?

After you've identified your tolerance for risk, above, you can determine what percentage of your money to put into stocks, bonds and cash, based on how long it will be until you need your money.

Following are two tables: one for investing for retirement and the second for investing to meet all *other* goals. Find the column that matches your tolerance for risk (as determined in the preceding quiz) and the row that matches the amount of time you have until you'll start drawing on your money. The point at which they intersect tells you what percentage of your total investment you should put into stocks. Invest the balance, if any, in bond funds.

Investing for retirement requires that you put a larger proportion of your money into stock funds than does investing for other goals. That's because you won't spend all your retirement money at once as you will for most other goals. (Chapter 5 is devoted to "Investing for Retirement.")

Table A:
How Much of Your Money to Invest in Stocks for Retirement

YEARS UNTIL RETIREMENT	TOLERANCE FOR RISK		
	LOW 60–70 POINTS	MODERATE 71–85 POINTS	HIGH 86–100 POINTS
More than 15	100%	100%	100%
10 to 15	70	80	100
6 to 10	60	70	100
0 to 6	40	50	85
Early retirement (65–75)	35	45	60
Late retirement (over 75)	30	40	50

Table B:
How Much to Invest in Stocks for All Goals *Except* Retirement

YEARS TO GOAL	TOLERANCE FOR RISK		
	LOW 60–70 POINTS	MODERATE 71–85 POINTS	HIGH 86–100 POINTS
More than 15	80%	100%	100%
10 to 15	60	80	100
6 to 10	55	70	90
4 to 6	30	40	60
2 to 4	10	25	35
0 to 2	0	0	0

your money to allocate to stocks is your time horizon, which we discussed briefly in the previous chapter, plus your tolerance for losses. The quiz on the preceding pages will help you judge your ability to withstand losses.

You probably already have a good idea of whether you're a conservative investor, who can barely stand to watch a fund you own decline by one penny per share, or whether you're a more aggressive investor, more willing to take risks. But what about your partner? Nancy DiBenedetto says she's pretty conservative. "One of the reasons we haven't invested is that we know that we're safe in the bank, and in investing there's always risk." But she adds, "It depends on how long I want my money to be tied up. If I'm interested in investing a certain amount of money for ten years, then I would be willing to take more risk." Paul is by nature more comfortable with risk. Before marrying, he and a buddy in Houston gambled on several "penny stocks"— extremely risky investments that typically lose money. That's just what Paul's stocks did. Nevertheless, he says, "I would be more of the risk taker than Nancy. I'm not really that conservative." It's important in investing to know not only your own risk tolerance but also that of your spouse. After all, when stocks are tumbling, it's best if you're both comfortable with the amount you have going along for the ride.

When Nancy and Paul took the test, she scored an 82 and he scored 94 out of a maximum 100 points. While the couple lacks investing experience, they are plainly pretty gutsy folks. Both of them love downhill skiing, and even Paul Jr., not yet three years old, has skied. Averaging their two scores, as a couple they get 88 points, which makes them aggressive investors. Accordingly, for their son's college money, which they won't need for more than 15 years, they could put 100% of the investments into stock funds. But the money for their new house, which they plan to buy in a year or so, belongs in a bank CD or money-market fund.

Not long before taking this simple test, Paul and Nancy felt overwhelmed by the task of trying to invest sensibly. Now, after beginning their investment education, they have made the most important decisions about how they should invest their money. Picking good mutual funds is the next step.

Key Points

- *Don't let your emotions keep you from being a successful investor.*
- *It's hard to stay invested in stocks during bear markets.*
- *The most important investment decision you make is what percentage of your assets to put into stock, bond and money-market funds.*
- *To allocate your money among stocks, bonds and money-markets, all you need to know is your time horizon and your risk tolerance.*
- *Dollar-cost averaging—investing small amounts regularly—is the best way to invest in stock funds.*

PART TWO

Putting Together Your Investment Plan

 ow that you know what percentage of your money to invest in stock funds, bond funds and money-market funds, it's time to assemble a portfolio of funds to meet your needs. While I claim no ability to pick "the best funds," this section of the book offers you solid portfolios of funds that work together in concert—the kind of mix discussed at the end of the book's opening chapter. By the time you finish Part Two, just 142 pages into the book, you'll have all the information you need to successfully manage your fund investments. The remainder of the book is for those who want to understand funds in more depth.

Keeping It *Really* Simple

Investing with index funds lets you save time, save money and match the markets performance

HILE YOU CAN LEARN A LOT ABOUT MUTUAL funds, you can also put together a solid portfolio of funds without knowing that much about funds. That's why this book is designed so that you don't have to master the art of picking mutual funds unless you want to.

In this chapter, moreover, I'll show you a way to invest that's even simpler than what's presented in the remainder of Part Two. Not only does this method take less time than the traditional way of selecting mutual funds, it requires almost no monitoring once you get it up and running. It employs just three funds: *Vanguard Index Total Stock Market, Vanguard Total International* and *Vanguard Index Total Bond Market.*

"Want to keep things *really* simple?" I asked Nancy DiBenedetto. "That sounds awfully tempting to me," she replies, "but will I have to give up any returns?" Read on and make up your own mind whether you are willing to accept, perhaps, a slightly lower investment return in exchange for the time savings of putting your fund investing on autopilot. (If you're investing for college or retirement, however, even if you do use index funds, be sure to read the following two chapters for other tips on meeting those investment goals.)

Index Funds

T HIS METHOD USES INDEX FUNDS, WHICH ARE DESIGNED TO mirror the market indexes, or averages. Indexes are used to take the temperature of the markets. They tell you how the stock or bond market as a whole has performed or how segments of the market have done. They also serve as the benchmarks against which fund performance is measured. So, rather than attempting to "beat the market," as most funds do, index funds aim to match the market's performance. They strive, in a sense, to be merely average.

The best-known index is the Dow Jones industrial average, which measures the performance of 30 of the largest U.S. companies. Even if you know nothing else about investing, you've probably seen news briefs relating the daily performance of the Dow Jones. A broader index, Standard & Poor's 500-stock index, provides a more accurate gauge of the stock market than the Dow, in part because it includes more stocks. The Wilshire 5000 is perhaps the most comprehensive index of the entire U.S. stock market. Specialized indexes include the Russell 2000, which measures the performance of stocks of small U.S. companies, and the Morgan Stanley Europe Australasia and Far East index, which tells you how major foreign stock markets have done.

Indexes are used to take the temperature of the market and serve as benchmarks for fund performance.

ARE THEY BETTER?

Many academics believe investors are best off in index funds. Why? Because, they say, fund managers can't consistently pick stocks or bonds that will beat their market's index. As a result, most actively managed funds will trail index funds, simply because they charge higher expenses than index funds. Instead of beating your head against the wall trying to choose funds that beat the indexes, these experts argue, you're better off simply investing in index funds.

Burton Malkiel, a Princeton University economics professor, may best make that argument, in his classic book, *A Random Walk Down Wall Street*. The "random walk" theory argues that the market efficiently (or rationally and fairly) prices stocks because it has already factored all the information about each stock into its price, and day-to-day changes are unpredictable. So, a blindfolded monkey throwing darts at the stock listings will be able to select a portfolio that performs as well as those managed by professionals.

While almost all fund managers devote their energies to beating an index (because their bonuses and ultimately their continued employment may depend on their doing so), Malkiel says most are doomed to fail. Better, he says, just to match the index—which index funds do by buying all, or substantially all, the stocks in an index.

Perhaps it's no surprise that Malkiel ended up on the board of directors of the Vanguard family of mutual funds, which have become synonymous with stock-market indexing. In 1976, Vanguard launched the *Vanguard Index 500* fund, which is designed to mirror Standard & Poor's 500-stock index, an index of stocks of mostly large companies. Indexing has been popular with some pension funds and other institutional investors for decades, but Vanguard was the first to offer these funds to individuals.

BEATING THE AVERAGES ISN'T EASY

In the mid 1990s, Vanguard Index 500 has been nearly impossible to beat, primarily because it invests in larger companies than almost all fund managers buy. From 1995 through 1997, only 6.5% of actively managed stock funds were able to best the S&P. It has likewise been difficult to outdo the S&P in other periods when big companies were the market leaders. Even in more normal times, when stocks of small- and medium-size companies outperform or match their big brothers, the S&P tends to beat the average fund. It's no secret why: Fund managers and other money managers, along with individual investors, *are* the stock market. It's unrealistic to expect more than half of them to beat a broadly based market index like the S&P.

Instead of trying to choose funds that beat the indexes, these experts argue, you're better off investing in index funds.

Think of it in baseball terms. All baseball players try to get the highest batting percentage they can each season. But no more than half will surpass the median batting percentage for all baseball players. After all, the median *is* the batting percentage that half the players exceed and the other half fall short of. Similarly, Garrison Keillor's Lake Wobegon, where "all the children are above average" can exist only in fantasy. Since the S&P and other stock indexes are stock-market averages, you can't expect more than about half of all fund managers to beat these indexes.

THE ADVANTAGE OF LOW EXPENSES

Expenses are the other reason more fund managers don't outperform the averages. The average stock fund charges 1.46% of assets annually in expenses to cover its costs and to earn a profit. (In other words, it has an *expense ratio* of 1.46%. That means $1.46 of every $100 invested in the fund goes annually to the fund company.) The S&P 500—and all other stock indexes, for that matter—have no expenses to subtract from their gain. Index funds do have some expenses, but these can be very low. After all, while it takes some computer muscle to track an index, there are no research analysts to hire, no companies to visit, no brokerage research reports to buy. Wisely, when Vanguard set up its Index 500 fund, it chose to assess very low expenses. Here's the bottom line: Vanguard Index 500 charges investors a mere 0.2% of assets annually, or $2 for every $1,000 invested.

Index funds do have some expenses, but these can be very low.

THE S&P 500: A VERY EFFICIENT MARKET

Swarms of analysts follow every hiccup of most of the companies in the S&P 500. When companies announce their earnings every three months, most of them hold conference calls with analysts. Investors often execute a blizzard of purchases or sales *during* these conference calls—propelling a stock up or down in moments. If ever there were a group of stocks that's thoroughly researched, it's those in the S&P 500. To use Malkiel's phrase, it is a very efficient market.

For that reason, any investor—not just those in search of simplicity—could do a lot worse than to buy Vanguard Index 500 or a similar low-cost index fund instead of an actively managed large-company fund. Over the long haul, the S&P 500 has beaten roughly two-thirds of all stock funds (even after subtracting Vanguard's 0.2% in expenses). I think an investor who takes the time to thoroughly research funds, or who uses a good source of information, like this book, may well select large-company funds that will consistently outperform the index. But almost no one is going to beat the index by much over the long term, and the average fund will likely continue to trail the index. (To learn when actively managed funds will almost certainly underperform the S&P 500, see Chapter 21, "Funds for Tax-Shy Investors.")

Expand Your Universe

I T's NOT A GOOD IDEA, HOWEVER, TO PUT ALL YOUR MONEY IN AN S&P index fund. Here's one reason: Since 1926, stocks of small companies have outperformed large-company stocks by about two percentage points annually, according to Ibbotson Associates, a Chicago-based research firm. Small companies, on the other hand, are inherently riskier than bigger companies; many have only a couple of products and lack the money to stay afloat through hard times. You wouldn't want to invest *all* your money in small stocks, but most investors should put 20% or more of their stock money into small stocks.

But the S&P contains hardly any small stocks, and furthermore it's composed almost exclusively of domestic stocks. Nearly half the world's stock-market value is outside the U.S. Why limit your choices? "We like to think of investing abroad as doubling our shopping aisles," says John Spears, co-manager of Tweedy Browne Global Value. Moreover, the ebbs and flows of the U.S. stock market often occur at different times than the ebbs and flows of overseas stock markets. By owning both foreign and domestic stocks, you'll smooth out some of the ups and downs in your overall investment portfolio. Investors with time horizons of ten years or longer could put 20% to 30% of their stock money abroad, depending upon their risk tolerance and preference.

Most actively managed small-company and international funds have beaten their indexes.

Most actively managed small-company funds have beaten the Russell 2000, a small-company index. Likewise, most actively managed foreign funds have beaten the Morgan Stanley Europe, Australasia and Far East index of foreign stocks. Why? These stocks are not as carefully researched as are large U.S. stocks, so it's easier for savvy managers to uncover bargains.

As a consequence, you can probably do better with actively

managed funds in these markets. But if you use actively managed funds, you need to spend some time monitoring them. They can't simply be bought and forgotten. Index funds can. Moreover, if your choice is between hiring an investment adviser to build a portfolio for you and buying index funds, you'll almost certainly do far better with index funds because your costs will be much lower. (Many investment advisers themselves employ index funds.) With index funds, there is only one thing you need to keep in mind:

Mind Your Costs

THERE'S NO EXCUSE FOR PAYING A SALES FEE (OFTEN CALLED A load) for an index fund. A commission is payment for an investment professional's advice, and no broker can provide much useful advice or insight about future performance of an index fund. (More on load and no-load funds can be found in Chapter 1.)

When comparing funds that follow the same or similar indexes, go with the one that has the lowest expense ratio. The average index fund that follows the S&P 500 has an expense ratio of 0.45%—less than one-third that of the typical U.S. stock fund. This difference, when compounded over time, gives index funds a sizable performance advantage over managed funds. Say $1,000 investments made by two funds earn 10% annually for ten years. The fund charging annual expenses of 0.45% will end up being worth $2,490, while the one charging 1.4% will be worth only $2,282. (You can find the expense ratio in the prospectus or by calling the fund's toll-free number.)

You might do best with Vanguard and USAA, which have long been low-cost providers.

In 1997, when the S&P 500 was hot, many companies launched low-cost index funds, or lowered the expense ratios on funds they already had, to attract more investor dollars. It's fine to buy one of these, but be sure to keep an eye on it. Some of these funds may later up the ante. When your semiannual reports arrive in the mail, look up the "annual expense ratio." If it has risen, consider swapping into a cheaper index fund. For index funds unlikely to raise their costs, you might do best with Vanguard and USAA, which have long been low-cost providers.

Which Funds to Buy

You can build a fine stock portfolio with just two funds:

Vanguard Index Total Stock Market (800–635–1511) seeks to track the Wilshire 5000 index, a broad U.S. stock-market index. While the fund emphasizes large stocks, it also holds many small stocks among its 1,900 issues. Expenses are 0.25% annually. If your account balance is less than $10,000, you also pay a $10 annual fee.

Vanguard Total International gives you the rest of the world by investing in other Vanguard index funds. Ninety percent of the fund seeks to replicate the Morgan Stanley Europe, Australasia and Pacific index by investing in Vanguard's Europe and Pacific index funds. The final 10% is in Vanguard's emerging-markets index fund, which invests in developing nations in Asia, Latin America, Eastern Europe and Africa. Total expenses of the underlying funds are about 0.35% annually, plus a $10 annual fee for accounts under $10,000.

How Much, Where?

Depending on your investment goal, your score on the risk-tolerance test on pages 28–29 and your time horizon (when you will need your money), you'll put all or part of your money in stock funds and the balance, if any, in more-conservative bond funds. The tables on page 29—one for retirement and one for all other goals—will help you determine what the breakdown of your investment should be.

Investing for Goals Other Than Retirement

For long-term goals, about three-quarters of the money you invest in stocks should go into *Vanguard Index Total Stock Market* and the remainder into *Vanguard Total International*. For example, say you're going to invest $200 a month and Table B (on page 29) tells you that you should invest 70% of your money in stocks, or $140 (.70 x $200). Of that, you would put $105 (.75 x $140) in Vanguard Index Total Stock Market and $35 (.25 x $140) in Vanguard Total International. (You may notice that the portfolios in this chapter offer slightly different proportions of funds that invest in stocks of large companies, small companies and foreign companies than do the portfolios for actively managed funds enumerated in the following three chapters. That's largely because of differences in risk among the recommended index funds and actively managed funds. All the portfolios, are designed to help you reach the same goals with roughly the same risk.)

Bond alternatives

If the table says you need to put some of your money in bonds—which are less volatile but also less rewarding than stocks—invest that portion in *Vanguard Index Total Bond Market*, which holds a representative sampling of all types of bonds. (In the example above, you would invest $60 (.30 x $200). Expenses are 0.2% annually plus a $10 annual fee for accounts under $10,000.

If you are in the 28% tax bracket or higher, and are investing outside of a tax-deferred account, use *Vanguard Municipal High Yield* instead of the bond index fund. The dividends from this fund are tax-exempt, and taxpayers in the 28% bracket or higher will end up with more money in their pockets with this fund instead of Index Total Bond Market.

With four to six years to go

For goals four to six years in the future, other than retirement, you'll want to limit risk by reducing your holdings in *Vanguard Total International* from 25% of your stock funds to about 10%.

With two to four years to go

For goals two to four years in the future, other than retirement, divide your bond money evenly between *Vanguard Index Total Bond Market* and *Vanguard Bond Index Short Term*. However, if you're investing outside a tax-deferred account and are in the 28% tax bracket or higher, split your money instead between *Vanguard Municipal Intermediate Term* and *Vanguard Municipal Limited Term*. Your stock money should be placed in *Vanguard Index Total Stock Market*.

With less than two years to go

Invest your money as follows:

Vanguard Bond Index Short Term (50%), or if you're in the 28% tax bracket or higher, *Vanguard Municipal Limited Term*.

Vanguard Money Market Prime (50%), or if you're in the 36% tax bracket or higher, *Vanguard Municipal Money Market*.

INVESTING FOR RETIREMENT

Portfolio for six or more years from retirement
Allocate your money between stocks and bonds as shown in Table A on page 29. Put 75% of your stock money in *Vanguard Index Total Stock Market* and 25% in *Vanguard Total International.* Any bond money should go into *Vanguard Index Total Bond Market,* or if you're in the 28% tax bracket or higher, into *Vanguard Municipal High Yield.* (*Note:* never buy a municipal bond fund inside a retirement account, because retirement accounts are already tax-exempt.)

Portfolio for zero to six years from retirement
Depending on your risk tolerance, put between 15% and 60% of your money into bond funds, as Table A advises. If your tax bracket is lower than 28%, use *Vanguard Index Total Bond Market* for your bond money. Otherwise, divide your bond money between *Vanguard Municipal High Yield* and *Vanguard Municipal Intermediate.*

Early retirement (up to age 75)
Invest 40% to 65% of your money in bond funds as indicated in the table. Invest your bond money as in the previous portfolio. Of your stock money, invest 85% in *Vanguard Index Total Stock Market* and 15% in *Vanguard Total International.*

Late retirement (over 75)
Put all of your stock money into *Vanguard Index Total Stock Market.* Invest between 30% and 50% of your portfolio in stocks as the table on page 29 advises. Put half your bond money into *Vanguard Bond Index Short Term,* leaving the remainder in *Vanguard Index Total Bond Market*—unless you are in the 28% tax bracket or higher, in which case you'll want to divide your bond money between *Vanguard Municipal Intermediate* and *Vanguard Municipal Limited Term.*

EASY MAINTENANCE

Once you've invested in your funds, you need only make sure they stay in proper proportions. In other words, if foreign stocks rally for several years, don't let them grow from the recommended 25% to, say, 50% of your portfolio. If your funds get way out of kilter, simply sell off some of the soaring fund and spread the proceeds among the laggards.

For instance, suppose you start out with $15,000 in Vanguard Index Total Stock Market, and $5,000 in Vanguard Total International, giving you 25% in foreign stocks. The U.S. stock market doesn't budge for two years, so your $15,000 remains unchanged in value. But foreign stocks double during those same years, giving you a total of $10,000 in Vanguard Total International. Instead of having 25% in foreign stocks, you now have 40% in foreign stocks ($10,000 divided by $25,000 equals 40%). In this instance, if you sell $3,750 of your foreign stocks and move that money into U.S. stocks, you will again have 20% of your money in foreign stocks (25% of $25,000 equals $6,250; $10,000 − $6,250 = $3,750).

Alternatively, instead of selling off part of your foreign stock fund, simply direct all your new investments to the U.S. stock index fund until your portfolio is rebalanced. This will minimize your taxes.

Another Approach

YOU DON'T HAVE TO USE INDEX FUNDS TO MAKE YOUR MUTUAL fund investing simple. *T. Rowe Price Spectrum* (800–638–5660) funds and *Fidelity Asset Manager* and *Fidelity Asset Manager Growth* (800–544–8888) funds offer equally good methods for making things really easy. While the future is impossible to predict, both Fidelity and T. Rowe Price have long histories of providing solid results. (All of these funds are no-load.)

T. Rowe Price Spectrum funds
The Price Spectrum funds are "funds of funds." Funds of funds invest in other funds, and most provide only anemic performance while charging an extra layer of expenses. But Spectrum funds charge nothing except the expenses of the underlying funds, and have produced solid results.

Spectrum Growth invests in six T. Rowe Price stock funds, including a small-company fund and a foreign fund. At times the fund even puts some assets in a money-market fund.

Spectrum Income invests in six bond funds and often places a little money in a conservative stock fund.

To invest using the Spectrum funds, turn back to the "How Much to Invest in Stocks" tables on page 29. Use Spectrum Growth in place of stocks and Spectrum Income in place of bonds. For example, if you're investing for retirement between six and ten years away, and you're a risk-averse investor (who scored between 60 and 70 points on the risk-tolerance test), you'll want to put 60% of your money in Spectrum Growth and the other 40% in Spectrum Income.

Fidelity Asset Manager funds

Fidelity Asset Manager Growth normally keeps about 70% of its assets in stocks, 25% in bonds and 5% in short-term investments. The managers adjust the mix depending on their view of market conditions. While it's more conservative than I would like for long-term investors, Fidelity's stock selection is usually good, and

Taxable Versus Tax-free Accounts

USING A BOND INDEX fund is all well and good if you're investing your money in a tax-sheltered retirement account, such as an IRA. But what if you're investing your money in an account that's subject to income taxes? In that case, a tax-exempt bond fund—whose dividends are free from federal taxes—is often a better bet than a taxable bond index fund.

That's because most ordinary mutual fund accounts are fully taxable. You'll pay 15% to 39.6% of your taxable bond-fund dividend income to the federal government in taxes.

Bond-fund investors who are in the 28% tax bracket or higher (single investors earning at least $25,351 annually or couples earning at least $42,351 in 1998) will generally do better in tax-exempt bond funds. These funds invest in municipal bonds. Their yields are lower than those of taxable bond funds, but after taxes you'll wind up ahead.

Tax-exempt accounts—such as IRAs, 401(k)s, 403(b)s and variable annuities—are a different story. If you're invested in these, you pay no taxes on earnings until you start to withdraw your money. In the case of Roth IRAs, earnings are generally tax-*free* if withdrawn after age 59½.

Here it's best to use taxable bonds so you can get the higher return within this already tax-sheltered environment. Usually, you'll want to keep stock funds in your retirement accounts whenever you can, because stock funds tend to have higher returns (which would be taxed in a taxable account) than do bonds funds.

One caveat: Tax-exempt money-market funds tend not to give as good an after-tax deal to investors. As a result, unless you're in the 36% bracket or higher, you should probably stick with taxable money-market funds rather than tax-exempt ones.

you'll likely do better in this fund over the long haul than you would paying an adviser. It's ideal for investors who have six to ten years before they need their money.

Fidelity Asset Manager normally holds 40% in stocks, 40% in bonds and 20% in short-term investments. It's well suited for investors with four to six years before they'll need their money.

Key Points

- *Index funds are the easiest way to invest, because you don't have to monitor the funds once you've selected them.*
- *Many academics believe low-cost index investing is likely to beat all other methods.*
- *You can put together an index portfolio with as few as two funds, or three if you need to invest in bonds as well as stocks.*
- *Fidelity and T. Rowe Price offer alternatives to index investing that also require little monitoring.*

Investing for (and in) Retirement

How to make sure your money will be ready when you are

HE SOCIAL SECURITY TRUST FUND WILL BE BANKRUPT in about three decades unless Congress fixes it. Most people aren't saving nearly enough for retirement. And fewer wage earners can expect monthly pension checks from their employers. Such discouraging news may tempt you to forget about retiring altogether and plan to work until you drop. Fight that pessimistic impulse. Yes, you'll need to save a lot more than your parents did to afford a comfortable retirement, but you have more tools than ever before. You just need to learn how to use them—and this chapter will give you that knowledge.

Mutual funds have become *the* way Americans are saving for retirement. A third or more of the assets at many fund companies are invested in retirement accounts. Moreover, the fund industry has made it easy and cheap for investors to set up different types of retirement accounts.

That's not to say you don't have a challenge ahead of you. Retirement is probably the main reason for investing, and it's also the trickiest goal to invest for. Unlike investing for shorter-term goals—such as a new car, a new house or even college for your children (discussed in the following chapters)—it's difficult to get a handle on how much money you'll need to afford a comfortable retirement. To invest for retirement, you need to figure out how much to put aside each year for decades—and how to invest it so that you will achieve the returns you want. Investing for retirement is kind of like launching a rocket; it has to fly straight and true for a long, long time—and you can't afford to undershoot your target by too much. But investing for retirement needn't be hard. We'll take you through the process step by step. And if you've already mapped out a retirement investing plan, this chapter will help you determine whether you're headed in the right direction and assist you in making any necessary course corrections.

In an hour or two, you'll have everything you need to know about investing for retirement.

Once you've read this chapter, completed the worksheet on pages 54–55 (which was prepared with the help of Karen Kratzer, a financial planner in Annapolis, Md., formally of Coopers & Lybrand), and consulted Table A on page 29, you'll know how much you need to save each year for retirement and what percentages of it to invest in stocks and in bonds. You'll find sample mutual fund portfolios appropriate for investors with different amounts of time left until retirement (see pages 65–70). In an hour or two, you'll have everything you need to know about investing for retirement—from soup to nuts. Here are the eight steps you need to take.

Step One: Get Serious

EVEN THOUGH THEY'RE STILL IN THEIR THIRTIES, PAUL AND Nancy DiBenedetto have been saving for retirement for several years. Paul has $27,000 in a 403(b) plan through the school system where he teaches. Nancy has saved up another $20,000 in a retirement plan at the hospital where she works as a recreation therapist. Still, after talking with me for months, Paul says, "You've opened our eyes about what we really need to do for ourselves." In truth, the couple needed only to invest more aggressively because their investments were too conservative for people their age.

As a rough rule of thumb, you'll be in fine shape for retirement if you:
• **you have a 401(k) or 403(b) tax-deferred retirement plan** at work that lets you put aside at least 10% of your income annually,
• **you contribute the maximum,** and
• **you put it into stock funds** starting in your twenties or early to mid thirties.

Starting in your early forties? You'll likely be all right if you contribute 10% annually to your 401(k) or 403(b) and also make the maximum $2,000 annual contribution to individual retirement accounts (IRAs). Whatever your age, if you're married be sure your spouse makes the same contributions you do, so far as he or she is allowed to. Of course, you're better off if you don't wait until your forties before you start putting money away for retirement. But even starting in your late forties or your fifties, your money will grow surprisingly fast if you invest regularly.

Step Two: Set Your Goals

ONCE YOU'VE MADE THE DECISION TO INVEST FOR retirement, it's time to set your income goal (line 1 on the worksheet in today's dollars and line 2 in inflation-adjusted dollars). The traditional guideline is that you'll need 70% to 80% of your preretirement income to live comfortably in retirement. That's a good benchmark for some people, but not for others. I've given you a broader range of 70% to 100%, because some people find they spend as much in retirement as they did when they were working.

If you're relatively close to retirement—say, within five to ten years—you'll have a better idea of what you'll *actually* spend in retirement, so you're best off using that estimate. Use your current income as a starting point, and add to or subtract from it based on these big-ticket items:

Your mortgage. Will you still be making mortgage payments after you retire?

College. Will the brain drain on your finances have ended?

Health insurance. If you retire before medicare kicks in (which is now at age 65, but in the future will likely be later), health insurance could cost $500 a month or more.

Work. Do you plan to work even part-time in retirement?

Taxes. Using government data, Stephen King, a retirement expert with Aon Consulting, found that a couple with one 65-year-old wage earner earning $80,000 annually pays an average of $21,000 in social security and income taxes. After retirement, the same couple pays only about $5,000 in taxes, on average, due to a drop in both income and taxes. While this is just one example, your taxes are likely to drop dramatically in retirement, mostly because your taxable income will decline markedly.

Lifestyle. How expensive a lifestyle do you want in retirement? Many people live parsimoniously in retirement, while others spend as much as or more than they did while working.

Paul and Nancy picked 80% of their pre-retirement income without much hesitation. Despite their relatively young ages, they're pretty clear about their priorities for retirement: to continue enjoying sports and outdoor recreation, to travel, and not to be too concerned about "a big house or a fancy car," as Paul puts it. They are also toying with buying some lake-front property at some point. "I'd love to live on a lake when I retire," Paul says.

Many people find that they spend more than they had anticipated in the early years of retirement.

Unlike the DiBenedettos, you may not be sure how much you want to spend in retirement. If you're like many people—particularly if you're decades from retirement—you may not have any idea how much you plan on spending, other than a vague notion that more will probably be better. As with other questions on the worksheet, if you aren't sure what to answer, make an educated guess. Later, you can always refine your answers and complete it again. Or try doing the worksheet twice—say, figuring 90% of your pre-retirement income the first time and 75% the second time. It's a good idea to make several photocopies of the worksheet beforehand so you can try out different scenarios.

Many people find that they spend more than they had anticipated in the early years of retirement. In the later years, people's spending tends to decline, at least until their health fails and medical bills increase.

Step Three: Add Up Your Pensions

START WITH SOCIAL SECURITY. YOU CAN APPROXIMATE YOUR social security benefits using the numbers provided with line 3 of the worksheet. For this exercise, I have assumed a retirement age of 65. Beginning with workers born in 1938, however, the retirement age for full benefits will gradually increase, eventually reaching 67 for people born in 1960 and later. Paul and Nancy hope to retire by the time they are 65 but are aware they may have to work longer to get full retirement benefits.

Reform proposals could push normal retirement age to 70.

While social security is not going to be eliminated, some cutbacks are inevitable. The worksheet assumes wage earners who are now around age 55 will get the full benefits at retirement that they are entitled to under current law. For workers around age 45, however, I have assumed a reduction of 15% from current law. And for wage earners around age 35, I have assumed a 30% reduction. These adjustments were made after consulting with numerous social security experts about how much benefits are likely to be reduced.

Direct from Social Security

You can obtain an official social security calculation by calling the Social Security Administration at 800–772–1213 and asking for the "Personal Earnings and Benefit Estimate Statement" (or by visiting www.ssa.gov on the Internet). After you fill out the form and mail it back, the Social Security Administration will tell you what benefits you will have earned if you work until full retirement age (65 to 67, depending on your current age). Be aware that the numbers you get from the Social Security Administration may be higher than what the worksheet shows because the agency doesn't assume any changes in current law. (The Social Security Administration will automatically mail annual estimate statements beginning in fiscal 2000, which begins in October 1999. Be sure to check yours over. If you have worked jobs that you have not received credit for from Social Security, you'll want to have your records corrected.)

Remember that if you change jobs you may end up with a lower pension than if you stay put.

YOUR PENSION

Next, estimate your pension benefits (line 4 on the worksheet). Your employee benefits office can provide this number. Most employers will give you the number in today's dollars. If yours does, be sure to use the appropriate inflation factor (from line 2 on the worksheet) to determine what your pension will likely be when you retire. Remember that if you change jobs you may end up with a lower pension than if you stay put. Also, many employers are skimping on pensions and leaving most of the work of saving for retirement to employees through 401(k) and 403(b) retirement plans.

Step Four: Add Up the Years

ARE YOU PLANNING TO RETIRE EARLY? IF SO, YOU WILL HAVE to make do with smaller social security checks—or do without them entirely until you reach the age at which you can receive full benefits. The same may go for your pension, depending on your employer. Plus, your savings will have to support you longer if you retire early. In doing the worksheet, you may find you have to readjust your retirement target age.

To figure how long you'll need to support yourself in retirement, you also need to estimate how long you'll live. No one, of course, can predict this with much accuracy. Lynn Hopewell of the Monitor Group, a financial planning firm in Fairfax, Va., says, only half in jest, "The objective of retirement planning is to run out of breath and money at the same time."

> **"The objective of retirement planning is to run out of breath and money at the same time."**

The table associated with line 7 of the worksheet shows how long the average man or woman can expect to live based on his or her current age. Remember that median life expectancy means that half the people live longer. And with advances in medicine, life expectancies will likely be greater by the time you retire. So you may want to plan for an extra five years in retirement beyond what the table suggests. If your health is particularly good and your relatives lived to ripe old ages, you might add even more. Paul and Nancy are both trim, active athletically and in good health. To be on the safe side, they estimate that at least one of them will live to be 95.

Step Five: Count Your Savings

TOTAL UP WHAT YOU'VE ALREADY SAVED. THAT MEANS everything you have in IRAs, 401(k) plans and other tax-deferred retirement accounts, other savings or investments earmarked for retirement, and any inheritances you're confident you'll receive. Be sure to include the *current* value of assets—such as the equity in your home, investment real estate or business—if you plan to sell those assets to help fund your retirement. Revise their value downward a bit if you think they won't appreciate at least 11% annually, which is the rate the worksheet assumes aggressive investors will earn (see line 8). The easiest way to do this is to use the worksheet's conservative investment assumption even if you plan to invest aggressively, that is, assume your total investments will earn 8% rather than 11%. If you already invest conservatively, reduce the *current* value of any low-returning assets by, say, 20% or 25%.

CONSIDER THE LIMITS OF THE EXERCISE

Please don't look on the worksheet as anything more than a good estimate of your retirement savings. An increase—or decrease— of one percentage point in inflation between now and when you retire could alter your bottom line considerably, as could a change of one or two percentage points in your investment return. Look at the DiBenedettos. Assuming they earn 11% annually (as the worksheet projects aggressive investors will) they need save just $3,685 annually to age 65 for a comfortable retirement. However, suppose stocks return only 8% annually (as we assume in the worksheet for conservative investors who own stocks and bonds in their retirement accounts). In that event, the DiBenedettos would need to save $13,778 annually—or almost four times the $3,685. The moral is clear: This worksheet can be a valuable planning tool, but it's only as good as its assumptions. You'll need to be flexible as you get closer to retirement, so that

Nancy and Paul's Results

NANCY AND PAUL DIBENEDETTO found filling out the table a simple matter. They want an annual income in today's dollars of 80% of their current income, or $63,200 *(line 1)* and would like to retire in 25 years.

Their desired income, when adjusted for future inflation, will need to be $149,152 *(line 2)*.

Social Security should pay them $40,361 in future dollars *(line 3)* and their pension should pay $43,487 in future dollars *(line 4)*, or a total of $83,848 *(line 5)*.

They'll need another $65,304 in future dollars from their investments *(line 6)*.

Since they are budgeting to live 40 years in retirement, they will need $1,048,128 at retirement from what they invest *(line 7)*.

But their current $47,000 in retirement savings should grow to $638,730 *(line 8)*.

That means they'll need to amass another $409,398 *(line 9)*.

To accomplish that, they need to save $3,685 annually *(line 10)*—or $307 per month. They're already saving $700 a month, or more than twice what they'll need. As I've emphasized, the earlier you save money, the less you'll need to save later on.

(continued on page 56)

How Much You Need to Save

THIS WORKSHEET will show you how much you need to save each year to retire in style. It assumes that you are saving in tax-deferred accounts, that inflation will average 3.5% annually and that, prior to retirement, conservative investors will earn 8% annually, while aggressive investors will make 11%. During retirement, conservative investors are assumed to earn 7% and aggressive investors, 9%.

1. Annual income in current dollars desired during retirement
Usually you'll need 70% to 100% of your current income. .... $ _____

2. Inflation-adjusted income desired
Multiply line 1 by the factor in the following table that corresponds most closely to the number of years you plan to work until retirement. ....$ _____

Years until retirement	5	10	15	20	25	30	35	40	45
Inflation factor	1.19	1.41	1.68	1.99	2.36	2.81	3.33	3.96	4.70

3. Annual social security benefits
Multiply the appropriate number from this table by the inflation factor from step 2 to get your approximate benefit in future dollars. If your spouse works, figure his or her benefits separately, and add both benefits together. Couples with a nonworking spouse should add the benefits for the nonworking spouse to that of the wage earner. .... $ _____

Current income	$36,000	$48,000	$65,400+
Current age, 55			
Worker benefits	$13,092	$14,556	$16,260
Nonworking spouse	6,444	7,164	8,004
Current age, 45			
Worker benefits	$11,087	$12,475	$14,423
Nonworking spouse	5,447	6,120	7,079
Current age, 35			
Worker benefits	$8,551	$9,635	$11,214
Nonworking spouse	4,108	4,629	5,384

4. Annual employer-paid pension benefits
Ask your employee benefits office for this number. If it isn't adjusted for future inflation, multiply it by the proper factor from step 2. .... $ _____

5. Income from pension and social security
Add lines 3 and 4. .... $ _____

6. Retirement income needed from your investments
Subtract line 5 from line 2. .... $ _____

7. Assets needed to generate required investment income during retirement
Multiply line 6 by the number in the table below that corresponds to how long a retirement you need to finance, based on your age now and your life expectancy. Choose the conservative or aggressive multiplier, depending on how you plan to invest. .... $ _____

How long in retirement?	Life expectancy							
This table offers a clue to how many years you can expect to live in retirement by showing average life expectancies. Subtract your planned retirement age from your life expectancy to estimate the length of your retirement.	AGE NOW	30	35 40 45	50 55	60	65		

How long in retirement?		Life expectancy						
	AGE NOW	30	35	40	45	50	55	60	65
	MEN	78	78	79	79	79	80	81	82
	WOMEN	84	84	85	85	85	85	86	86

Years in retirement	15	20	25	30	35	40	45
Conservative	11.52	14.21	16.48	18.39	20.00	21.36	22.50
Aggressive	10.04	11.95	13.41	14.53	15.39	16.05	16.55

8. Total nest egg for retirement
Add present tax-deferred and taxable retirement savings (including any real estate or business that will be sold to fund your retirement) and multiply by the appropriate number from this table. As in line 7, choose either conservative or aggressive investments. .... $ _____

Years to retirement	5	10	15	20	25	30	35	40	45
Conservative	1.47	2.16	3.17	4.66	6.85	10.06	14.79	21.72	31.92
Aggressive	1.69	2.84	4.78	8.06	13.59	22.89	38.57	65.00	109.53

9. Additional capital needed
Subtract line 8 from line 7. .... $ _____

10. Annual savings needed to meet your goal
Multiply line 9 by the appropriate number from this table, based on how you plan to invest. .... $ _____

Years to retirement	5	10	15	20	25	30	35	40	45
Conservative	0.170	0.069	0.037	0.022	0.014	0.009	0.006	0.004	0.003
Aggressive	0.161	0.060	0.029	0.160	0.009	0.005	0.003	0.002	0.001

you can adjust your goals to reflect changes in inflation and your investment returns—and in your own personal situation. Even during retirement you may have to do some fine-tuning.

Because the worksheet—or any retirement-planning worksheet or software—can't do more than provide an estimate, I've deliberately chosen to make this one easy to complete—even at the expense of precision in a few places. Most important, I have assumed that you've invested almost all your retirement assets in tax-deferred vehicles, such as 401(k)s, variable annuities or tax-managed funds (more on these last two in a minute). If you're 20 or more years from retirement and you've invested a large portion of your retirement money in ordinary taxable accounts, consider adding an extra five years onto your years in retirement to counterbalance the taxes you'll pay along the way.

And other retirement-planning tools

If you want a worksheet that takes a more exacting look at retirement planning, T. Rowe Price (800–638–6550) offers one of the most comprehensive, at no charge. In addition, they sell retirement planning software for $19.95.

Don't be fooled, though. Staying up half the night completing a worksheet or working with a computer program doesn't necessarily make the numbers you come up with any more meaningful. I've tested the retirement software from several companies. All give you significantly different results, simply because they make different assumptions about such things as inflation, social security and your future investment return. For most investors, I think the worksheet here provides all the information you need.

Step Six: Just Do It

THE WORKSHEET GIVES YOU A GOOD IDEA OF HOW MUCH YOU need to save each year. All you have to do now is start investing. In saving for retirement, several tax-deferred options are available.

TAX-DEFERRED SAVINGS AND INVESTING

All of the plans described below let your money compound tax-free until you take it out in retirement (or, in the case of a Roth

IRA, forever). Here are brief descriptions of these different retirement-savings vehicles, and whom they suit best.

401(k)s

401(k)s are the most ubiquitous retirement accounts. They are available to employees of most for-profit corporations. 401(k)s allow you to invest only in the funds or other investment choices your employer offers. Generally, employers (and federal restrictions) limit your annual contributions to 10% or 15% of your salary—with a maximum annual contribution for 1998 of $10,000 (which increases with inflation). Often the company provides some match of, say, the first 6% of your salary that you contribute. 401(k) plans may allow you to borrow money. When you repay the loan, with interest, all the money goes right back into your account. When you borrow money from a plan, however, you don't earn any investment return on that sum until you repay it. For that reason, it's best not to dip into your 401(k) unless you have no better choice.

The Power of Tax-Deferred Compounding

LEARN HERE HOW quickly your money grows in a tax-deferred account without the drag of paying taxes every year. This table compares returns in a tax-deferred account versus a taxable account. The table assumes a $2,000 annual investment, a 9% annual rate of return and a 28% tax rate. (The final column actually understates the true value of tax deferral, because it assumes withdrawal of the entire amount at once. In reality, you'll withdraw money from tax-deferred retirement accounts gradually over many years during retirement.)

YEARS	VALUE OF TAXABLE ACCOUNT	VALUE OF TAX-DEFERRED ACCOUNT BEFORE TAXES	VALUE OF TAX-DEFERRED ACCOUNT AFTER PAYING TAXES UPON WITHDRAWAL
15 years	$51,400	$64,000	$54,500
20 years	82,500	111,500	91,500
25 years	125,100	184,600	146,900
30 years	183,300	297,200	230,800

SOURCE: T. Rowe Price Associates Inc.

403(b)s

403(b)s are like 401(k)s except they are offered to employees of public school systems and other nonprofit enterprises. In most cases, the 403(b) is offered by an insurance company the employer has selected. That adds a needless layer of expenses. For details on switching your 403(b) investment to any mutual fund you would like, see the discussion beginning on page 70.

IRAs and Roth IRAs

IRAs, short for individual retirement accounts, allow you and your spouse each to save $2,000 annually in pretax income (if you qualify to make deductible contributions) with whatever mutual fund company, brokerage, insurance company or bank you choose. The money is taxed as ordinary income when you withdraw it during retirement.

Contributions to Roth IRAs are not deductible, but the long-term tax benefits are enormous.

In 1997, Congress increased the maximum amount of federally adjusted gross income (found on the first page of your tax return) you may earn and still remain eligible for making a contribution to a fully tax deductible IRA. If you are covered by a pension plan, you can make a fully deductible contribution so long as your adjusted gross income is below a certain level. For 1998, the threshold is $30,000 for a single person or $50,000 for a couple. If you're married and are not covered by a pension plan but your spouse is, you can make a fully deductible contribution if your combined income is less than $150,000. If neither you or your spouse (if you're married) are covered by a pension plan, you can make a deductible contribution regardless of your income.

Congress also created Roth IRAs, which, like regular IRAs, allow an individual to contribute $2,000 annually if his or her adjusted gross income is under $95,000; the maximum contribution phases out gradually as income rises to $110,000. Married couples who file joint returns can each invest up to $2,000, so long as their combined adjusted gross income is less than $150,000; their maximum contribution phases out gradually as income rises to $160,000. For example, if the adjusted gross income on a joint return is $155,000, that's halfway through the phaseout zone, so each partner's maximum contribution would be cut in half, to $1,000. (Married taxpayers who file separate returns may not open Roth IRAs.)

The Roth advantage. While contributions to these accounts are not tax-deductible, the long-term tax benefits are enormous: You don't pay any taxes when you take the money out. For nearly all *investors,* Roth IRAs are a much better deal than regular IRAs. (The main exception is investors who plan to leave their money invested for less than about ten years and who, therefore, may benefit more from the initial tax break—the deductibility of contributions—to a regular IRA.) That's because the money you withdraw in retirement from regular IRAs is taxed as ordinary income in your usual tax bracket, so you lose a big chunk of your IRA to Uncle Sam. By contrast, Roth IRAs will never be taxed, no matter how much your money grows before and during retirement.

Moreover, Roth IRAs allow you to decide when to withdraw money in retirement, while strict and complicated rules govern retirement withdrawals from traditional IRAs. Be sure to make the full $2,000-per-individual contribution to a Roth IRA even if you have to cut back a bit on your other retirement savings, including 401(k) or 403(b) plans for which you are not receiving an employer match.

Convert to a Roth? Another option worth considering is to convert your current IRAs to Roth IRAs. This option is available only to individuals *or* married couples whose adjusted gross income is $100,000 or less. You'll have to pay taxes now on your existing IRAs (Uncle Sam lets you spread the cost of these taxes over four years if you convert during 1998), but you'll never have to pay taxes on future earnings. If you can afford to pay those taxes with money from outside your IRAs, and you're roughly 20 years or more away from retirement, you'll probably be better off converting to Roth IRAs.

Early withdrawals. The 1997 Congress also made it easier under most circumstances to take money out of IRAs at any age to pay for college expenses, a first home or certain other expenses without paying the usual 10% early-withdrawal tax penalties. Use these provisions only if absolutely necessary, though. Why? You'll still have to pay taxes on the contributions and earnings you withdraw from a deductible IRA and on the earnings you withdraw from a nondeductible IRA or Roth IRA. (*Note:* Withdrawals from a Roth for a first home can be tax-free.) And the money

(continued on page 61)

Funds' Investment Objectives and Styles

YOU'LL SMOOTH THE volatility of your overall portfolio if you choose funds for your retirement from a variety of investment objectives and, in the case of stock funds, from a cross section of investment styles (see also Part Three, Chapters 13, 14 and 15). An investment objective tells you *what* the fund does; its style tells you *how* it aims to accomplish that objective. Following are thumbnail descriptions of the major investment objectives and styles of stock funds.

Major investment objectives

Aggressive-growth funds try to achieve maximum growth and are usually extremely volatile (meaning their investment results bounce around a lot from month to month and year to year).

Long-term-growth funds also aim for growth, but are less volatile.

International stock funds invest overseas.

Emerging-markets funds invest in foreign countries with underdeveloped economies in regions such as Latin America, Asia and Eastern Europe.

Growth-and-income funds seek both growth and income, and are among the least-volatile stock funds. They may contain bonds as well as stocks.

Balanced funds are the most conservative funds with any stocks in them. Their managers try to earn high yields and decent returns—but take special care to try to avoid big losses.

High-quality bond funds invest in taxable bonds with high credit ratings. They differ from one another primarily on how long it will be until the average bond in their portfolio reaches maturity and pays back to the fund all the money it originally borrowed. The longer a fund's average maturity (the more long-term it is), the more risky it is.

High-yielding bond funds invest in high-yielding, low-quality "junk" bonds. These funds can be nearly as risky as stock funds, but in reasonable quantities they provide diversification and high income.

Municipal bond funds earn tax-exempt income by investing in bonds issued by states and municipalities and their agencies. Most invest in high-quality bonds, but some invest in high-yield bonds. As with taxable bonds, funds with longer average maturities tend to be more risky.

Investing styles of stock funds

Large-company value funds buy stocks of large companies (often household names such as Sears, Ford and Caterpillar) that are selling at low prices relative to their current earnings or assets and are unpopular among most investors, usually because of fears that earnings won't grow rapidly.

Large-company growth funds invest in stocks of large companies with rapidly increasing earnings (such as Coca-Cola, Johnson & Johnson, and Microsoft). These stocks are often glamour issues and sell at high prices relative to their current earnings.

Small-company value funds invest in stocks of small companies that sell at low prices relative to their earnings or assets. Bad news about these neglected companies, such as forecasts of slow earnings growth, is often already reflected in their stock price.

Small-company growth funds invest in stocks of small companies with rapidly growing earnings. These stocks tend to sell at the highest prices relative to their current earnings. They are among the riskiest of all stocks.

won't be there to fund your retirement—which was the whole point of funding an IRA in the first place.

SEP-IRAs

SEP-IRAs are similar to IRAs, but they're for people who are self-employed or who own very small businesses. They allow self-employed people to deduct about 15% of their earnings and put it into a SEP-IRA. The advantage of SEP-IRAs is that they generally let you put away far more tax-deductible income in a tax-sheltered account than do ordinary IRAs.

Keogh plans

Keogh plans are also for people who are self-employed or in partnerships. They allow you to contribute up to 20% of your earnings to a tax-deferred plan. But Keoghs involve more paperwork than SEP-IRAs.

SIMPLE IRAs

SIMPLE IRA plans are for businesses of up to 100 employees that want to offer a 401(k)-like plan without some of the administrative costs. They allow employee contributions of up to $6,000 and employer matches of up to 3% of contributions. They can be a good option for self-employed people.

GETTING STARTED

Start by contributing the maximum to your 401(k) or 403(b) that your employer will match.

Next, fully fund Roth IRAs for yourself and your spouse, if you are eligible.

If you can afford to, contribute the maximum allowed to your 401(k) or 403(b), or to a SEP-IRA, SIMPLE or Keogh plan if you're self-employed. All except the Roth IRAs allow you to stash pretax money in retirement plans. If your combined federal and state tax rates total 35%, by investing pretax money you can put $1,000 into your retirement account for every $650 in after-tax income you forgo. Moreover, the employer match of at least a portion of your contributions to 401(k) and 403(b) plans is too good to pass up. If your company offers a 50% match, based on the preceding example, you could squirrel away $1,500 in your retirement plan for every $650 in after-tax income you forgo.

You've more than doubled your money even before your investment starts growing.

Next, if you're not eligible for a Roth IRA, consider a nondeductible IRA. While you don't get the initial tax break, your money still compounds tax-deferred.

If you need to save even more, think about investing in a tax-managed fund. *Vanguard Tax-Managed Growth & Income* (800–635–1511) is designed to mirror the Standard & Poor's 500-stock index but without producing any taxable capital gains. (For details on how tax-managed funds work, turn to Chapter 21.) Tax-managed funds are ideal for money you can't stash in a tax-deferred account. Make sure, however, that you plan to leave your money invested for 15 to 20 years or more.

Or consider a low-cost variable annuity (see the discussion beginning on page 72).

Step Seven: Put It on Automatic

BY NOW, YOU MAY BE SAYING: ALL THESE IDEAS SOUND wonderful, but where in the world am I going to find the extra money to invest for retirement? Especially if you're already saving for college for your children, extra money is a scarce commodity. No one would suggest that you give up activities you love, such as travel and hobbies. After all, life is short, and there's no point depriving yourself.

We can't help you find extra cash, but we can suggest a way to make saving less painful. As discussed in Chapter 1, many investors have found that the key to investing for retirement is to have money automatically withdrawn from their paychecks. Most mutual funds will debit your checking account for monthly investments in IRAs, SEP-IRAs or taxable accounts.

Step Eight: Choose Your Funds

YOU'LL LIKELY LIVE MANY YEARS IN RETIREMENT, SO YOU'LL tap your money gradually instead of all at once. Because the rate of return on your money must at least keep up with the rate of inflation before and during retirement. you'll want to keep a large portion of it in stock funds. Table A on page 29 indicates what percentage of your retirement assets to put in stock funds based on your risk-tolerance score. But you'll notice that when investing for retirement, I encourage you to put much more money into stock funds than when investing to meet all other goals.

How much you can afford to invest in stock funds as you near retirement and during retirement, however, will also depend in part on how financially secure you are—rather than solely on your time horizon. If you have a generous pension, or a more-than-adequate amount of savings socked away already, you can afford to put more of your money into stocks and keep less in bonds and other lower-risk investments. Even if the stock market suffers a prolonged fall, you'll be able to ride it out comfortably. But if your pension and other retirement savings are meager and you'll be more dependent on income from your investments, invest more conservatively.

> **How much you can afford to invest in stock funds as you near retirement will depend, in part, on how financially secure you are.**

If you aren't financially secure as you near or live in retirement, you may want to reduce by 10% the amount of stock funds the table recommends (see page 29) and invest that money in bond funds instead. Otherwise, a bear market could depress the value of your savings, leaving you in a precarious situation. Conversely, if you are financially quite well off—as you get close to retirement and while living in retirement—I'd suggest you increase the percentage of assets you invested in stocks by 10% over the table's recommendation.

Regardless of your financial wherewithal as you get within a couple of years of retirement and after you retire, be sure to keep enough money in a money-market fund or a low-risk bond fund (such as *Vanguard Municipal Limited Term*) so that—combined with your other sources of income—you can support yourself for two or three years. Do this even if you need to sell some stocks. Such a cushion can help prevent you from having to sell stocks when the market is depressed.

SOME SUGGESTED PORTFOLIOS OF FUNDS

I have devised portfolios that embody these principles of diversification among objectives and styles. The portfolios vary among each other in their aggressiveness. Keep in mind that they are merely suggestions for how to deploy your money. You can build equally good investment plans by choosing other funds that use the same objectives and investment styles (such as those described in Part 4) or by selecting your own funds based on performance, costs, consistency and other factors (to learn how to pick your own funds, see Chapter 15).

In truth, the particular fund you choose is rarely paramount. What *is* important is to pick funds that invest in different types of stocks—small companies, large companies, growth companies, value companies and foreign companies. For that reason, if one of the funds I recommend is closed to new investors by the time you read this book, simply turn to Chapter 17, "Great Stock Funds," and substitute any fund that has the same investment objective and invests in the same type of stocks. For instance, if *Berger New Generation* were closed, you could instead use *PBHG Emerging Growth,* which is also an aggressive-growth fund that specializes in small growth companies.

Moreover, if you are investing for more than one goal at once—say, for retirement and college—you don't have to invest in all the funds listed in the retirement portfolio *and* all the funds listed in the college portfolio. While there's nothing wrong with doing that, you'll have to keep track of a lot of funds. Instead, you might use funds from one of the portfolios, say the retirement portfolio, for both college and retirement. Just earmark the proper proportion of your money for each goal. Also, be sure that for each goal, your percentage of stock funds, bond funds and money-market funds is appropriate given your time horizon and tolerance for risk (see pages 28–29). You can use the same technique to reduce the number of funds you invest in for all your goals. If you can, aim to build one overall portfolio that suits all your needs. However, if one or more

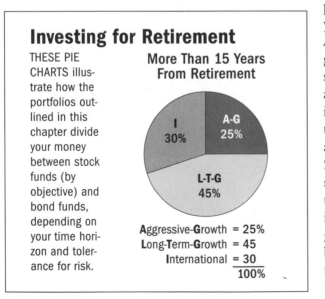

Investing for Retirement

THESE PIE CHARTS illustrate how the portfolios outlined in this chapter divide your money between stock funds (by objective) and bond funds, depending on your time horizon and tolerance for risk.

More Than 15 Years From Retirement

I 30%
A-G 25%
L-T-G 45%

Aggressive-Growth = 25%
Long-Term-Growth = 45
International = 30
100%

of your goals is less than ten years away, be careful not to elimi-nate funds described as "low risk" in the text.

However you put together your retirement portfolio, don't let the proportions of fund types get too out of whack over time. If one fund does so well that it becomes a much bigger part of your portfolio than you had intended, sell some of it and put the proceeds into your lagging funds—or at least redirect your future contributions to the laggards until your allocations are back in line. (See the example of how this works on page 43.) Also, as you get closer to retirement, *gradually* move the appro-priate portion of money from stock funds to bond funds; avoid doing it in one fell swoop.

All the funds are no-load, that is, they have no sales charges. (See Chapter 8 for details on purchasing funds through discount brokers and directly from fund companies.) Since they are decades from retirement, the DiBenedettos chose the portfolio for investors more than 15 years from retirement.

More than 15 years from retirement

Skyline Small Cap Value Plus (15% of your money; 800–458–5222) is an aggressive-growth fund that invests in stocks of small, undervalued companies (for more information on this fund, see page 205).

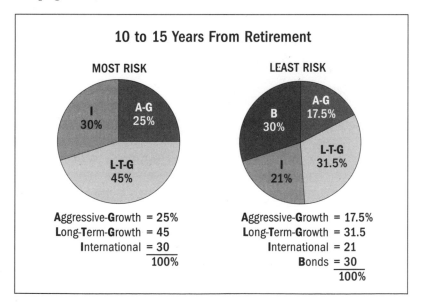

10 to 15 Years From Retirement

MOST RISK

- I 30%
- A-G 25%
- L-T-G 45%

Aggressive-Growth = 25%
Long-Term-Growth = 45
International = 30
100%

LEAST RISK

- B 30%
- A-G 17.5%
- L-T-G 31.5%
- I 21%

Aggressive-Growth = 17.5%
Long-Term-Growth = 31.5
International = 21
Bonds = 30
100%

Berger New Generation (10%; 800–333–1001), an aggressive-growth fund, invests in fast-growing small companies (page 204).
Harbor Capital Appreciation (25%; 800–422–1050) is a long-term-growth fund that hunts for large companies that are growing rapidly (page 212).
Selected American Shares (20%; 800–243–1575) is a long-term-growth fund that invests in stocks of undervalued large companies (page 223).
Artisan International (30%; 800–344–1770) invests in foreign stocks (page 226).

10 to 15 years from retirement

If you had a score of 86 or higher on Table A, "How Much to Invest in Stocks for Retirement," on page 29, your funds and their allocations will remain unchanged from those in the portfolio just discussed. But if you had a lower score, put 20% to 30% of your total portfolio—a little from each of your funds—in *Loomis Sayles Bond*, which holds long-term bonds (the riskier side of bond investing, but more conservative than stocks; see page 236). Investors must purchase shares through a discount broker such as Charles Schwab (800–435–4000).

If you're investing the bond money outside of a retirement account, use *Vanguard Municipal High-Yield* (800–635–1511; see

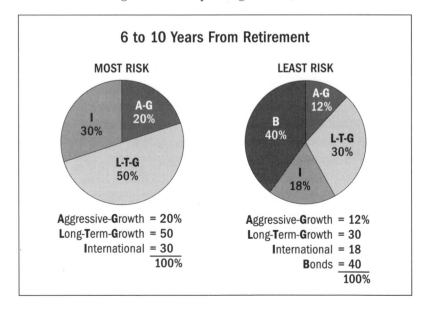

6 to 10 Years From Retirement

MOST RISK

I 30%
A-G 20%
L-T-G 50%

Aggressive-Growth = 20%
Long-Term-Growth = 50
International = 30
100%

LEAST RISK

A-G 12%
B 40%
L-T-G 30%
I 18%

Aggressive-Growth = 12%
Long-Term-Growth = 30
International = 18
Bonds = 40
100%

page 242), a tax-exempt fund that invests in long-term bonds, instead of Loomis Sayles.

Whether in a tax-deferred or taxable account, keep your holdings in the stock funds in the same proportions as before.

Six to ten years from retirement

Invest your stock money as follows:

Berger New Generation (10% of your money; 800–333–1001) is an aggressive-growth fund that buys stocks of fast-growing small companies (for more information on this fund, see page 204).

Skyline Small Cap Value Plus (10% of your money; 800–458–5222) is an aggressive-growth fund that invests in stocks of small, undervalued companies (see page 205).

Montag & Caldwell Growth (25%; 800–992–8151), is a long-term-growth fund that hunts for large, fast-growing companies (see page 214).

Oakmark (25%; 800–625–6275), is a long-term-growth fund that invests in undervalued midsize to large companies (see page 215).

Artisan International (30%; 800–344–1770), invests in foreign stocks (see page 226).

If you had a high score on the risk-tolerance test, continue to invest all your money in stock funds. But if you had a lower score, put 30% to 40% of your total portfolio in *Loomis Sayles*

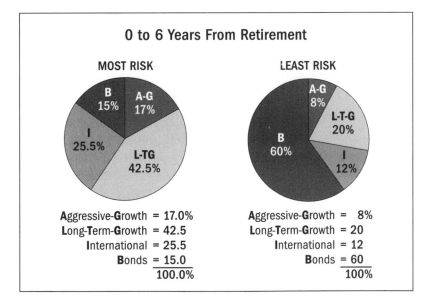

0 to 6 Years From Retirement

MOST RISK

B 15%
A-G 17%
I 25.5%
L-TG 42.5%

Aggressive-Growth = 17.0%
Long-Term-Growth = 42.5
International = 25.5
Bonds = 15.0
100.0%

LEAST RISK

A-G 8%
L-T-G 20%
B 60%
I 12%

Aggressive-Growth = 8%
Long-Term-Growth = 20
International = 12
Bonds = 60
100%

Bond, see page 236, which invests in long-term bonds.

If you're investing in a taxable account, use tax-exempt *Vanguard Municipal High-Yield* (800–635–1511; page 242) instead.

Zero to six years from retirement

Use the same stock funds as in the previous portfolio (for investors who are six to ten years from retirement). Depending on your tolerance for risk (see Table A on page 29), put between 15% and 60% of your money into bond funds, split evenly between *Loomis Sayles Bond* (see page 236), and *Harbor Bond* (800–422–1050; see page 235), a fund that holds bonds with medium-term maturities. If you're investing in a taxable account, instead of using Loomis Sayles and Harbor, divide your bond money between *Vanguard Municipal High-Yield* (800–635–1511; page 242) and *Vanguard Municipal Intermediate-Term*.

Early retirement (up to age 75)

Invest 40% to 65% of your money in bonds, depending on your results from the "How Much to Invest in Stocks" table (page 29). Invest your bond money in the same proportions as in the previous portfolio. Invest your stock money as follows:

T. Rowe Price Equity Income (35%; 800–225–5132), a growth-and-income fund that invests in large, undervalued companies (see

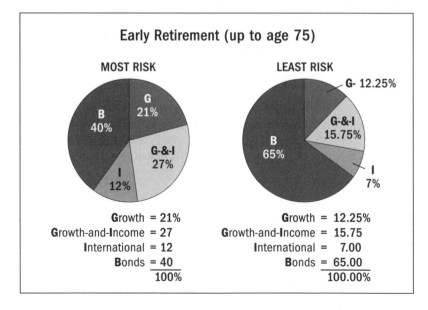

Early Retirement (up to age 75)

MOST RISK

B 40%
G 21%
G-&-I 27%
I 12%

Growth = 21%
Growth-and-Income = 27
International = 12
Bonds = 40
100%

LEAST RISK

G- 12.25%
G-&-I 15.75%
B 65%
I 7%

Growth = 12.25%
Growth-and-Income = 15.75
International = 7.00
Bonds = 65.00
100.00%

page 222 for more information on this fund).

Yacktman (35%; 800–525–8258), a fund that invests in growth stocks but buys them at cheap prices (see page 218).

Greenspring (10%; 800–366–3863), a growth-and-income fund that invests in low-risk, undervalued small companies and high-yielding bonds (see page 225).

Tweedy Browne Global Value (20%; 800–432–4789), a fund that invests in foreign companies (see page 230).

Late retirement (generally ages 75 and older)

Invest 50% to 70% in bonds. Divide your bond money as follows:

Harbor Bond (50%; 800–422–1050), a fund that invests in bonds with medium-term maturities (see page 235).

Vanguard Short-Term Corporate Bond (25%; 800–635–1511), a fund that invests in short-maturity bonds (see page 240).

Loomis Sayles High Yield (25%; 800–633–3330), a high-yielding "junk bond" fund (see page 237).

If your bond money is in a taxable account and your tax bracket is 28% or higher, use the following in place of the first two funds: *Vanguard Municipal Intermediate-Term,* which invests in medium-term tax-exempt bonds (page 242), and *Vanguard Municipal Limited-Term* (page 243), which invests in short-term

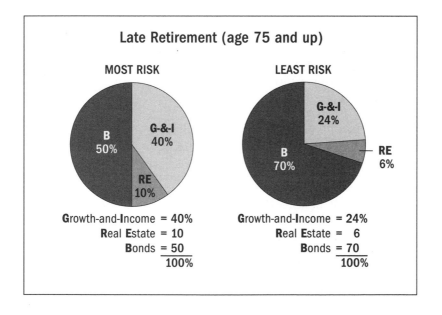

Late Retirement (age 75 and up)

MOST RISK

B 50%
G-&-I 40%
RE 10%

Growth-and-Income = 40%
Real Estate = 10
Bonds = 50
100%

LEAST RISK

G-&-I 24%
B 70%
RE 6%

Growth-and-Income = 24%
Real Estate = 6
Bonds = 70
100%

tax-exempt bonds. Hold on to *Loomis Sayles High Yield* for the income it produces.

Invest your stock money as follows:

T. Rowe Price Equity Income (60%; 800–225–5132), a growth-and-income fund that invests in undervalued large companies (see page 222).

Greenspring (20%; 800–366–3863), a growth-and-income fund that invests in low-risk, undervalued small companies and high-yielding bonds (see page 225).

Fidelity Real Estate (20%; 800–544–8888), a fund that invests only in real estate companies (see page 247).

IF YOUR RETIREMENT PLAN DOESN'T OFFER THESE FUNDS

This chapter gives you a simple way to put together an investment plan for retirement. If your employer-sponsored retirement plan doesn't offer the funds in the suggested portfolios, though, you'll have to do a little more work. Start by looking at the funds listed in Chapters 17 and 18 to see whether they match funds offered in your retirement plan. If they do, you may be able to construct at least part of your portfolio from them, substituting funds that match the investment objectives and styles of those you must replace. Otherwise, you'll want to read Parts Three and Four to learn the ins and outs of picking funds. That way you'll be able to construct a portfolio on your own within the limits of what your 401(k) program offers. You might also ask your employer to add more and better funds. Show your benefits department this chapter if you'd like.

> If your 401(k) plan doesn't offer the funds in the suggested portfolios, you will have to do a little more work.

403(B)S: HOW TO GET OUT OF MEDIOCRE ONES

403(b)s are similar to 401(k) plans, though they are offered only to people who work for nonprofit and educational institutions. Unfortunately, insurance companies dominate the 403(b) market, and most charge high fees—often one percentage point annually more than a mutual fund charges. That's because these insurance companies generally sell variable annuities rather than plain mutual funds to 403(b) members. Over a long period, those extra charges can put a big dent in your retirement savings. Exceptions to this rule include: *TIAA-CREF* (800–223–1200) and

VALIC (800–448–2542) which offer 403(b)s. They also sell annuities, but their costs are low.

Paul DiBenedetto bought into one of the high-priced plans without even knowing it. There were virtually no other options. "I had no idea how much I was paying for the annuity," he says. Fortunately, a list of approved 403(b) vendors for the Arlington, Va., school system included USAA, a solid, low-cost fund company. So he switched his 403(b) savings into USAA funds, and he puts his new 403(b) investments directly into USAA funds. That saves Paul a bushel of money because the funds are not in an annuity and because USAA charges low expenses on its funds.

Insurance companies dominate the 403(b) market. Most charge high fees. Those can put a big dent in your retirement savings.

If you're investing in an annuity in your 403(b) plan, call your benefits department to see if any no-load (no-sales-charge) mutual fund companies are approved vendors at your place of work. Or call a few of the big fund companies, which offer low-cost annuities and good funds, to see if they are approved vendors with your employer. Try Fidelity (800–544–8888), T. Rowe Price (800–638–5660) or Vanguard (800–635–1511). If that fails, ask your employee benefits department if it will add one of these fund companies to its list of approved vendors.

Still no luck? There is one more way, though it's a little more cumbersome and some employers forbid it. Contribute to your employer's plan (if you can, to avoid fees, choose a money-market option) and then transfer the money to a 403(b)(7) custodial account that you set up with a fund. That strategy will keep your money out of an annuity. But be careful to avoid surrender charges; your old company may bill you when you take your money out. Also, find out whether your plan will impose any restrictions. Some plans won't match 403(b) contributions made to an outside mutual fund, and it's not worth transferring your money if you lose a match. If you follow this course, you'll have to arrange the transfers yourself. But it might be well worth the effort. Contact the above-named fund companies to begin the process. Be persistent. Ask specifically for a phone representative who handles 403(b) accounts. Even some 403(b) telephone representatives don't know it's possible. But if you find a good rep, he or she will steer you through the process.

If You've Maxed Out on Tax-Deferred Saving: Variable Annuities?

I F YOU HAVE PUT THE MAXIMUM IN ALL YOUR TAX-DEFERRED retirement accounts (including 401(k)s, 403(b)s, IRAs, Roth IRAs, SEP-IRAs, Keoghs and SIMPLE plans) and you still need to save more for retirement, a variable annuity may be an option. Variable annuities work a lot like nondeductible IRAs. Your contributions are not tax-exempt, but your money compounds tax-deferred until you withdraw it, at which time it is taxed in your top tax bracket. There are important differences, however. One plus of variable annuities is that you can invest as much as you want in them. But there are several minuses:

Expensive insurance you don't need. Variable annuities gain their tax deferral by having a thin layer of insurance wrapped around them. All it insures is that your heirs will get at least as much back as you invested if you die before making withdrawals. Since the stock market tends to go up over time, this is not usually worthwhile insurance. But the insurance costs money, raising the costs of your investment.

Higher taxes. Variable annuities convert capital-gains income, which is taxed at a lower level, into ordinary income, which is taxed at a higher level. If you pay taxes as you go in an ordinary taxable account, most of your earnings are capital gains, which are taxed at a maximum 20% rate for assets held more than 12 months. When you withdraw money from a variable annuity (or an IRA, for that matter), all of it is taxed as ordinary income, which for higher-income taxpayers means the tax rate can be as high as 39.6%.

A high cost at death. Variable annuities are a lousy way to leave money to your heirs. They are heavily taxed upon your death or, depending on how your contract is written, upon the death of both you and your spouse. For that reason, make sure to take your money out of a variable annuity in a stream of income payments that will last throughout your lifetime(s). That's the only way to get their full benefit assuming you don't die too soon—payments stop when you die. Don't use a variable annuity as emergency cash to tap when you need it. And don't plan to leave money in a variable annuity to your children.

All that said, if you are young enough and are already contributing the maximum to all other available retirement plans, variable annuities can be a decent choice for saving more. (You may not have time to overcome the expenses and tax disadvantages unless you start early, before, say, age 45.) Be sure you want a variable annuity before you buy, though. Buying one is a little like getting married: Changing your mind later can be an expensive proposition.

The plans offered by Fidelity, T. Rowe Price and Vanguard are all reasonably priced. Plans sold by insurance agents are almost all too expensive. (If you're already in a poorly performing, overpriced variable annuity, call Fidelity, T. Rowe Price or Vanguard to inquire about a tax-free exchange.)

Unfortunately, most variable annuities are sold rather than bought. Want proof? Half the money in variable annuities is inside tax-deferred retirement accounts, which is a little like wearing a raincoat indoors.

Key Points

- *Get started now.*
- *The worksheet on pages 54–55 will help you determine how much you need to save each month.*
- *Use tax-sheltered retirement plans whenever possible.*
- *Roth IRAs are almost always better than regular IRAs.*
- *Choose a solid mix of funds, like those listed here.*
- *Get out of bad 403(b) plans if you can.*
- *Be wary of variable annuities.*

Investing for College

Or other goals (except for retirement) more than ten years in the future

EW THINGS CAN BE SCARIER TO A PARENT THAN THE thought of simultaneously saving for retirement and trying to salt away enough money to pay the sky-high costs of college one reads about. But here's a secret: Investing for college isn't as difficult as it's made out to be. This chapter will show you how to do it. (The fund mixes on pages 81–83 are also appropriate for any other savings goals *more* than ten years in the future—except for retirement, which was covered in Chapter 5.) If your son or daughter will be going to college in less then ten years—or you'll need money that soon for any reason other than retirement—consult the next chapter, "Investing for the Short-Term." Here's why the hype about college is worse than the reality:

College doesn't cost as much as you might think.
The *average* private college costs about $21,500 annually, and the average state college costs about $10,000 once you include tuition and fees, room and board, books and supplies, transportation, and personal expenses, including visits home. That's not cheap, but it's less than the $33,000 figure bandied about so much, which is the cost of the most expensive private colleges.

College-cost increases are slowing.
For years, college costs rose at annual rates of about 7% to 9%. The main reason: Colleges had too few students, so they made up the difference by charging the students they had higher prices. With baby-boomers' children now reaching college age,

enrollment is climbing and will continue to increase well into the next century. As a result, college-cost increases have dropped to about 5% annually and will likely continue to rise at no more than that rate.

The new education savings plan may help.
In 1997 Congress created a new kind of IRA for education to which parents earning less than $150,000 (or $95,000 for a single parent) may contribute $500 per child. Other relatives may also make contributions—but annual contributions per child from all sources can't total more than $500. While contributions aren't tax-deductible, the earnings on the money are tax-free if used for education. You must withdraw the money by the time your child turns 30. You won't fund college with $500 a year, but it will help.

Congress now also allows you to withdraw money from your own IRA, penalty-free, for college costs (excluding room

What College Will Cost

THE TABLE BELOW gives you an idea of what total college costs will be (tuition and fees, room and board, books and supplies, and personal expenses) assuming costs rise 5% annually. It also takes into account increases during college years. If your child begins school in ten years, for instance, add the annual costs for years ten through 13 to get the total cost. If you think a child will attend an elite private college, use the $33,000 figure. For a state college, use the $10,000 figure. Use the $21,500 number if you're not sure.

TODAY	1 YEAR	2 YEARS	3 YEARS	4 YEARS	5 YEARS	6 YEARS	7 YEARS
$33,000	$34,650	$36,383	$38,203	$40,113	$42,119	$44,225	$46,436
$21,500	22,575	23,704	24,889	26,133	27,440	28,812	30,253
$10,000	10,500	11,025	11,576	12,155	12,763	13,401	14,071

TODAY	8 YEARS	9 YEARS	10 YEARS	11 YEARS	12 YEARS	13 YEARS	14 YEARS
$33,000	$48,758	$51,196	$53,756	$56,444	$59,266	$62,229	$65,340
$21,500	31,766	33,354	35,022	36,773	38,612	40,543	42,570
$10,000	14,775	15,513	16,289	17,103	17,959	18,856	19,799

TODAY	15 YEARS	16 YEARS	17 YEARS	18 YEARS	19 YEARS	20 YEARS	21 YEARS
$33,000	$68,607	$72,037	$75,639	$79,421	$83,392	$87,562	$91,940
$21,500	44,699	46,934	49,281	51,745	54,332	57,049	59,901
$10,000	20,789	21,829	22,920	24,066	25,270	26,533	27,860

and board) for yourself, your spouse, your child or your grand-child. But you will still owe taxes on any deductible contributions and earnings you take out of an IRA to pay college costs.

You don't have to pay the full sticker price.
More than half of families receive a discount on college costs based on their ability to pay—and you needn't be poor to qualify. A family with a $50,000 income will almost certainly qualify for generous assistance for a child attending an expensive private college—even with significant assets, such as $150,000 in home equity and $50,000 in mutual funds. And a family with two children at such a college should qualify for aid even with a $100,000 income.

Non-need-based aid is available from colleges, too. A 1996 study by the National Association of College and University Business Officers found that 60% to 82% of freshmen were receiving some sort of institutional grant that reduced college tuition by 28% to 38%. Many of those grants were not based on need, but rather targeted students who might otherwise not enroll.

You don't have to save everything in advance.
A typical student can borrow $17,125 over four years, sometimes with no interest payments on the loan during college years. Larger loans are available to parents to cover the balance. Plus, many students work part-time during college.

How Much Should You Save?

WHILE THERE'S NO ONE-SIZE-FITS-ALL ANSWER TO THE question of how much to save, you'll likely be in great shape if you save 75% of what you'll need for college—and in good shape if you save 50%—by the time your son or daughter is halfway through college. You don't need all your child's college money saved by freshman year. Once you've completed the worksheet below, you'll have a better idea of how much to save.

The key to investing for college, as for other goals, is to automate your investing: Have money withdrawn monthly from your checking account and sent directly to a mutual fund.

What You Should Save Each Month

THE TABLE ON page 75 gives you a good idea of total college costs for one child anywhere from one to 21 years from now. After you've found your estimated costs on the table, complete the following worksheet to get an idea of how much to save monthly.

A. Savings goal
Multiply your anticipated college costs from the table on page 75 by the percentage of costs you want to have saved in advance. If you don't know, pick a number between 50% and 100%. The DiBenedettos picked 50% for Paul Jr. He will start college in 15 years, so adding the costs for that year and the following three years—$44,699 plus $46,934 plus $49,281 plus $51,745—means his total college will be $192,659.

Your expected college cost x _____ % = $_____

B. Estimate your investment return
If most or all of your money is in stocks (based on Table B, "How Much to Invest in Stocks for All Goals *Except* Retirement," on page 29) you can expect to earn about 10% annually. If you're investing more conservatively, with 55% to 70% in stocks, figure a return of 7.5% annually. The DiBenedettos have all their college money in stocks; they're estimating a 9.5% annual return.

Your estimated investment return_____%

C. Figure your after-tax return
Multiply your pretax return by 1 minus your highest tax rate. For instance, the DiBenedettos are in the 28% federal tax bracket and pay a 6% state income tax, so their after-tax return on a 9.5% investment is: $1 - 0.34 = 0.66 \times 0.095 = 0.0627$, or 6.3%.

1 – _____ your federal tax bracket –_____ your state income tax
x _____% (from Step B) =_____%

D. Count what you've already saved
Take any money you've already accumulated for college and find out what it will be worth by the time your son or daughter is halfway through college (see the table on page 78). Subtract this number from your "Savings Goal" (Step A) to determine what you still need to save. The DiBenedettos haven't saved anything yet.

$_____your savings goal (from Step A) – $_____ your savings to date
= $_____what you still need to save

E. Determine your monthly savings
Paul Jr., 2½, will be roughly halfway through college some 17 years from now. On the table on page 10 (Chapter 1), the DiBenedettos found where 17 years intersected with 6% (the closest whole percentage point to 6.3%; see Step C, above). The result is $28—what they need to save monthly to end up with $10,000. By dividing $10,000 into $96,000, the total amount they want to save, and multiplying the result by $28, the DiBenedettos know they need to save $269 monthly for college for Paul Jr.

$_____total amount you want to save ÷ $10,000 x
$_____monthly amount needed to save $10,000 (from table on page 10)
= $_____amount you need to save monthly to achieve your goal

Also take a minute to flip to the table on pages 10–11 (in Chapter 1) showing how long it takes to save $10,000 at different rates of return. You can see the importance of earning a high return, sure, but the table also vividly shows how much it helps to start saving and investing early. If you have 20 years to save $10,000 and assume you'll earn an 11% return, you have to invest only $12 per month. But you won't be able to invest wholly in stock funds for the entire time you're saving for college. As

What You've Saved Already

HAVE YOU ALREADY put some money aside for your children's college? If so, you have a big head start. The table below illustrates how much $1,000 will grow to at different rates of return, depending on how many years you have until you'll need the money.

(For an idea of what return you can expect to earn on your money, see the discussion in the text above.)

Saved more than $1,000? Find the number at the intersection of the rate of return you expect and the number of years you

| | RATES OF RETURN | | | | | | |
YEARS	5%	5.5%	6%	6.5%	7%	7.5%	8%
1	$1,050	$1,055	$1,060	$1,065	$1,070	$1,075	$1,080
2	1,103	1,113	1,124	1,134	1,145	1,156	1,166
3	1,158	1,174	1,191	1,208	1,225	1,242	1,260
4	1,216	1,239	1,262	1,286	1,311	1,335	1,360
5	1,276	1,307	1,338	1,370	1,403	1,436	1,469
6	1,340	1,379	1,419	1,459	1,501	1,543	1,587
7	1,407	1,455	1,504	1,554	1,606	1,659	1,714
8	1,477	1,535	1,594	1,655	1,718	1,783	1,851
9	1,551	1,619	1,689	1,763	1,838	1,917	1,999
10	1,629	1,708	1,791	1,877	1,967	2,061	2,159
11	1,710	1,802	1,898	1,999	2,105	2,216	2,332
12	1,796	1,901	2,012	2,129	2,252	2,382	2,518
13	1,886	2,006	2,133	2,267	2,410	2,560	2,720
14	1,980	2,116	2,261	2,415	2,579	2,752	2,937
15	2,079	2,232	2,397	2,572	2,759	2,959	3,172
16	2,183	2,355	2,540	2,739	2,952	3,181	3,426
17	2,292	2,485	2,693	2,917	3,159	3,419	3,700
18	2,407	2,621	2,854	3,107	3,380	3,676	3,996
19	2,527	2,766	3,026	3,309	3,617	3,951	4,316
20	2,653	2,918	3,207	3,524	3,870	4,248	4,661
21	2,786	3,078	3,400	3,753	4,141	4,566	5,034

you get closer to the time you'll need the money, you'll want to put more and more into safer, but lower-returning, bonds and money-market funds. So your return over 20 years—even if you start by investing aggressively—is likely to be about 10%. Conservative investors will likely earn closer to 7.5%.

If you have only ten years, you'll have to invest nearly four times as much—$46 per month at 11%, but you might want to assume a return of 8.5% if you're an aggressive investor with ten

have to invest. Then multiply that number by the multiple of $1,000 that you've saved. For instance, if you've saved $15,000 already and anticipate earning 8% on that money over 20 years, find the point where 8% and 20 years intersect, and multiply the result ($4,661) by 15 ($15,000 divided by $1,000), which equals $69,915. When you've finished, insert the result in line D of the worksheet on page 77.

			RATES OF RETURN				
8.5%	9%	9.5%	10%	10.5%	11%	11.5%	12%
$1,085	$1,090	$1,095	$1,100	$1,105	$1,110	$1,115	$1,120
1,177	1,188	1,199	1,210	1,221	1,232	1,243	1,254
1,277	1,295	1,313	1,331	1,349	1,368	1,386	1,405
1,386	1,412	1,438	1,464	1,491	1,518	1,546	1,574
1,504	1,539	1,574	1,611	1,647	1,685	1,723	1,762
1,631	1,677	1,724	1,772	1,820	1,870	1,922	1,974
1,770	1,828	1,888	1,949	2,012	2,076	2,143	2,211
1,921	1,993	2,067	2,144	2,223	2,305	2,389	2,476
2,084	2,172	2,263	2,358	2,456	2,558	2,664	2,773
2,261	2,367	2,478	2,594	2,714	2,839	2,970	3,106
2,453	2,580	2,714	2,853	2,999	3,152	3,311	3,479
2,662	2,813	2,971	3,138	3,314	3,498	3,692	3,896
2,888	3,066	3,254	3,452	3,662	3,883	4,117	4,363
3,133	3,342	3,563	3,797	4,046	4,310	4,590	4,887
3,400	3,642	3,901	4,177	4,471	4,785	5,118	5,474
3,689	3,970	4,272	4,595	4,941	5,311	5,707	6,130
4,002	4,328	4,678	5,054	5,460	5,895	6,363	6,866
4,342	4,717	5,122	5,560	6,033	6,544	7,095	7,690
4,712	5,142	5,609	6,116	6,666	7,263	7,911	8,613
5,112	5,604	6,142	6,727	7,366	8,062	8,821	9,646
5,547	6,109	6,725	7,400	8,140	8,949	9,835	10,804

SOURCE: KAREN KRATZER, CFA

or fewer years to go, and a return of 6% if you're a conservative investor. By the time you are two or three years from needing your money, you shouldn't expect to earn more than 5% or so annually.

Nancy and Paul DiBenedetto aren't overly concerned about the costs of college for their children, Paul Jr., age 2½, and a second child they're expecting. Nancy finished getting her master's degree in health administration from the University of Maryland in 1997, so she knows the ins and outs of paying for education. She was lucky, too. Her employer paid $2,000 per year of her tuition—more than half of what it cost her, so she graduated without taking out any loans.

As for the children, Nancy says, "The bottom line is, we want them to go where they want to go. That's why it's so important to save as much money as possible. But I'm not worried about it. Whatever money we have, we'll be able to offer to them. But it still may mean taking out loans depending on what colleges they want to go to."

Nancy and Paul are saving $269 per month for college. They aim to save $96,000 for Paul Jr.'s college, which would pay

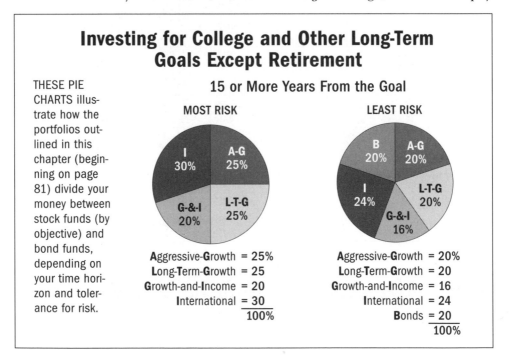

Investing for College and Other Long-Term Goals Except Retirement

THESE PIE CHARTS illustrate how the portfolios outlined in this chapter (beginning on page 81) divide your money between stock funds (by objective) and bond funds, depending on your time horizon and tolerance for risk.

15 or More Years From the Goal

MOST RISK

- I 30%
- A-G 25%
- G-&-I 20%
- L-T-G 25%

Aggressive-Growth = 25%
Long-Term-Growth = 25
Growth-and-Income = 20
International = 30
　　　　　　　　100%

LEAST RISK

- B 20%
- A-G 20%
- I 24%
- G-&-I 16%
- L-T-G 20%

Aggressive-Growth = 20%
Long-Term-Growth = 20
Growth-and-Income = 16
International = 24
Bonds = 20
　　　　　　100%

half the four-year bill at an average private college starting in 2013. Nor do they worry about saving "too much" for college. Unfortunately, there's a dangerous notion afoot that parents are penalized for saving for college. In fact, college-aid formulas place much more weight on your annual income than they do on your assets. Of your taxable savings, roughly the first $20,000 (for a young single parent) to the first $70,000 (for a two-parent family where one parent is 65 or older) isn't even considered in calculating what share you should pay of your children's college education. Amounts above those are tapped at a maximum of 5.6% annually so long as assets are held in a parent's name.

The Portfolios

FOLLOWING ARE TWO PORTFOLIOS—ONE FOR PEOPLE SUCH AS the DiBenedettos whose son is more than 15 years from college, and the other for people with children ten to 15 years from college. Bear in mind that I've designed these portfolios for children who will be *halfway* through college in more than 15 years or ten to 15 years, respectively. These two portfo-

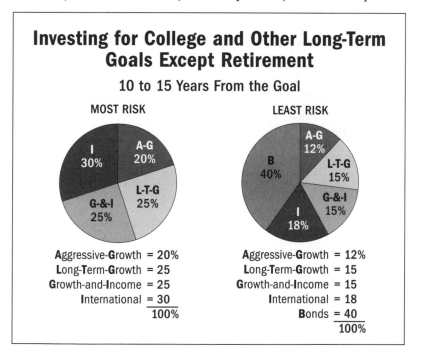

Investing for College and Other Long-Term Goals Except Retirement

10 to 15 Years From the Goal

MOST RISK

- I 30%
- A-G 20%
- L-T-G 25%
- G-&-I 25%

Aggressive-Growth = 20%
Long-Term-Growth = 25
Growth-and-Income = 25
International = 30
100%

LEAST RISK

- A-G 12%
- L-T-G 15%
- G-&-I 15%
- I 18%
- B 40%

Aggressive-Growth = 12%
Long-Term-Growth = 15
Growth-and-Income = 15
International = 18
Bonds = 40
100%

lios are also suited for any other goals more than 15 years in the future or ten to 15 years in the future, respectively. (Fund mixes for college and other goals less than ten years away are in the following chapter). Remember that the portfolios in these chapters are only ideas; you can do just as well by picking a variety of funds from Chapter 17, or by using other top-performing funds.

Also keep in mind, if you are investing for more than one goal at once—say, college and retirement—you don't need to buy each fund in each portfolio. Instead, you can use funds from one of the portfolios, say the retirement portfolio, for both college and retirement. Just be sure that for your college savings, your percentage of stock funds, bond funds and money-market funds is appropriate given your time horizon and tolerance for risk.

15 OR MORE YEARS FROM THE GOAL

Westcore Small-Cap Opportunity (15% of your money; 800–392–2673) is an aggressive-growth fund that invests in stocks of small, undervalued companies (for more information on this fund, see page 208).

Berger New Generation (10%; 800–333–1001) is an aggressive-growth fund that invests in fast-growing small companies (see page 204).

Harbor Capital Appreciation (25%; 800–422–1050) is a long-term-growth fund that hunts for large companies that are growing rapidly (page 212).

Babson Value (20%; 800–422–2766) is a growth-and-income fund that invests in stocks of undervalued large companies (page 219).

Artisan International (30%; 800–344–1770) invests in foreign stocks (page 226).

If Table B, "How Much to Invest in Stocks for All Goals Except Retirement," on page 29 indicates you should own some bond funds, keep the above stock funds in the same proportions, but use *Loomis Sayles Bond* (or, if you're investing in a taxable account and your tax bracket is 28% or higher, *Vanguard Municipal High-Yield*) for the bond portion of your investment plan. You can find more information on these two funds on pages 236 and 242 respectively.

10 TO 15 YEARS FROM THE GOAL

Berger New Generation (10% of your money; 800–333–1001) is an

aggressive-growth fund that buys stocks of fast-growing small companies (for more information on this fund, see page 204).
Third Avenue Small Cap (10%; 800–443–1021) is an aggressive-growth fund that invests in undervalued small companies (see page 217).
Harbor Capital Appreciation (25%; 800–422–1050) is a long-term-growth fund that hunts for large, fast-growing companies (see page 212).
Dodge & Cox Stock (25%; 800–621–3979) is a growth-and-income fund that invests in undervalued large companies (see page 221).
Artisan International (30%; 800–344–1770) invests in foreign stocks (see page 226).

If Table B on page 29 indicates you should own some bond funds, keep the above stock funds in the same proportions, but use *Loomis Sayles Bond* (or, if you're investing in a taxable account and your tax bracket is 28% or higher, *Vanguard Municipal High-Yield*) for the bond portion of your investment plan (see pages 236 and 242).

Whose Name Should You Save In?

THE TAX CODE GIVES YOU A BREAK FOR SAVING IN YOUR children's names. In 1998, the first $700 of investment income earned in a child's name each year is tax-free. Assuming your child is in the 15% tax bracket, as most are, the next $700 is taxed at 15% (just 10% if it's a long-term capital gain). Anything more than that first $1,400 is taxed at your rate when your child is under 14. After your child turns 14, moreover, everything after the first tax-free $700 is taxed at his or her rate, so you may save even more on taxes.

To save in your child's name, check the box on a fund application form that indicates you want to open a custodial account, and then fill in the box that says you want to open a Uniform Gift to Minors Act (UGMA)/Uniform Transfer to Minors Act (UTMA) account. Then fill in the box that tells what state the child lives in. Be aware, though, that some states allow children to do as they please with the money as soon as they turn 18; others make them wait until they're 21. If given the option, always choose 21. This will help avoid the dreaded Ferrari scenario, in which your child gets his or her hands on tens of thousands of dollars and instead of college—well, you get the idea. For assistance in completing the form, see Chapter 8 or call the fund's toll-free number.

The other drawback to putting money in your child's name is that college-aid formulas consider 35% of a student's savings to be available each year to pay for college. If you save in your name, no more than 5.6% of your assets will be considered available annually to pay for college.

HERE'S HOW TO DECIDE

If your taxable income is $100,000 or more, you'll probably be better off saving in your child's name. That's because you're unlikely to qualify for much financial aid in any event.

If you're in the 15% tax bracket, you'll get little tax break from saving in your children's name(s), so you might as well keep the money in your name.

Anywhere in between is a tougher call. Consider how responsible your child is likely to be at age 18 or 21, and guesstimate what your income and tax bracket will be when your child reaches college age. Then use your best judgment.

Key Points

- *Investing for college is not as hard as it's made out to be because you may not have to pay full price, your child's college will likely cost less than the highest-cost schools, college-cost increases are slowing, and you don't need to save everything before your child's freshman year.*
- *Invest in solid portfolios of funds, like those listed above. The fund mixes in this chapter are also useful for other long-term goals.*
- *Use the worksheets to help you figure out how much you need to save each month for college.*
- *Whether you should save in your name or your child's name depends largely on your income.*

Investing for the Short-Term

Portfolios for intermediate- and short-term goals other than retirement

ITH TEN YEARS OR LESS TO INVEST TOWARD A goal, you'll want to be more conservative than when investing for longer periods. That means you'll need a mix of stock funds and bond funds. And the stocks funds you buy should be more conservative than the ones listed in the previous two chapters for longer-term goals. If the overall market crashes, your stock funds will still go down, but probably not nearly as far as the market averages.

Following are portfolios for goals up to ten years away. If you're investing for longer periods or for retirement, you'll want to read Chapters 5 and 6. The portfolios in this chapter are ideal for saving for college, a new house, a car—in fact, any relatively short-term goal except retirement.

Note that if you're now ten years from your goal, you'll want to readjust your portfolio every few years. For instance, when you have only six years to go, switch to the appropriate portfolio provided below. Another adjustment makes sense when you are two to four years from your goal. These shorter-term portfolios emphasize bond funds and low-risk stock funds. While they are less risky, they probably won't earn the high returns that an all-stock portfolio can.

The funds listed in this chapter are only suggestions. You can construct equally solid portfolios by choosing other funds that use the same objectives and investment styles (see Chapters (17 and 18) or by identifying your own funds (see Chapter 15).

For goals six to ten years in the future
Depending on your tolerance for risk and Table B, "How Much to Invest in Stocks for All Goals *Except* Retirement," on page 29, invest 10% to 45% of your money in bonds. Put half your bond money in *Loomis Sayles Bond* (800–633–3330; see page 236 for more information on this fund) and the rest in *Harbor Bond* (800–422–1050; see page 235).

If you're investing in a taxable account and are in the 28% tax bracket or higher, split your bond money instead between *Vanguard Municipal High Yield* (800–635–1511; page 242) and *Vanguard Municipal Intermediate Term*.

Allocate any stock-fund money as follows:

T. Rowe Price Equity Income (35%; 800–225–5132), a low-risk, growth-and-income fund that buys undervalued large companies (page 222).

Yacktman (30%; 800–525–8258), a long-term-growth fund, which invests in undervalued mid-to-large size companies (page 218).

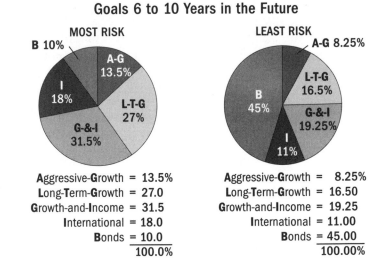

Investing for Intermediate and Short-Term Goals Other Than Retirement

THESE PIE CHARTS illustrate how the portfolios outlined in this chapter divide your money between stock funds (by fund objective) bond funds and money-market funds, depending on your time horizon and tolerance for risk.

Goals 6 to 10 Years in the Future

MOST RISK
B 10%
A-G 13.5%
L-T-G 27%
G-&-I 31.5%
I 18%

Aggressive-Growth = 13.5%
Long-Term-Growth = 27.0
Growth-and-Income = 31.5
International = 18.0
Bonds = 10.0
100.0%

LEAST RISK
A-G 8.25%
L-T-G 16.5%
B 45%
G-&-I 19.25%
I 11%

Aggressive-Growth = 8.25%
Long-Term-Growth = 16.50
Growth-and-Income = 19.25
International = 11.00
Bonds = 45.00
100.00%

T. Rowe Price Small Cap Stock (15%; 800–225–5132), an aggressive growth fund that buys stocks of small companies (page 206).
Tweedy Browne Global Value (20%; 800–432–4789), a relatively low-risk fund, which invests in foreign stocks (page 230).

For goals four to six years in the future

Bond funds will make up 40% to 70% of your total investments, depending on where you fit in the "How Much to Invest in Stocks" table on page 29. Put one-quarter of your bond money in high-yielding *Northeast Investors Trust* (800–225–6704; see page 238 for more information on this fund). Invest the remainder in *Harbor Bond* (800–422–1050; see page 235) or, if you're investing in a taxable account and are in the 28% tax bracket or higher, in *Vanguard Municipal Intermediate-Term* (800–635–1511; page 242).

Allocate your stock money as follows:

T. Rowe Price Equity Income (60%; 800–225–5132), a low-risk, growth-and-income fund that invests in large companies (see page 222).
Royce Premier (20%; 800–221–4268), a low-risk fund despite its classification as an aggressive-growth fund. It invests in under-

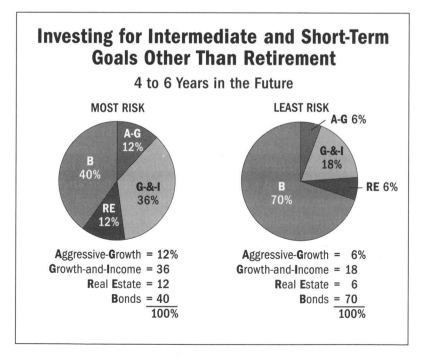

Investing for Intermediate and Short-Term Goals Other Than Retirement

4 to 6 Years in the Future

MOST RISK

A-G 12%
B 40%
G-&-I 36%
RE 12%

LEAST RISK

A-G 6%
G-&-I 18%
B 70%
RE 6%

Aggressive-Growth =	12%
Growth-and-Income =	36
Real Estate =	12
Bonds =	40
	100%

Aggressive-Growth =	6%
Growth-and-Income =	18
Real Estate =	6
Bonds =	70
	100%

valued small companies (page 207).

CGM Realty Fund (20%; 800–345–4048), which invests in real estate companies, which are fairly low risk (page 247).

For goals two to four years in the future

Divide your bond money—between 65% and 90% of your investments—evenly among *Harbor Bond* (800–422–1050; see page 235), *Loomis Sayles High Yield* (800–633–3330; page 237), and *Vanguard Short-Term Corporate* (800–635–1511; page 240). If you're investing in a taxable account and your tax bracket is 28% or higher, use *Loomis Sayles High Yield,* but substitute *Vanguard Municipal Intermediate-Term* (800–635–1511; page 242) and *Vanguard Municipal Limited-Term* (page 243) for the other two funds.

Divide your stock money as follows:

Greenspring (65%; 800–366–3863), a very low-risk balanced fund which invests in undervalued stocks and bonds (page 225).

Fidelity Real Estate (35%; 800–544–8888), which invests in real estate companies, which are fairly low risk (page 247).

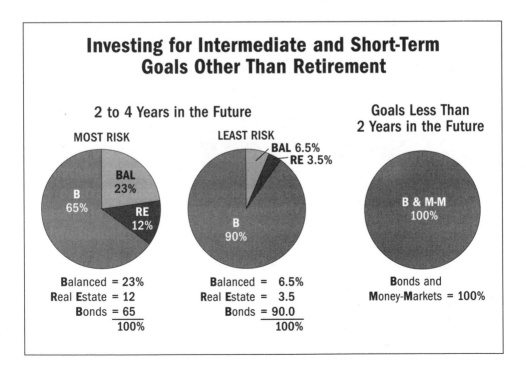

Investing for Intermediate and Short-Term Goals Other Than Retirement

2 to 4 Years in the Future

MOST RISK

BAL 23%
B 65%
RE 12%

LEAST RISK

BAL 6.5%
RE 3.5%
B 90%

Balanced	= 23%
Real Estate	= 12
Bonds	= 65
	100%

Balanced	= 6.5%
Real Estate	= 3.5
Bonds	= 90.0
	100%

Goals Less Than 2 Years in the Future

B & M-M 100%

Bonds and
Money-Markets = 100%

For goals less than two years in the future

Invest your money as follows:

Strong Advantage (50%; 800–368–1030), an ultra-short-term bond fund (see page 239). If you're in the 28% tax bracket or higher, substitute *Vanguard Municipal Limited-Term* (800–635–1511; see page 243).

Vanguard Money Market Prime (50%; 800–635–1511), a money-market fund. If you are in the 39.6% tax bracket, substitute *Vanguard Municipal Money Market.* (For more on money-market funds, see pages 241–242.)

Key Points

- *These portfolios are appropriate for shorter-term goals than those listed in the previous two chapters.*
- *The closer you are to needing your money, the more conservative you'll want to be. That means putting less in stock funds and more in bond funds and money-market funds.*

How and Where to Buy Funds

Filling out fund application forms, tracking your funds' progress, using a mutual fund "supermarket," and transferring retirement accounts to funds

 HEN I DROPPED BY THE DIBENEDETTOS IN LATE spring, their condominium looked surprisingly spacious. Nancy explained that it was on the market and the real estate agent had suggested rearranging some furniture to make it look bigger. The couple had decided the two-bedroom condo was just too small.

Over in a corner of the living room, Paul had neatly stacked a growing pile of investment literature—prospectuses, annual reports and account applications—they had received from funds, based on my suggestion of investment choices for Paul Jr.'s college and for their retirement. (For details on the funds, see Chapters 5 and 6.) It wouldn't be a neat stack for long, though. On this Saturday afternoon, Paul Jr., not yet 3, found playing with the forms more interesting than watching Barney on television. With Paul Jr. "helping," Nancy and Paul began to fill out the forms.

Almost immediately, Nancy complained about the growing quantity of junk mail they had been receiving since they called the fund companies' toll-free numbers to request applications. "They send us this all the time," Nancy says. "It's just more and more paper in the mail. Who has time to go through all this? I just want to invest quickly and get it over with.

I am beginning to feel a little uneasy. Here I am on a mission to show how easy it is for beginners to invest in funds, and Paul and Nancy are finding it harder than I thought they would. "Well," I tell them, "there is an even simpler way. Let's see if you can buy your funds through a discount broker."

Buying Through a Discount Broker

O NE OF THE NICE THINGS ABOUT THE FINANCIAL-SERVICES industry is that, because there is so much competition, you can reach many discount brokers in the evenings and on weekends.

Charles Schwab

For starters, I called Charles Schwab (800–435–4000; www. schwab.com), which runs the biggest "mutual fund supermarket" in terms of total client dollars invested. (All transaction fees listed in the following discussion are for buying and selling over the phone unless otherwise noted.)

The Schwab program gives you access to some 2,300 funds, just under half without any sales charges or transaction fees. The other funds are available for relatively low transaction fees—a minimum of $39. As long as you don't plan to buy or sell often, that's not much to pay for the convenience of getting one consolidated monthly statement for all your funds and being spared an avalanche of mail from fund companies.

Schwab, the Neiman Marcus of discount brokers, also shines when it comes to service. Schwab provides probably the best telephone service of any discount broker.

Another big plus: Schwab provides a free annual tax summary for all funds you've sold in the previous year. This can save a lot of time and aggravation when doing your taxes (see Chapter 9 for details on doing your fund taxes).

And, more

Fidelity Discount Brokerage (800–544–8888; www.fidelity.com) offers Fidelity funds without transaction fees—something you can't find anywhere else. Overall, the brokerage offers 1,300 no-load funds, three-fifths of them without a transaction fee. Fidelity's service is fairly good, and its transaction fees, as of this

---

Sales Charges and Transaction Fees

DISCOUNT BROKERS sell mostly funds that have no sales charges, although you can buy load funds (as well as stocks and bonds) from them if you wish. On many funds without sales charges, a discount broker charges you nothing: The fund pays the broker to sell the fund. On some other no-load funds, however, discount brokers assess investors a small transaction fee—less than 1.0% of the amount you invest except on very small purchases. The difference between a sales charge and a transaction fee may seem like a distinction without a difference—either way you're paying money to buy a fund. But keep this in mind: Sales charges tend to be much, much higher than transaction fees.

---

writing, are slightly lower than Schwab's: The company charges a minimum of $35. Fidelity also provides its customers a free yearly tax summary.

Jack White (800–233–3411; www.jackwhiteco.com) is the Kmart of discount brokers: Don't expect a lot of patient explanations. But it's hard to beat the selection and the price. San Diego–based White offers nearly 2,200 no-load funds, three-fifths without any transaction fees. On funds for which it does assess transaction fees, Jack White charges a flat $27, regardless of the size of the trade. The firm does not provide yearly tax summaries, so it makes the most sense for tax-deferred accounts, which require little record keeping.

Waterhouse Securities (800–431–3500; www.waterhouse.com) offers 1,300 no-load funds with no transaction fees and 6,700 load and no-load funds with a flat $25 fee. Like Jack White, Waterhouse is a bargain-basement operation. No hand-holding here either. Waterhouse doesn't provide yearly tax summaries.

SHOPPING STRATEGY

Prices, selections and services change so frequently that you'll find it worthwhile to call all four of these brokers—and perhaps a few of those listed below. Find out which one currently has the best deals and offers more of the funds you want without fees. If you reach the brokers via the Internet, your brokerage transaction fees, if any, may be even lower. Other brokerages, such as AmeriTrade (www.ameritrade.com), E*Trade (www.etrade.com),

Datek (www.datek.com) and SureTrade (www.suretrade.com) operate primarily or exclusively over the Internet. They tend to offer few frills but charge even lower prices.

Whether you use the Internet or the telephone, be sure *not* to limit yourself to no-transaction-fee funds. Funds that charge a low transaction fee are sometimes better than their no-fee competitors—and very often cheaper (in terms of annual expenses), because they don't pay discounters to hawk them. If you are buying and holding for a long period, as all savvy investors should, the small transaction fee will make very little difference.

If you pay a $25 transaction fee on a $100 investment every month, you're paying a 25% transaction fee— a huge drag on your returns.

Unfortunately for Nancy and Paul, Schwab and its lower-cost competitors levy transaction fees on every purchase of several funds they want to invest in. While a small fee on a one-time or occasional basis isn't a big deal, such a fee charged every month on a purchase of only $50 to $200 *is* a big deal. If a fund charges you a $50 fee for investing $50,000, that equals just one-tenth of one percent. But if you pay a $25 fee on a $100 investment every month, you're paying a 25% transaction fee—a huge drag on your returns. So Paul and Nancy went back to filling in the forms from the fund companies. They made it through the forms for four funds in about 30 minutes. Once they had begun, they didn't find it all that difficult— even with Paul Jr.'s help.

Step by Step Through the Forms

APPLICATIONS FORMS PARTICULARLY FOR REGULAR, TAXABLE accounts, usually aren't difficult to fill out—and you can always call the fund's toll-free number if you get stuck. Most application forms will be similar, and in this section, I discuss the elements that you can expect to find on any company's forms.

STEP ONE: WHOSE ACCOUNT?

Step One asks you to fill in your name and social security number. If you're opening an individual account, or an account you'll own jointly with your spouse or someone else, that's easy. Nancy is investing for Paul Jr.'s college, however, which is a little trickier. The DiBenedettos have already decided to put the money in Paul Jr.'s name under the Uniform Gift to Minors Act/Uniform Transfer to Minors Act (UGMA/UTMA), as described on pages 83–84. Nancy can't find a box to fill in her choice, and is flummoxed that she's stuck on Step One. "Instead of going through all this, I would rather have someone sit down with me and say, 'This is what this means. This is what that means,'" she says. I try to let her find her own way, and soon she figures out she needs to fill out the box for a custodial account. She lists herself as the custodian (the one who can move the money around until Paul Jr. comes of age). Paul Sr. could have listed himself as custodian if the couple had preferred, but only one adult can be listed as custodian. The form also requires Paul Jr.'s social security number and date of birth.

STEP TWO: WHERE ARE YOU?

Step Two requires your address and statement of citizenship. The fund company usually asks for your day and evening phone numbers. These are optional; leave them blank if you like. It's not a bad idea to list your work phone number, however. If you make a mistake on your application, the fund company can call and clear it up. I have never had a fund company call me for any other reason, much less to sell products.

STEP THREE: WHICH FUNDS?

Step Three asks you to select your funds. Make sure that you list each fund by its precise name. Many funds within the same fund family have very similar names. For instance, Vanguard has a fund called Windsor and another called Windsor II.

Be sure to write your personal check (no traveler's checks or third-party checks) and fill in the blank on the form for at least the minimum initial investment required. Minimum investments range from $100 to $100,000, but typically are between $1,000 and $3,000. As discussed earlier, if you can't afford the minimum, many funds will let you start with less so long as you join an automatic investment plan (see Step

---

Mutual Fund Mail

IF YOU DON'T WANT to receive a bunch of mailings from the mutual fund companies you contact, ask them not to mail you anything except the prospectus and application. Many fund companies will honor such a request.

Five, below). Funds also usually have lower initial minimums for IRAs, generally $500 to $1,000.

STEP FOUR: TO RECEIVE OR REINVEST?

Step Four asks you how you want your capital gains and dividends handled. Unless you check one of the boxes indicating that you want your dividends or capital gains paid in cash, the fund will reinvest your dividends and capital gains in additional shares. I discuss the reinvesting your dividends and capital gains on page 103.

STEP FIVE: FLIPPING THE SWITCH

Step Five contains instructions on how to set up an automatic investment plan, allowing the fund to automatically debit your checking account every month for an amount of money you specify, down to a minimum set by the fund company. You'll have to fill in bank information and attach a voided check.

STEP SIX: CHECK WRITING

Step Six gives directions on how to set up check-writing if you are opening a money-market or bond-fund account. Check writing is a valuable convenience in a money-market fund, but to avoid tax headaches you may not want to use it for bond funds (see page 109 for details). If you need money from a bond fund, you may minimize tax headaches by transferring a relatively large amount, say $5,000, to a money-market fund in the same fund family, then writing checks on the money-market fund. That way you'll have only one taxable sale to report to the IRS, rather than the several you would have to report if you wrote checks on your bond fund. You usually can't write money-market checks for less than $250 or $500, though some funds are beginning to offer lower check-writing minimums.

STEP SEVEN: OTHER CONVENIENCES

Step Seven gives you the option to sell one fund and buy another one in the same fund family simply by calling the fund company's toll-free number. You can also redeem your shares in the fund with a phone call and have a check mailed to your home address. These are handy options.

STEP EIGHT: SKIP THIS QUESTION

Step Eight is a request for information about your employer, occupation and work address. The fund company doesn't require you to answer these questions, and I see no benefit in answering them.

For regulatory reasons, the National Association of Securities Dealers requires fund companies to ask whether you work for a stock broker or related firm. But you don't have to answer them either.

STEP NINE: STRAIGHT TO AND FROM THE BANK?

Step Nine asks if you want to establish the ability to wire money from the fund company to your bank or vice versa. This can save you a little time when you want to redeem or purchase shares, but check first to see whether your bank will charge to send or receive money in this manner. If there is a charge, the service is probably not worth it.

STEP TEN: A FINAL FLOURISH

Step Ten is your signature. There's a lot of legal mumbo jumbo beforehand telling you that by signing you certify that the information on the form is correct and that you are not subject to IRS backup withholding (if you are, you know it). Just sign and date the application, enclose your check, and send off the application.

IRA Applications

FOR THE MOST PART, IRA APPLICATIONS ARE SIMILAR TO regular account applications. I'll highlight the differences here and focus particularly on questions related to transfers.

WHAT KIND OF ACCOUNT AND HOW MUCH TO DEPOSIT?

Check "individual account" for yourself, if you're employed. Check "spousal account" for a spouse who is not employed. Each spouse can contribute up to $2,000 in earned income annually, so long as your combined earned income is at least $4,000. You can contribute for, say, calendar year 1998 from January 1, 1998, until the day you file your taxes in 1999, usually no later than April 15—or as a late as October 15 if you request two filing extensions. The earlier you contribute, the better; it gives your money that much more time to grow. Make sure to specify the correct year for your contribution. Otherwise, the IRS might think you didn't contribute anything for one year and contributed twice what's allowed the following year.

Also give your birth date, which will become important when you begin withdrawing money from your IRA, sometime between ages 59½ and 70½.

As with regular accounts, most IRAs give you the option of having your bank account debited every month until you hit the $2,000 mark. Don't contribute more than the $2,000 legal maximum. A monthly contribution of $166.66 will keep you under the $2,000 maximum.

> **Usually, you will want the old trustees to convert all your assets to cash before transfer.**

ROTH IRAS

Opening one of the Roth IRAs is virtually the same as opening a regular IRA. The forms are essentially identical to the forms for the old IRAs, so they'll be no trouble to fill out. In many instances, the form simply asks you to check a box saying whether you want to open a Roth IRA or a regular IRA.

HOW TO HANDLE A TRANSFER

If your contribution to an IRA is annual, as most are, check that box on the form. But if you're moving your IRA from a bank or other custodian to the mutual fund, you'll want to check the box that indicates it's a transfer from an existing IRA. Be sure also to complete the "IRA Transfer Form," which you may have to specially request from the fund company. Be sure to print your name exactly as it was on the old IRA (including your middle name or an initial), and staple a copy of a recent statement to the transfer form.

Check with your current trustees to see whether they require a signature guarantee—a signature from a bank or a broker (not a notary public) verifying that you are who you say you are. Usually, you'll want the old trustees to convert all your assets to cash before transferring them to the new trustee. Otherwise, the mutual fund you're moving your IRA to will likely sell the securities and bill you for the brokerage transactions— or reject your application.

Other kinds of transfers

Whether you are transferring your account from another mutual fund, a bank, an insurance company or a brokerage, the process is pretty similar.

From multiple trustees. If you are transferring IRAs from more than one trustee, make sure to ask for enough forms to handle each transfer.

From a bank CD. If you are transferring from a bank CD, you will generally come out ahead by asking—in the appropriate space on the transfer-of-assets form—that the money be transferred upon maturity, thereby avoiding any early-withdrawal penalties.

From a former employer's 401(k) plan. If you want to transfer your retirement assets to an IRA, you're likewise best off having your previous employer send the check directly to the mutual fund company or mail you a check made out to the mutual fund company. The procedures and forms are quite similar to those for direct transfers from one trustee to another.

BENEFICIARIES

Make sure to designate your beneficiaries—the people you want to receive the proceeds if you die (usually your spouse or children). This is usually on the back of the IRA application or on a separate page.

FEES AND FINE PRINT

The information you get with the application from the fund company, or from a discount broker, will include a lot of legalese about the IRA, most of which you can ignore. Be sure to find out, however, what fees the sponsor charges for an IRA. You can find these in the small print, on the IRA application (sometimes), or by calling the fund. Some fund companies charge annual fees, sometimes for each fund account. Some charge a small fee to open an account, and some even charge to close your account. Many funds don't charge anything anymore, because these fees irritate consumers. Don't stay away from a good fund company, however, simply because of a niggling $10 or $20 annual IRA fee. If the company has solid funds with low annual overall expenses, you'll more than make up the difference.

> **Make sure to designate your beneficiaries—the people you want to receive the proceeds if you die.**

What Your Fund Sends You

FUNDS SEND AN ACKNOWLEDGMENT OF EVERY INVESTMENT YOU make. Save each one at least until the next statement comes. Usually statements are cumulative, listing all transactions for the calendar year. At the end of each year, most funds send you statements summing up your activity. When these arrive, you can throw all the monthly and quarterly statements away for that year, but, make sure to keep each yearly statement for at least three years after you *sell* all your shares and file your tax return reporting the sale. Otherwise, keep yearly statements indefinitely.

If you have sold any funds in a taxable account during the year, many fund companies will send you a separate annual tax statement, which is a blessing when you do your taxes. Besides itemizing your transactions, these summaries show the tax basis of any fund shares you sold during the previous year—this is information the IRS demands on Schedule D of your tax return. Again, keep these about three years. Fund companies also send you annual Form 1099-DIV statements, showing dividends and other distributions that you must report on your income tax.

> **Make sure to keep each yearly statement for at least three years after you *sell* all your shares and file your tax return reporting the sale.**

The year-to-year paperwork is less onerous in IRAs and other tax-exempt accounts. Once a year the fund company will send you Form 5498 that tells you how much your IRA is worth (a copy also goes to the IRS). Keep these forms in a folder against the day you begin making withdrawals from your IRAs.

Read All About It

WANT TO SEE HOW YOUR FUND IS DOING? THE EASIEST WAY is to look it up in the newspaper mutual fund tables or on the Internet. Not all newspapers carry all funds, so you may have to get a weekly *Barron's* or Friday *Wall Street Journal* for complete fund information. You can usually find a fair amount of information about most funds in any newspaper. Not all newspapers list the same data, nor do they list it the same way. But following is a guide to the fund listings of many newspapers. Even if yours is different, this guide should help you navigate the fund tables.

The fund name

First look for your fund alphabetically. Usually this is a straight-forward process, but not always. For instance, if you own EuroPacific fund, you'll have to know to look it up under the American family of funds—in the As, not the Es.

The NAV

Next find the NAV—that's the *net asset value* per share of the securities held in the fund. If the fund lists a different *offering price* (the price at which it will sell to new investors), that means it assesses a sales charge. Usually, no-load funds will contain the abbreviation NL in that space. *NAV chg, daily chg* or *net chg* tells you how much the fund went up or down in value from the previous day. Some fund listings, including those in the *Wall Street Journal* and *Barron's,* also tell you how many percentage points a fund has risen or fallen since the start of the year, over the past 12 months, and sometimes over the past three and five years.

A quick note on your *real* rate of return

Just because a fund is up, say, 20% so far this year doesn't mean you've made 20% on your investment. You may have bought the fund on a different day than Dec. 31 of last year, or on several different dates. This can change your personal rate of return significantly. (I get more angry letters on this subject than perhaps any other, and, alas, the fund companies are almost invariably right.) Figuring out your personal rate of return, unfortunately, takes more mathematical computations than most people want to undertake. There is hope for change, though. Barry Barbash, head of mutual fund enforcement for the Securities and Exchange Commission, proposes that funds furnish each investor with his or her personal rate of return. Meanwhile, some money-management software such as *Quicken* will compute your personal rate of return.

Performance ratings

In some newspapers, fund-research firms such as Morningstar and Lipper also provide ratings of how well a fund has done in the past. These are superficial and not worth attention. Similarly, ignore fund advertisements boasting that Morningstar rated a fund "Five Stars." Morningstar maintains that the star system

A Sample Mutual Fund Listing

KEY TO THE TABLE See the accompanying text for further explanation of each of these items.

A: Fund Name   D: Year-to-date return
B: NAV   E: 12b-1 and other fees (p)
C: Net chg   F: Redemption charge (r)

Ranges for investment companies, with daily price data supplied by the National Association of Securities Dealers and performance and cost calculations by Lipper Analytical Services Inc. The NASD requires a mutual fund to have at least 1,000 shareholders or net assets of $25 million before being listed. NAV–Net Asset Value. Detailed explanatory notes appear elsewhere on this page.

Name	NAV	Net Chg	YTD %ret
AAL Mutual A:			
Balance p	10.62	−0.05	+ 6.5
Bond p	10.04	...	+ 2.5
CGrowth p	28.55	−0.23	+ 9.8
HiYBdA	10.24	...	+ 3.3
Intl p	11.23		+11.1
MidCap p	14.77	−0.06	+ 1.9
MuniBd p	11.58	−0.01	+ 2.1
SmCap p	12.47	−0.08	+ 0.2
EqInc p	14.03	−0.10	+ 7.0
AAL Mutual B:			
CGrowth p	28.27	−0.22	+ 9.4
EqInc p	14.03	−0.09	+ 6.6
HiYBdB p	10.24	−0.01	+ 2.9
Intl p	11.12		+10.5
MidCap	14.62	−0.06	+ 1.4
SmCap p	12.36	−0.07	− 0.2
AARP Invst:			
	~~n~~ 06	+ 6.9	
CAInsLT ~~r~~		2.8	
Convrt	12.32		
EqInc	24.05	−0.1/	
Explr	55.66	−0.13	+ 0./
FLInsLT	11.36	−0.01	+ 2.1
GNMA	10.44	...	+ 3.0
GroInc	29.02	−0.23	+12.9
HYCor r	8.12	...	+ 4.1
HzAgGr r	15.20	−0.06	+ 4.1
HzCpOp r	11.35	−0.09	+11.3
HzGlAA r	11.05	+0.03	+ 7.5
HzGlbEq r	13.47	+0.01	+12.4
IntlGr	18.81	+0.14	+14.8
IntlVal	26.70	+0.28	+19.8

Name	NAV	Net Chg	YTD %ret
SpectmB p	16.47	−0.09	+ 6.0
VentureA	12.98	+0.09	+ 4.2
Aetna Class A:			
Aetna t	13.03	−0.05	+ 7.7
Bond t	10.29	...	+ 3.0
Grow t	16.58	−0.15	+16.9
GrInc t	16.43	−0.06	+ 8.9
IntlGr t	13.42	+0.08	+23.1
SmCo t	11.78	−0.04	+ 5.5
Aetna Class I:			
Aetna	13.04	−0.05	+ 7.8
Ascent	12.41	...	+ 6.8
Bond	10.29	...	+ 3.1
Crossrds	12.17	...	+ 6.1
Grwth	16.82	−0.15	+17.1
GrwIncm	16.48	−0.06	+ 9.0
IntlGr	13.44	+0.07	+23.3
Legacy	10.76	+0.01	+ 5.4
SmCoGr	12.10	−0.04	+ 5.5
Alger Funds A:			
CapApr	27.04	−0.19	+10.6
Growth	11.61	−0.06	+14.8
~~Gl	21.47	−0.11	+11.1
Bala~~~~	~~~~	' 0.02	+ 3.1
EmgMktA	10.~~.~~		
EmgMktY	10.52	+0.0~~~~	
EquityA	14.97	−0.13	+ ~~~~
EquityY	14.98	−0.13	+ 8.4
EqIndexA	20.90	−0.22	+11.9
EqIndexY	20.93	−0.21	+12.1
FixedInY	9.93	...	+ 3.0
GrIncA	21.80	−0.15	+10.5
GrIncY	21.80	−0.16	NA

REPRINTED WITH PERMISSION OF THE WALL STREET JOURNAL ©1998 DOW JONES & COMPANY, INC.

gives you only a few clues about a fund. I agree. To pick funds, you'll want to dig much deeper. For that, you'll want to look in Part Three, particularly Chapter 15, "How to Pick Winning Stock Funds."

12b-1 and other fees

The letter *p* or *b* next to the fund's name usually means it charges a *12b-1 fee,* which funds use to cover marketing and other expenses. No-load funds can't charge a 12b-1 fee of more than 0.25% of assets.

An *r* stands for *redemption charge.* Most no-load funds that levy these charges, designed to discourage short-term trading, impose them only if you sell a fund within say, a year of buying it. Load funds, however, may assess sales charges whenever you redeem shares, even years after investing.

Ex-dividend

An *x* next to a fund stands for *ex-dividend,* meaning only current shareholders will get the next dividend or capital-gains payout, which is imminent. New buyers won't get the dividend.

Key Points

- *Don't let the blizzard of mail that mutual fund companies may send distract you. Some companies will heed requests to reduce mail.*
- *Filling out fund forms is an easy matter if you follow the directions in this chapter.*
- *Buying funds through a discount broker can save a lot of time and trouble, but may cost a little money.*

Paying Uncle Sam

Six rules for minimizing your tax bills—
and tax headaches

ANY FUND INVESTORS PAY MORE THAN THEIR FAIR share to Uncle Sam. That's not just my opinion. It's the belief of no less an authority than Fred Goldberg, former head of the Internal Revenue Service (and no relation to yours truly). In this chapter, I'll show you six ways you can minimize the income taxes on profits from your taxable funds. (Funds in tax-deferred accounts require little tax record keeping until you begin withdrawing money, usually between ages 59½ and 70½.) The most important thing is to keep good records—whether on a computer or with pencil and paper. That'll keep you from overpaying your taxes. However, if you're like many people who find keeping detailed records burdensome, I'll also describe some shortcuts. Some of these may cost you a tiny bit in return, but they'll save you time. And, after all, one of the main advantages of mutual funds is that they make your investing life simpler.

Rule 1:
Keep Careful Records

THE BIGGEST MISTAKE MANY FUND INVESTORS MAKE WHEN they pay their income taxes is suffering amnesia about their reinvestment of dividends and capital gains in additional shares of a fund. Let's say you buy 100 shares of the Makemerich stock fund at $10 per share, for a total of $1,000. At the end of the year Makemerich pays you a distribution of $1 per share in long-term capital gains (profits on stocks the fund sold after holding them for more than 12 months) and 50 cents per share in dividends—or a total of $150, which is reinvested in additional shares. The fund company sends you a 1099-DIV form listing those distributions, and you dutifully copy the numbers onto your income-tax return for that year. (Funds that hold bonds and some income-oriented stock funds often pay distributions quarterly or monthly.)

The following year, you sell your shares of the Makemerich fund and replace them with the Pot of Gold fund. The Makemerich fund sends you a final 1099 form—this one listing the total amount you received when you sold the fund. Let's say you sold your shares for $1,500. When you sit down to do your income taxes for that year, you record that you paid $1,000 for your shares of Makemerich and sold them for $1,500. Therefore, you have a capital gain of $500—from which Uncle Sam gets his cut. Not so fast!

When they sell, many investors neglect to add to the cost of their original investment the value of the money they reinvested.

The problem here is that many investors forget about the $150 in capital gains and dividends that they had reinvested in additional shares. *You've already paid taxes on that $150.* Since you reinvested that money in extra shares, you really paid $1,000 *plus* $150, or $1,150, for the shares you sold. Subtracting $1,150 from $1,500, your real capital gain on selling the fund is not $500, but only $350. Many investors hold a fund five, ten or 20 years, reinvesting dividends and capital gains every year. Unfortunately, when they sell their shares, they neglect to add to the cost of their original investment (called the *cost basis* in tax lingo) the value of all the money they reinvested over the years.

On page 107 is a worksheet that shows you how to keep a pencil-and-paper record of all purchases, sales and reinvestments in each mutual fund you own. If you use *Quicken* or any other financial record-keeping software, you'll need to enter the same numbers to avoid overpaying taxes.

Record keeping, however, can be a minor nightmare because funds tend to pay these distributions in dribs and drabs. For instance, a fund might pay you:

- **1.4414 shares in dividends** worth $34.91,
- **0.4806 shares in short-term capital gains** (gains on securities held

by a fund for a year or less) worth $11.64 (short-term gains distributed from your fund are treated just like dividends on your tax return and are taxed as ordinary income), and

• **3.6837 shares in long-term capital gains** (gains on securities held more than 12 months) worth $89.22.

Anyone who owns funds can attest that—whether transcribed with pencil and paper or on computer software—it is a tedious job to enter all those numbers. (Most people who use computer software—and remember to back up their work—find the job less of a hassle.) Also, remember you'll need to track the reinvestment dates to determine your holding periods.

I've labeled this section Rule 1. If you keep good records you'll have no need for the shortcuts described in some of the following sections. You do need to make a choice, however: Either resolve to keep good records, or follow the shortcuts.

Rule 2:
Use the Average-Cost Method

THE IRS ALLOWS YOU TO USE ANY ONE OF THE FOLLOWING three methods for calculating the cost basis of fund shares that you sell.

FIRST-IN, FIRST-OUT

This method assumes that the *first shares* you bought are the first shares you sell. Say you bought your first 100 shares of the Makemerich fund at $10 a share (for a total of $1,000) and then bought 60 more shares at $15 (for a total of $900). If you sold 40 shares at $20 a share (for a total of $800), you would owe taxes on a capital gain of $400—that is, the $800 you sold your 40 shares for minus the $400 you paid for 40 shares (40 of the first 100 that you bought at $10 apiece). Unless you choose otherwise, the IRS assumes you're using the first-in-first-out method.

SPECIFIC IDENTIFICATION

If you keep good records, this is the method to use. You'll delay paying some of your taxes. When you sell, the IRS allows you to designate *which shares* in a fund you are selling. By choosing the highest-cost shares to sell first, you can cut your tax bill for that year. In the example above, this is clearly to your advantage

unless you have a loss to absorb. Flexibility is key to specific iden-
tification. Instead of selling the first 40 shares you bought at a
lower price, you can sell the 40 shares you bought at the higher
price—in this instance, 40 of the 60 shares you purchased at $15
per share. Your cost basis on these shares is $15 times 40 shares,
or $600. Since you sold your 40 shares for $800, you now have a
taxable gain of just $200—half what you'd have using
first-in-first-out.

Many mutual funds (and some discount brokerages) provide you with average-cost-basis information.

The specific-identification method will add to
your paperwork. Each time you sell shares, you have
to write a letter to the fund company stating which
shares you are selling and asking for a written confir-
mation. You also must keep track of which shares you
sold when for your own records.

For all that paperwork, your savings from using
the specific-identification method are likely to be
minuscule unless you hold your remaining shares for
15 years or more. (For evidence of how little you will save, see
Chapter 21 on tax-efficient investing.) Why? Because when you
sell your remaining shares in the fund, the tax bite you so artfully
dodged will catch up with you—since you've already sold your
high-cost shares.

AVERAGE COST

This is far and away the easiest method for most taxpayers to use.
You simply average the cost of the shares you bought and use
that as your cost basis. You bought 100 shares of Makemerich at
$10 per share, and 60 shares at $15. You compute average cost
by taking the $1,900 you invested altogether and dividing by the
160 total shares you bought, which gives you an average cost of
$11.875 per share. Since you sold 40 shares, you multiply 40
times $11.875 to get your cost basis, which is $475. Subtract that
from the $800 you made from selling your 40 shares, and you
have a capital gain of $325.

Doesn't sound so simple? Well, it's not. But the trick is that
many mutual funds (and some of the discount brokerages from
which you can buy funds) automatically provide you with
average-cost-basis information. All you have to do is copy onto
your tax form the information from the statement the fund sends
you at the end of each year in which you've sold shares—and,

Tracking Your Funds

YOU CAN USE the worksheet below to track your mutual funds—that is, unless your fund supplies you with average cost basis and you plan to employ it.

The example filled in below uses the average-cost method, although the worksheet can be used with any of the three IRS-approved methods. Using first-in-first out, the sale would have resulted in a $23.80 gain. Using specific identification, and selling from the lot purchased on 6–15–98, when the price was highest, you'd have a loss of $23.82. (*Note:* The purchase on 12–28–98 was a dividend reinvestment.)

Date	Buy/ sell	Dollar amount	Number of shares	Share price	Share cost basis	Total basis	Total shares owned	Average basis	Dollar gain (or Loss)
3–15–98	Buy	$1,000	100	$10.00	$10.00	$1,000	100	$10.00	
6–15–98	Buy	1,000	90.91	11.00	11.00	2,000	190.91	10.48	
12–28–98	Buy	99.76	8.56	11.65	11.65	2,099.76	199.47	10.53	
4–15–99	Sell	500.00	47.62	10.50	10.53	1,598.32	151.85	10.53	–$1.44

voilà, you've satisfied the IRS. "You might as well use the funds' figures," says Tom Ochsenschlager, a partner with the accounting firm of Grant, Thornton. "You'll usually end up with the same money, and you'll save a lot of work."

Before you rely on a fund to provide you with average-cost data, make sure your fund does, indeed, provide average-cost-basis information. And, to be safe, keep at least each year-end statement from your funds—just in case something goes wrong. Fund companies will usually be able to send you old records if you lose them, but they'll often charge a fee for this service.

Also, keep in mind that the IRS lets you switch between first-in-first-out and specific-identification methods, but once you choose the average-cost method, you're stuck with it until you sell all the shares of that fund.

The average-cost information that many funds give you includes data on reinvested dividends and capital gains. If you could be sure that all the funds you own would provide you with this data, you would be freed of all the record keeping involved in tracking reinvested dividends and capital gains. Alas, many good funds still don't provide this information, and until they do, it's better to be safe than sorry: Keep your own records.

Rule 3:
If You're Going to Sell a Fund, Sell All of It

THE MORE TRANSACTIONS YOU HAVE IN ANY INDIVIDUAL mutual fund account, the more complicated your tax preparation becomes. If a fund company provides you with average-cost tax information, that's no problem. But if it doesn't, you will have to be mighty good with a calculator—or have software to do the job for you. Things get the diciest when you decide to sell off a portion of your holdings in a fund and hold on to the rest. By the time you decide to sell off the third or fourth lot of shares, you may be ready to pull your hair out unless you've kept scrupulous records.

The easiest solution: When you sell shares in a fund, sell all of them. Then you don't have to worry about which accounting method to use. Your cost basis is simply the total amount you invested in the fund. In the example above, you have invested a total of $1,900, which is your cost basis. Instead of selling just 40 shares, sell the entire 160 shares at $20 per share, or $3,200. Your capital gain is $3,200 minus $1,900, or $1,300. Even true math phobics can do that calculation with aplomb. Then, to maintain the proportions in your portfolio, invest your money in a similar fund.

WHY IT PAYS TO HANG ON

Selling all your shares can be tricky, or impossible, if you are invested in a fund that is closed to new investors and you wish to keep your place in the fund. Call the fund and ask whether there's a minimum number of shares you must hold in order to remain an investor. Even if you sell all your shares, some funds will give you several months to buy back in. Of course, the easiest way to reduce your tax record keeping is to avoid selling funds if you can. Don't hold on to a lousy fund, but being a long-term investor makes sense for lots of reasons, including making your taxes simpler. If you want to routinely switch from fund to fund, at least confine those activities to a tax-deferred account such as an IRA.

Changes to the tax law made in 1997 and 1998 provide more incentives for staying put. If you hold fund shares for more than 12 months your maximum tax rate when you sell is 20% (10% if you're in the 15% tax bracket). As under the old law, if you sell a fund after owning it 12 months or less, you'll have to pay taxes on it as ordinary income. Ordinary rates range from 15% to 39.6%.

Rule 4:
Don't Write Checks on Bond Funds

IT'S SO EASY TO SWITCH FROM ONE FUND TO ANOTHER WITH A telephone call, or to withdraw money simply by writing a check on many bond funds, that it's easy to lose sight of the fact that the IRS considers each of those transactions a "taxable event." If you have a bond fund and write a dozen checks on it over a couple of years, your tax records may well become impenetrable, unless you keep careful records.

If you know that you don't keep good records, take the checkbook your fund company sends you when you open a bond fund and tear it into little pieces. Keep a money-market fund at the same fund company and hold on to that checkbook. If you need money, transfer a big, round number, say $10,000, from your bond fund to your money-market fund. Then write checks on that fund. Since money-market funds endeavor to keep a constant price of $1 per shares, and pay only dividend income, you don't need to worry about capital gains or figuring a cost basis on these funds.

Rule 5:
Don't Buy a Fund Just Before It Distributes Gains

FUNDS ARE REQUIRED TO DISTRIBUTE ALMOST ALL OF THEIR capital gains and dividends to shareholders every year. Most stock funds make distributions just once, usually in December. The date the fund declares the dividend is known as its *ex-dividend* date. If you have the misfortune to buy shares just before that date, you will immediately get hit with a taxable distribution from the fund.

For this reason, it's best to be wary of investing large amounts in funds late in the year. Call a fund's toll-free number and ask for its ex-dividend date. Then make sure to buy after that date. Some funds are considerate enough to estimate, in advance, how big a distribution they intend to declare on the ex-dividend date. If the distribution is a small one, say 5% or less of the fund's net asset value, you might want to go ahead and buy the fund anyway. But if it's a big one, you're better off delaying your investment.

(Late-year distributions can sometimes add insult to injury. Sometimes funds that have had a horrible year will, nevertheless, have large taxable distributions. This is a matter of fund accounting, and there is little that funds—or shareholders—can do to control it.)

If you do have the misfortune to buy a fund just before it goes ex-dividend, there is some solace. When you eventually sell your shares, your cost basis will be higher than it would otherwise have been, because you bought your shares at the higher price. But you will have lost use of the money you paid in taxes-for the time you hold the shares.

For instance, suppose you buy the Makemerich fund at $10 a share just before it declares a $2 distribution. The share price will drop to $8. You'll pay taxes on the $2 distribution the next time you file your income taxes. But when you sell the fund, say a year later, your cost basis on your original shares will be $10 rather than the $8 it would have been had you bought it *after* the ex-dividend date. That will save you money on taxes.

In other words, when you buy a fund before it goes ex-dividend, you pay some of your taxes up front. If you buy after it goes ex-dividend, you don't have to pay those taxes until you sell the fund.

Rule 6:
Dealing With the IRS Is Never Really Simple

OKAY, THIS LAST RULE DOESN'T MAKE THINGS SIMPLER. BUT it's the truth: As you've seen already in this chapter, investing in mutual funds (or anything else, for that matter) requires that you learn some arcane rules (or pay an accountant to do the work for you). Here are some of the less simple things you need to know about funds and taxes:

INHERITED OR GIFT FUNDS
While your cost basis is usually the amount you invested in a fund, that's not the case if you inherit fund shares. In that event, your basis is generally the value of the shares on the date of the death of the person who bequeathed you the shares.

However, if you receive shares as a gift and sell them at a loss, your basis is whichever is *lower*: the value of the shares on the day you were given them, or the price that your benefactor paid for them. In other words, you don't get to deduct any decline in value before you got the gift. If you sell for a profit, your basis is the same as your benefactor's.

MUNICIPAL MISCELLANY
Income from municipal bond funds is exempt from federal tax, but it must be reported on your federal return. Many states and localities make you pay taxes on some or all income from muni funds. Also, a muni fund can realize a capital gain if it sells bonds for a profit. These capital gains are taxable. In addition, to avoid Alternative Minimum Tax complications, try to steer clear of muni funds that hold so-called "private-activity bonds," which

might be taxable to you under the Alternative Minimum Tax.

DIVIDENDS, NOT INTEREST

Income from mutual funds, even money-market funds and bond funds, is dividend income, not interest income, as far as the IRS is concerned. This is so even though these funds generally hold debt instruments that pay interest to the funds. Remember this when you're filling out your tax return so you don't enter the information in the wrong place.

A TAX BREAK FOR FOREIGN TAXES

If you own a fund that invests some or all of its money in foreign securities, you can get a tax break for foreign taxes paid by the fund; those taxes should be reported on the 1099-DIV forms your fund mails you. You can take this amount as a deduction if you itemize deductions. Or you can take it as a tax credit, which is usually worth more. Taking it as a credit, however, requires filling out an additional tax form (IRS Form 1116, *Foreign Tax Credit for Individuals*).

Selling Your Losers?

HAD A BAD YEAR in the markets? Uncle Sam wants to help—really. If you own a stock or bond fund that gets pummeled to a level far below what you originally paid for it, consider selling it and buying a similar fund. You can deduct the loss when you file your taxes. (IRS wash-sale rules, however, prevent you from taking a tax loss if you sell a fund at a loss and rebuy the same fund before 31 days have elapsed.) Assuming you buy a similar fund (for instance, replace an aggressive-growth fund with another aggressive-growth fund), you won't lose an opportunity to make money when the market rebounds.

Selling a losing fund and buying another is most easily done with bond funds because it's usually an easy matter to find another bond fund that's almost identical to your loser. You could sell Vanguard Municipal Long Term, for instance, buy Vanguard Municipal High-Yield, and have little change in your portfolio. It's trickier with stock funds, though—it's often very difficult to find two that are almost identical because their portfolios are likely to be diverse, even if their goals are similar.

Bear in mind, that selling a losing fund and buying a winner will likely yield you only a very small savings because you'll eventually sell the winning fund and owe taxes on its gains. Moreover, selling your losers will complicate your financial record keeping. So use this technique sparingly.

SALES CHARGES

Any initial sales charge you pay (called a *front-end load* in fund-speak) is included in your cost basis, because it's part of the cost of your shares. If you invest $1,000 in a fund with a 4.5% front-end load, your cost basis is $1,000, even though you will have bought only $955 worth of shares. Similarly, brokerage transaction fees are deductible.

FUNDS THAT INVEST IN U.S. GOVERNMENT SECURITIES

If you own a fund that gets all or part of its income from investing in U.S. government securities, you'll have to pay federal tax on the income, but you usually don't have to pay state or local tax on it. However, interest on securities issued by government agencies—such as federally insured mortgage-backed securities and student loans—is not exempt from state taxes. When you receive your Form 1099 from a fund, you'll also receive an accounting what percentage of income came from government securities of various types.

Key Points
- *Keeping careful records, on a computer or with pencil and paper, is essential to managing the tax aspects of fund investing. Computers are the best method for most people.*
- *If you don't want the aggravation of keeping good records, there are some shortcuts you can employ. They include:*
- *Using the "average cost" method of accounting (with the fund doing the record keeping).*
- *Selling all shares of a mutual fund if you sell any.*
- *Even with these shortcuts, complying with IRS rules on funds is tedious.*

13 Investment Pitfalls

And how to avoid them

S YOU CAN SEE FROM THE PRECEDING CHAPTERS, investing wisely isn't that difficult. All you need to do is determine your time horizon and tolerance for losses; decide how much you're going to invest in stocks, bonds and cash; pick solid funds; and invest regularly. Unless you want to learn more of the nitty-gritty about funds, you don't need to read beyond this chapter to create a first-class investment plan.

However, gremlins lurk to throw you off course—largely because, when it comes to investing your money, your emotions tend to come into play as much as your brain. Here are 12 pitfalls that can snare investors—novices and veterans alike—and tips on how to avoid them.

Pitfall 1: Waiting for Stocks to Fall

THIS TRAP CAN BE ESPECIALLY EASY TO FALL INTO FOR fledgling investors who are afraid to get their feet wet—especially if they have a large sum to invest. At the end of 1994, for instance, the dividend yield on the average stock in Standard & Poor's 500-stock index fell below 3% of the average stock's price. The only other times that had happened were a few months prior to the 1929 crash, just before the onset of the 1973–74 bear market, and a few months preceding the 1987 crash—the worst three markets of the century. It seemed prudent to put off investing until stock prices fell, which would push up yields. When dividend yields are low compared with stocks' prices, it traditionally means companies don't have the confidence to share much of their profits with shareholders. But those who waited for yields to fall watched as the S&P 500 soared 37.5% in 1995, 23% in 1996 and 33.4% in 1997. The lesson is clear: If you are going to invest, put in a little bit regularly; don't wait for stocks to get cheaper.

Pitfall 2: Timing the Market

WHAT IF YOU KNEW IN ADVANCE WHEN STOCKS WERE GOING to plunge? What if you could step to the sidelines in advance of the bruising bear markets that take the market down by 20% or more? The answer, of course: You could do wonderful things. James Stack, editor of the investment letter *InvesTech*, calculates that an investor who buys the stocks Standard and Poor's 500-stock index and holds them for the long term would have earned 317% in the ten years that ended in mid 1994. But if that same investor had presciently jumped out of the market on just the ten worst days each year, he or she would have earned 4,576%!

Even after following the market for more than 20 years, I find market timing beguiling. It is nearly as satisfying to sit safely on the sidelines in a money-market fund while stocks plunge as it is to watch your stock funds rise. I experienced it once. I sold all my stocks just days before the 1987 crash. Unfortunately, it took me one and a half years to fully reenter the market because I kept waiting for the market to fall again. As a result, I ended up no better off than if I had patiently stayed in stocks through the crash and the subsequent recovery.

Advocates of market timing counter that the mettle of most buy-and-hold investors hasn't really been tested.

The sad fact is, no one has ever been able to time the stock market well enough and consistently enough to outperform long-term holding. Says John Markese, president of the American Association of Individual Investors: "Good timing can't be beat." The problem is, "It just can't be done."

Advocates of market timing counter that the mettle of most buy-and-hold investors hasn't really been tested by a nasty, drawn-out bear market. The overwhelming majority of assets in stock funds has been poured in since the last bear decline in 1990 and that one lasted only three months, and many investors have never experienced a drop of anywhere near 20%. Market timers doubt that buy-and-holders will hang tough in a protracted down market. Indeed, when stocks fall, mutual fund investors, on the whole, tend to slow their investing. If a market decline extends over a long period, fund buying tends to dry up and investors begin redeeming shares, several studies show. Then, when the market is buoyant again, investors flock back into stocks. It's not just individual investors who fall victim to this buy-high, sell-low malady; professional investors do it, too. Mutual fund managers, as a whole, tend to hold the highest percentage of assets in cash on the eve of bull markets; conversely, they tend to have little cash just before bear markets begin.

Years ago timers promised that they could outperform the market with lower risk. In recent years they've lowered their claims by promising good returns adjusted for the risks they take. In other words, they say, they'll produce decent returns and keep you safely in cash during bear markets—and make it easier to sleep at night.

Many Investors Fall Into Traps

UNFORTUNATELY, MANY INVESTORS—whether employing a broker or other financial adviser or investing on their own—fail to avoid investment pitfalls. And their returns show it. From 1984 through 1997, the average stock-owning domestic mutual fund gained an annualized 13.6%. But most fund investors fared much worse.

A study by Dalbar, a Boston-based investment-research firm, found that the average stock-fund investor earned a mere annualized 6.7% over those 14 years—not much better than the return for supersafe Treasury bills (6.0%). Investors, on average, whether they used financial advisers or chose funds on their own, achieved roughly the same poor returns. Why? Many investors buy and sell funds at the wrong times, so funds tend to have more assets when they're falling in price and fewer when they're rising. A similar study by Morningstar showed that over a five-year period ending March 31, 1995, the average stock fund returned 63%, while the average investor earned only 52.1%.

Dalbar and Morningstar arrived at their conclusions by tracking each dollar invested in stock funds, then assigning each dollar its proper weighting. For instance, if a fund gained 4% in a month but had only $50 million in assets, the performance of that fund counted only half as much as a fund that gained 1% in the same month and had $100 million in assets. Since twice as many investor dollars were in the larger (and poorer-performing) fund, that fund's results were given twice the weighting of the smaller (and better-performing) fund.

Luckily, the remedy for this investment pitfall is not difficult: Just follow the guidelines laid out in this chapter.

But before you engage in market timing, be clear about what you're getting into. From the highest-paid, most-quoted brokerage strategists on Wall Street to the shoeshine boys, no one really knows what the stock market is going to do today, tomorrow, next month or next year. The best way to invest for maximum gain is to buy stock funds (or individual stocks) and hold them. Consider the flip side to Stack's perfect market timer: If you missed the ten best days in the market each year during the decade ending in mid 1994, you wouldn't have profited at all. *Not* to be invested in stocks is risky.

If you missed the ten best days in the market each year during the decade ending in mid 1994, you wouldn't have profited at all.

In addition to the poor record of market timers, timing presents another problem: It's a lot of work. While good performance is anything but guaranteed, it's a certainty you'll spend hours listening to market timers' telephone hotlines, or fiddling with computer programs. If you're timing in a taxable account, moreover, you condemn yourself to more agony at tax time each year.

Avoiding market timing is easy intellectually, though sometimes terribly difficult emotionally. If you are tempted to try it, remind yourself of the long-term gains of the stock markets and the difficulty of anticipating market turns.

STILL WANT TO TIME THE MARKET?

If you want to lower your risks, and are willing to accept lower-than-stock-market returns, you may want to consider hitching your star to one of the timers in this section. First, though, here's some advice on timing:

• **Don't do it by hunch,** word of mouth or somebody's hot tip that "the market looks ripe for a 10% fall" or "a quick 10% rise."

• **Instead, use a systematic approach** that makes you rely on hard and fast rules rather than emotions.

• **Use a mutual fund or a newsletter** that has a decent record at market timing (you won't find any with great records).

• **Do it with only a portion of your money.** You might, say, put 60% of your money into buy-and-hold stock funds, funnel 20% into bond funds, and time the market with the final 20%. That way, even if you're wrong, you won't have given up all your opportunities for gain.

Following are two timers with decent long-term records.

The Zweig Strategy Fund (5.5% maximum sales charge, 800–444–2706) has trailed the S&P 500 most years, but it has exhibited little more than half the index's ups and downs. In other words, in periods when the S&P fell 10%, the fund dipped only about 5%, on average. This fund should do well in bear markets. Martin Zweig, who determines how much of the fund's assets should be in cash or stocks, has a relatively good record stretching over 20 years.

Fabian's Investment Resource ($100 per year for new subscriptions, $149 for renewals; 800–950–8765) uses a simple 39-week average. When the market is selling above its average weekly closing price of the past 39 weeks, editor Douglas Fabian recommends stock funds. When the market (Fabian uses several indexes to represent "the market") falls below its 39-week average, he retreats to cash. Such an approach would have nearly equaled buying and holding the S&P 500-stock index since 1926, because it would have sidestepped the 1929 crash and much of its aftermath, as well as most of the brutal 1973–74 bear market.

But beware: When the market zigzags over a period of years, either Zweig's or Fabian's approach can be a death of a thousand tiny cuts; they often sell just before the market heads up and buy just before it starts down.

A better approach than either of these two

Follow this rule: Invest conservatively for the short term and aggressively for the long term, and forget about what the market may or may not do, because you're covered either way.

Pitfall 3: Chasing Performance

PICK UP *KIPLINGER'S PERSONAL FINANCE MAGAZINE* OR ANY other personal-finance publication and you'll see advertisements for funds that have shot the lights out over the past year. These funds aren't spending their money on ads for nothing: They know that great results attract money.

Take Wasatch Mid-Cap. In 1994, it was a sleepy little fund with just over $1 million in assets and fund manager Karey Barker piloted it to an 8% return while the S&P 500 gained just 1%. Then, in 1995, the fund erupted. It rose 59%—beating the S&P by more than 20 percentage points. Money flooded in. By the end of 1995, the fund had $130 million in assets. But just as quickly, Barker's hot hand turned ice cold. Wasatch Mid-Cap earned just 4% in 1996, while the S&P rose 23%. Shareholders jammed the exits, and by the end of the year the fund held only $100 million. Assets have since dwindled to $57.6 million.

What went wrong? Barker hadn't proven in 1995 whether her performance was due to talent or luck. In fact, her fund had badly lagged the indexes in 1993, her first year running the fund. Nor had she shown she could run a $100 million fund—which is much harder that managing $1 million. (For more detail on the difficulties of running bigger funds, see Chapter 16.)

> **Buying a top performer isn't necessarily a bad idea—just look for at least three and preferably five years of good numbers.**

Buying a top-performing fund isn't necessarily a bad idea—just look for one with at least three and preferably five years of good numbers under its belt. (These numbers are available for many funds in Chapter 17 of this book, as well as in personal-finance magazines.)

MOMENTUM INVESTING

As with so many investment rules, the rule against chasing performance has a caveat. One style of fund investing, known as momentum investing, buys funds that have chalked up the best performance over relatively short periods. You hold those funds as long as they continue to outperform their peers. When they lag, you switch to other top performers.

If you want to employ momentum investing, do it with only some of your money, because it's a fairly risky strategy. The bulk of your money belongs in good, solid funds that you can hold for years and years. Also, to keep your tax preparation manageable, practice momentum investing only in a tax-deferred retirement account. For best results, subscribe to a good newsletter that exploits momentum investing in a disciplined way; don't simply try to wing it. Perhaps the best of the momentum newsletters is *Equity Fund Outlook* ($125 per year; for a sample issue, send a $2 check or money order to P.O. Box 76, Boston, MA 02117; 800–982–0055). Edited by Thurman Smith, this newsletter is very technical and can be hard to understand. But its model portfolios are easy to read and follow, and they gained an annualized 42.1% from 1995 through 1997. Smith recommends top-performing funds in a variety of investment styles to minimize the risk in the overall portfolio.

ADHERE TO YOUR STRATEGY

A variation of chasing performance is hopping from strategy to strategy. Some investors will be fans of buy-and-hold investing only as long as the market is going up. When it starts going down, they decide to become market timers. They might then subscribe to the hottest-performing newsletter for the previous couple of years, only to switch to another newsletter when the first newsletter's performance wanes. Next, they may decide they should hire a broker instead of going it alone. Hopping from one approach to another is a recipe for lousy returns. Pick your investing strategy and stay with it through thick and thin. Why? Because all too often investors switch approaches at just the wrong time—when their method has been out of favor for a long period and is about to rebound.

Pitfall 4: Putting Too Much Money in One Industry Sector

PBHG EMERGING GROWTH HAD A WONDERFUL RUN IN THE mid 1990s. It rose 23.8% in 1994 (a bad year for most funds) and 48.5% in 1995. In the first months of 1996 it did well, too, rising 30.7% through May 24 compared to a rise of 10.9% by the S&P 500. But then the fund lost its way. It fell 10.4% from May 24 to the end of the year, versus the S&P 500's gain of an additional 12.1%. What went wrong?

It's a huge mistake to concentrate your assets in one or two industries.

Though this fund, like Wasatch Mid-Cap, was co-managed by a relatively inexperienced manager, Christine Baxter was implementing a well-thought-out strategy engineered by other managers at PBHG funds. Moreover, she had senior manager Gary Pilgrim looking over her shoulder. This fund was a dud in late 1996 and early 1997 largely because 40% of its assets were in small technology stocks, which took a shellacking beginning in May 1996. The fund doesn't say technology in its name. But careful investors knew this fund bought risky small companies, many of them in the high-tech arena.

There's nothing wrong with taking some of your more

aggressive investment money and putting it into a fund like PBHG Emerging Growth, knowing it's chock full of risky technology stocks. (*PBHG Emerging Growth* is included in Chapter 17 as one of our "Great Stock Funds.") In investing, high risks are often the price you pay to reap high rewards. But investors make a huge mistake if they concentrate massive portions of their assets in one or two industries. After all, one of the biggest advantages of mutual funds is diversification. When you concentrate your investments in one or two industries, you're defeating that purpose. Putting too much into an industry sector can be a problem whether you invest through a sector fund (see Chapter 14), or in a diversified fund that is really a "closet" sector fund (see Chapter 19).

How can you protect yourself? Before you buy a fund, check out its description in this book or look at another source, such as *Morningstar Mutual Funds*. Or just call the fund and request either a list of its investments by industry sector or an annual report, which will contain this data.

Pitfall 5: Falling in Love With a Fund (or Failing to Clean Out Your Attic)

SCUDDER DEVELOPMENT HAD SOME GOOD YEARS. IT BEAT THE S&P 500 every year from 1976 through 1981. That was enough to attract some favorable attention and cause assets to rise to a then-respectable $80 million. But since 1982, Scudder Development has bested the S&P in only three years and the Russell 2000, an index of small-company stocks, in only six years. A fund that once was excellent has been mediocre, at best, for a long time. Yet, despite its below-par performance, assets have grown to more than $900 million. For investors fortunate enough to have bought Scudder Development in the 1970s, there was an understandable reluctance to pull the plug. But when a fund loses its touch and shows no sign of regaining it— except for an isolated year of decent performance—it's time to cash in your chips. There's no need to wait 15 years, either!

A fund that fails to keep up with its peers for a year or two should be watched carefully. If it doesn't turn around fairly quickly, it should be sold—unless you can satisfy yourself that the problems are, indeed, temporary (for more detail on when to sell a fund, see Chapter 16). Of course, if a fund's manager has a long and superior record or is investing in a part of the market that is out of favor, you'll want to give it the benefit of the doubt. But eventually, you have to bail out.

Don't let fear of a taxable capital gain stop you. As I explain in Chapter 21, *when* you sell usually makes little difference from a tax standpoint.

Too many investors, once they buy a fund (or even inherit it) can never quite bring themselves to sell it. Don't fall into that trap. Look on your mutual funds for what they are—investments, not a cherished possession to be held on to forever. And if their best times have passed, it's time to let them go.

Pitfall 6: Following Your Instincts

L ETTING YOUR EMOTIONS CONTROL YOUR INVESTMENT decisions can lead to trouble. Are you a worrier? If so, you scored fairly low on the risk-tolerance test in Chapter 3. But once you've decided what percentage of your money to invest in stock funds, bond funds and money-market funds, don't let the ups and downs of the market spook you into selling or slowing your buying. Don't look at what's happening to the Dow Jones industrial average or the S&P 500. Remember that your own carefully constructed portfolio will probably fall a lot less than the Dow or the S&P in a bear market. Moreover, you are probably considerably ahead of where you started when you first got into the market. And, if you keep investing money regularly, you will almost certainly be well ahead by the time you need your money.

Are you a person who gets depressed easily, who thinks the worst is likely to happen to you? Again, your score on the risk-tolerance test probably has you partly invested in bonds for all but the longest-term goals. Remind yourself, whenever you feel like selling, that the market goes up most of the time. Over the long run, the bulls tend to beat the bears. Hold a steady course.

Are you an optimistic person? Then, like the DiBenedettos, you probably have the bulk of your money in stock funds. Don't get too carried away, though, and be tempted to overload on speculative funds. Don't use borrowed money to invest. Remember to pay off your credit cards and other bills before putting more money into stocks. And don't keep money in stocks that you may need to spend within a year or two.

Pitfall 7: Holding On Until You Get Even, and Selling Too Soon

MANY INVESTORS HAVE A TENDENCY TO WANT TO "LOCK IN" their profits. If a fund goes up 20% or 30%, they may decide it's time to bail out. But a rise in a fund's price shouldn't prompt you to sell if the reasons you bought the fund are still in place: The fund has a good manager and a good long-term record, it still fits into your investment program, and your goals haven't changed. You should generally hold on at least until a fund shows signs of weakening—such as a long-term deterioration in performance when compared with similar funds or the departure of a good manager. Many people sell funds too quickly.

Conversely, as I mentioned in Chapter 3, it can be hard to trim losers from your portfolio. If a fund you buy swoons immediately, you may be tempted to hold on at least until you get even. But sometimes that can take years—years in which you could have been profiting in a better fund. The question to ask yourself when deciding whether to sell a fund is: Would I buy this fund today? If you discover the answer is no, you should generally pull the plug.

Pitfall 8: Being Too Plugged In

WHILE YOU NEED TO BE WELL INFORMED, DON'T PUT MUCH stock in day-to-day market moves. It's the news media's job to tell you what's new. If you hang on every word, you can miss the real message—that over the long term the market's direction is always up and stocks will appreciate more than bonds or short-term investments.

Former psychologist turned money manager Paul Andreassen once performed an experiment with graduate business students at the Massachusetts Institute of Technology. Half the students got frequent news bulletins about stocks, and the others got no information at all. Those who got no news were more successful stock traders. "People are paralyzed by fear caused by too much information," says Bob Wacker, a financial planner in San Luis Obispo, Cal. "I have clients putting their retirement savings into money-market funds because they just get so many conflicting reports."

The remedy: Limit yourself to one or two good sources of current investing information, and don't spend too much time even with them. For instance, CNBC might be a good source of current market movements, but if you watch it all day, you can drive yourself crazy. Several studies have shown that the more information investors take in, the more frequently they tend to buy and sell stocks and funds. And the more frequently investors trade, the less money they tend to make.

Pitfall 9: Remembering Too Well

WE DEVELOP OUR ATTITUDES ABOUT INVESTING FROM OUR parents, and we rarely examine those attitudes," says Rennie Gabriel, a financial planner in Encino, Cal., and self-described "financial coach." Many of today's investors grew up hearing stories about how the 1929 market crash wiped out a relative. Such family legends can lead people to avoid stocks altogether. "The average American has a Great Depression mentality," adds financial planner Harold Evensky of Coral Gables, Fla. "Ask people what's safe and they'll say Treasury bills, bank certificates of deposit and money-markets." Those types of investments were safe during the Depression, but they're less so today, when the bigger threat is inflation. Don't confuse safety with an investment that doesn't change much in value. When investing for the long term, the ups and downs of the stock market generally work to your advantage.

I have a good friend who keeps all of her money in real estate, even though she hates renting out the properties she has bought. When I asked her why she invests in real estate, she explains how well her grandfather did in real estate. Such family stories are often handed down from parents to children, and they dictate how people determine whether an investment is a good one, or whether it is one to be avoided. Instead of relying on what you heard around the dinner table decades ago, look at what has really worked over the long run. There's nothing wrong with investing in real estate, by the way: It's just a lot of work.

Pitfall 10: Seeking Perfection

WITH THOUSANDS OF INVESTMENTS TO CHOOSE FROM, YOU can search forever for a flawless fund. Call off the hunt. "Every investor has to be prepared to lose money," says Maury Elvekrog, a former psychologist who's now an investment adviser in Detroit. "If you're not, you're not doing much of a job of investing." Don't expect to own *the* top-performing fund. Be satisfied with a solid portfolio of funds—some of which will lag the market averages at any given time.

Many investors grew up hearing stories about how the 1929 market crash wiped out a relative, leading them to avoid stocks altogether.

One sure-fire way to raise your investment comfort level—and increase your odds of success, to boot—is to have a friend or relative with whom you talk at least occasionally about your investments. Warren Buffett, probably the most successful investor of our time, never makes a move in the market without talking to his alter ego, Charlie Munger, vice-chairman of his firm. Talking over ideas with someone else can prevent you from acting impulsively and help you make sound decisions. Many people hire a financial advisor solely for the handholding he or she can provide. Barton Biggs, a global investment strategist at Morgan Stanley, once observed: "It may seem corny, but when the market or a stock goes against you, it always seems to help to have someone else to complain to and commiserate with."

Pitfall 11: Owning Bear-Market and All-Market Funds

CRABBE HUSON SPECIAL EQUITY MADE HUGE GAINS IN THE early 1990s. It beat the S&P 500 by 25.8 percentage points in 1992, 24.5 percentage points in 1993, and 10.4 percentage points in 1994. Like a lot of people, manager James Crabbe got nervous toward the end of 1995. He decided to wager that some of the high-flying technology stocks would fall on their keisters. Investors bet that a stock will go down by a complicated process known as "short selling." A short seller borrows shares of stock from one investor and then sells it to a second investor, hoping he or she can buy it back later at a lower price. Crabbe put a large proportion of his fund's assets in these short sales—which turned out to be a disaster, as the stocks continued to climb higher. Crabbe Huson Special Equity proceeded to trail the S&P by 26.7 percentage points in 1995, 17 percentage points in 1996, and 22.1 percentage points in 1997.

Since the stock market has a long-term upward bias, betting that it will go down—or even that certain stocks will go down—is like casino gambling: The odds are not on your side, because stocks go up more than down.

A number of funds (such as Lindner Bulwark, Rydex Ursa and Prudent Bear) put all or part of their money into investments that will profit only if stocks decline. Or they may put their assets into gold, which, although it's supposed to do well during times of inflation and global uncertainty, hasn't delivered on that promise in many years. Ignore these funds. You can tell if a fund is a bear-market fund by calling the toll-free number and asking what percentage of the fund is in gold stocks and what percentage is in short sales or in index *puts*—bets that a market average will decline. Anything over 10% of assets in these usually indicates a bearish fund. They offer the *illusion* of insurance against market declines—although many of them, surprisingly, have failed to do well even in market plunges—and retard your overall returns.

Although gold is supposed to do well during inflationary and uncertain times, it hasn't delivered on that promise in many years.

If you feel you want some protection against inflation by investing in natural resources' stocks, T. Rowe Price New Era, and perhaps, Robertson Stephens Contrarian (which also shorts some stocks) are the best of the lot. But keep these to a tiny percentage of your portfolio, or, better still, don't buy them at all.

Pitfall 12: Owning Too Many Funds (or, How Many Are Enough?)

MONEY MANAGER ROGER GIBSON LIKES TO COMPARE unskilled fund investing to a ramble on the beach picking up shells: "That's a pretty one; I'll pick that one up. And that's a pretty one, too." Trouble is, if you buy too many funds, your portfolio can become so unwieldy that you may find it difficult to tell how you've really deployed your money. Your holdings in stocks, bonds and cash can be out of kilter without your even knowing it. And you're unlikely to do as well as the market averages when you own dozens of funds.

How many funds are enough to reduce risk without sacrificing performance? There's no magic number. Most financial planners and money managers believe a portfolio should contain at least three but probably no more than a dozen funds, and money managers who invest in funds generally recommend a number in the middle of that range. Or as Tim Medley, a financial planner and asset manager in Jackson, Miss., puts it: "The ideal number is somewhere between a basketball squad and a baseball team." The portfolios in this book are generally in Medley's ballpark. For beginning investors, even fewer funds may suffice. Investors with large portfolios, on the other hand, might want to own more funds.

> **Over the long haul, your biggest enemy isn't the loss of money in stocks, but the whittling away of your purchasing power through inflation.**

If you suspect that you own too many funds, go back over them one by one and try to recall why you bought each one. Are those reasons still valid? Would you buy the fund today? If not, the fund is a candidate for selling. Do you own two funds that seek largely the same objective and go about it in largely the same manner? Sell one or the other of them.

Funds should make life simpler. Don't buy so many that you defeat that purpose.

Pitfall 13: Not Investing Enough in Stock Funds

ONE OF THE BIGGEST MISTAKES MADE BY MANY INVESTORS with long-term goals is putting too little into stock funds. The stock market may be too high, or too low, or too frightening to invest more of your money. But remember, over the long haul, the biggest enemy you face is not the loss of money in stocks, but the slow whittling away of your purchasing power through inflation. Only stock funds can afford you long-term protection against that unhappy outcome.

Every year or so, check your funds. Ask yourself: Do you have enough in stock funds? If you're not sure, take the risk-tolerance test and look at the "How Much to Invest in Stocks" tables on pages 28–29. Of course, this advice applies mainly to long-term investing. When investing for short- and intermediate-term goals, you'll want to trim your stock exposure gradually as you get closer to your deadline.

Key Points
• *Don't try to time the market.*
• *Don't chase short-term, top-performing funds.*
• *Don't invest too much in one industry sector.*
• *Don't fall in love with a fund.*
• *Don't let your emotions get in the way of sound decisions.*
• *Do invest enough in stock funds.*

Want Someone to Do It for You?

How to find a good planner or broker, or to get help from a mutual fund company

HILE I WAS WRITING THIS BOOK, I SPOKE OFTEN with Nancy and Paul DiBenedetto to see whether they—as busy, intelligent people with virtually no knowledge of mutual funds—could easily understand the points I was making. For the most part, they did quite well. But one topic—the different types of funds—totally bewildered them. "I am definitely confused," Paul said after I attempted to explain them. "I am so confused I want to just take my money and hire someone, and pray I don't lose my shirt. This is just too mind-boggling." Fortunately, the more Nancy and Paul learned, the more their fears subsided. They had simply hit a temporary roadblock. You may hit a roadblock or two yourself and decide, for at least a moment, that you don't want to go it alone.

It's the raison d'être of this book that almost anyone can do his or her own investing. This book gives you all the tools you need to accomplish that task. And investing on your own should consume little, if any, more time than you would spend finding and working with a broker or financial planner. Plus, investing on your own guarantees you will save a ton of money in commissions and fees. (Not only that, you'll be in control, and you won't have to take a close-your-eyes-and-hope-for-the-best attitude.)

However, lots of people who invest in mutual funds don't do all the work themselves—determine their goals; figure their time horizon; estimate their tolerance for risk; decide how much to invest in stock funds, bond funds and money market funds; and select their mutual funds. For a variety of reasons, you may decide you want to hire a professional to handle your money. You may be too busy to do your own investing. You may feel you'll make mistakes if you invest on your own. You may think you'll panic and sell when the market falls. You may look on investing as a chore that you want someone else to handle. Whatever your reason, this chapter will help you find a good professional.

Still, I'd suggest you continue to learn about investing. After a year or two of working with a broker or financial planner, you'll likely feel more confident about handling things on your own. So, whatever you do, hold on to this book. Even if you decide to let someone else make your decisions for you now, you may well change your mind.

A HYBRID STRATEGY

What if you feel nervous about investing on your own but aren't sure you want to turn your affairs over to a financial planner, either? Here's an excellent way to become more confident about investing and keep your costs down, as well: Pay an hourly fee to meet two or three times, for an hour or two each time, with a planner—and implement his or her recommendations on your own. Expect to pay about $100 to $150 per hour. Tell the planner up front that you want temporary help. Most will be glad to oblige you.

If you proceed this way, make sure you have all your financial files organized before you go visit the planner, and, once the clock starts, spend all your time discussing your financial affairs. Don't get distracted by other topics. Don't get talked into turning all your affairs over to the planner, which is much more lucrative for the planner.

In a year or two—or sooner if you feel adrift—visit again for an update. "Renting a planner" is a good course of action if you feel you need a little advice or handholding before putting an investment plan into action, or if you don't have a lot of money to invest. Many planners don't want long-term relationships with clients who have less than $100,000 to invest. Many advisers and virtually all brokers welcome clients with significantly less.

Finding the Right Adviser

ONCE YOU'VE DECIDED YOU NEED HELP, THERE ARE HUNDREDS of thousands of people—bankers, insurance agents, stockbrokers, financial planners, mutual fund representatives and money managers—who would love to handle your investments for a fee. It sometimes seems as if everyone is hanging out a shingle these days and offering to help you invest in mutual funds.

Unfortunately, it doesn't take any training whatsoever to call yourself an investment adviser or financial planner. Those who manage more than $25 million of clients' money—or work for a firm that does—must register with the federal Securities & Exchange Commission (SEC). That involves filling out a voluminous (and revealing) form called an ADV (short for "adviser") that includes information about an adviser's education, compensation and investment strategy. All the SEC requires is full disclosure. So if a financial adviser is a convicted felon, that's fine—as long as the ADV notes it. If he or she picks mutual funds by using a Ouija board, that's okay, too, if it's disclosed on the ADV.

Advisers or planners managing less than $25 million need not register with the SEC. Instead, state regulations cover them. To locate the state agency that can give you information about a financial adviser or planner, call the North American Securities Administrators Association at 202-737-0900 or visit its Web site at www.nasaa.org.

Rent a planner if you need advice or handholding before putting an investment plan into action, or if you don't have a lot of money to invest.

PLANNER, ADVISER OR BROKER?

To find an honest, competent adviser with whom you can work well, you're probably best off seeking a good financial planner, investment adviser, or a good stockbroker, in that order. While planners, investment advisers and brokers all offer financial expertise, brokers make most of their money by getting you to buy or sell stocks, bonds or mutual funds. Many planners and advisers make their money the same way.

But a growing number of "fee-only" planners and advisers will give you advice for an hourly fee or manage your portfolio for an annual fee of 0.5% to 3% of the assets you place under their management. The advantage of a fee-only planner is that he or she is "on the same side of the table" as you are. In other words, the bigger your portfolio grows, the more money the planner makes. Some planners call themselves "fee-based," which means they derive some of their compensation from fees but the rest from commissions.

Brokers and commission-based planners and advisers can make money simply by persuading you to buy or sell. They generally get a commission on everything you trade—whether it's stocks, bonds or mutual funds. Commission-based planners and advisers, like stockbrokers, typically make their money from mutual fund companies, which pay them around 5% of the amount you invest in a fund.

Stockbrokers are less popular than they used to be. As a result, many have taken to calling themselves by all manner of other titles: financial consultant, financial planner, account executive, vice-president—anything, it seems, but stockbroker. Because fee-only planners and advisers are growing in popularity, many brokers are migrating into that business. That doesn't mean good brokers aren't out there; they're just difficult to find. If you decide to use a broker, see the discussion, "Checking On a Broker," beginning on page 138.

Both fee-only planners and fee-only advisers make most of their money by charging you an annual percentage of the assets they manage. But planners typically offer far more than money management, and may charge little or nothing extra for their extra services. They look at your entire financial situation— estate planning, insurance, the value of your home and other assets, taxes, and so on. In most instances, this may make them a better choice, particularly for beginners, than investment advisers—who may offer additional services, but focus on money management. Investment advisers, on the other hand, argue that they are better at investing simply because it's their primary endeavor.

WHERE TO LOOK

Try any of these leads:

Family and friends

The best way to find a good broker, planner or adviser is to talk with your friends and relatives about who helps them manage their money. If a friend has someone he likes a lot, try to find out if your friend's ideas about investing are similar to yours. Is your friend a fund investor? Does he buy and hold funds for long periods—as opposed to trading frequently, which is usually a money-losing strategy? Also, ask other questions: Does the broker or planner return his calls promptly? Does the adviser seem to understand your friend's investment needs and temperament?

Accountant or lawyer

Lacking a friend who is happy with a broker, adviser or planner, your next step may be to turn to your accountant or lawyer for a recommendation. Be aware that a lawyer or accountant may regularly send clients to the same investment professional, who in turn may send clients to the lawyer or accountant.

Referral services

Still running into a brick wall? At this point, if you haven't already, you may want to cross stockbrokers off your list. If you contact a brokerage firm, or reply to a solicitation from a firm, you may end up with a beginning broker who is just starting to hone his or her skills.

A better strategy may be to contact professional associations that will provide you with lists of credentialed financial planners in your area:

The Institute of Certified Financial Planners (3801 E. Florida Ave., Suite 708, Denver, CO 80210; 800–282–7526; www.icfp.org)

The American Institute of CPAs (Personal Financial Planning Division, 1211 Avenue of the Americas, New York, NY 10036; 800–862–4272; www.aicpa.org)

The National Association of Personal Financial Advisors (fee-only planners; 355 W. Dundee Road, Suite 200, Buffalo Grove, IL 60089; 888–333–6659; www.napfa.org)

The problem with these referral services is that they don't give you any idea which planners are good and which are mediocre. But membership in the National Association of Personal Financial Advisors is particularly meaningful because a screening committee takes a close look at prospective members. It requires them to have clean disciplinary records and to produce a financial plan that passes muster with the organization's membership committee.

A rating service

You can also locate a financial planner through Dalbar Inc. This Boston-based research firm rates financial planners (as well as other money managers) on performance, trustworthiness, and the quality and scope of services provided. It rates only planners with clean regulatory records, and at least 50 clients and $15 million under management. The information is available on the Internet at www.dalbar.com or you can call 617–723–6400.

Although Dalbar provides the service free to consumers, planners pay Dalbar to rate them. "People are reluctant to check references, and to the degree that the ratings provide that, they offer some potential information," says Barbara Roper, director of investor protection for the Consumer Federation of America. "But any time we have people buying ratings, it raises questions." Well-respected planners with booming businesses may be unwilling to pay for inclusion on Dalbar's list.

Charles Schwab

Discount broker Charles Schwab will help you find a planner or investment adviser in your area if you call 888–774–3758. Schwab makes no effort to ensure that the planners it refers you to have had good past performance. It does insist that they have at least five years of experience managing money and have at least $25 million under management. As with Dalbar, managers pay Schwab for referrals.

A First Interview

If you use Schwab, Dalbar or one of the associations above to find a financial planner or investment adviser, make sure to interview at least three. The first interview should be free. Try to get a feel for whether the planner's personality and approach to investing matches yours. If you're not comfortable with a planner when you talk, you're not going to be comfortable with his or her investment recommendations. Here are some things to ask a planner about at a first meeting:

His or her educational background

While education is no guarantee of competence, a certified financial planner (CFP) designation shows the planner had a willingness to get an education, as opposed to simply hanging out a shingle. Other credentials that reflect training are the chartered financial consultant (ChFC), which is the insurance-industry equivalent of a CFP, and the personal financial specialist (PFS) designation awarded to certified public accountants.

A résumé

You're mostly looking for evidence that this person isn't just getting his or her feet wet. While an ex–real estate agent may become a top-flight financial planner or adviser, let him or her make the rookie mistakes with other people's money. Look for someone who's been in financial planning for at least five years.

An investment strategy

Look for evidence that a planner's or adviser's main concern isn't "beating the market," but rather learning your goals and assembling a good, long-term portfolio for you. Get nervous if a planner or adviser spends time bragging about the investment returns of his or her clients. Run if he or she promises to outperform the market. Steer clear of planners who try to "time the market" by guessing when to sell stocks or bonds. Likewise, it's time to end the interview if a planner talks of frequent moves among funds. Good planners and investment advisers generally hold funds for years, not months.

A sample investment plan

It should show evidence of a well-thought-out, long-term approach to investing.

Amount of interaction

Ask how often your planner or adviser will be in contact with you, and what sort of ongoing monitoring of your portfolio he or she will do. He or she should send you at least quarterly reports showing how your portfolio is doing, and should be available to discuss your portfolio whenever you feel it's necessary.

A Form ADV

Ask to see a planner's ADV form, if he or she has one (refer back to the discussion on page 131 for more on this). If a planner or the firm he or she works for manages less than $25 million and, therefore, is not registered with the SEC, the planner must have a similar form filed with the state. The planner must give you Part II of the ADV or its state equivalent, but not Part I, which records any disciplinary actions. If the planner or adviser doesn't voluntarily give you Part I, it's time to look elsewhere. (Both parts of the ADV are also available from the SEC if you submit a written request. You can send a letter to the Securities and Exchange Commission, 450 Fifth Street, N.W., Washington, DC 20549; fax it to the SEC at 202–942–9634; or email it to: help@sec.gov.)

References

A planner or adviser should give you several references to satisfied clients. Naturally, he or she won't refer you to someone who has had a bad experience. But when you call references, ask detailed questions about the kind of assistance they have received. By probing a bit, you may learn useful information. For instance, ask whether they feel the planner has put them into good mutual funds or merely adequate ones. Also ask if they've been able to get through to the planner easily to discuss their investments or changes in their financial situations. Ask whether the planner seems on top of their financial situation and keeps in touch on a regular basis.

Bonding

Before you sign on the dotted line, make sure a planner or adviser is bonded, meaning you're insured if he or she walks off with your money. That protects you if you give the planner or adviser direct access to your money. In rare instances, crooked planners and advisers have vanished with their clients' money. (You're a smidgen safer if a discount broker, like Schwab, holds your money. The planner or adviser has access to the money to make trades, but can't withdraw money without your knowledge and approval.)

Compensation

Be sure you understand precisely how you will pay the planner or adviser. Will you pay only a percentage of assets (fee-only), commissions, or some combination of the two? You can sometimes bargain for lower fees. *Don't hire anyone who will charge you more than 1% annually.* One advantage of fee-only planners and advisers is that you can tell what your costs will be in advance. With a commission-only planner or fee-based planner, you'll pay part of your money in sales charges on investments your planner gets you into and out of. Most of these fees are invisible to you, so you may not really know how much you are paying.

Many fee-only financial planners and advisers have Charles

Getting Help From Newsletters

MOST MUTUAL FUND newsletters are mediocre at best, but a handful provide solid advice, including funds to consider and portfolios of funds for conservative, moderate and aggressive investors.

Before you subscribe, request a sample issue. Is this a newsletter you feel comfortable with and will use? If you can't read, understand and agree with the logic of its investment strategy, the newsletter is not for you.

Also consider cost. If a newsletter costs $200 and you're investing just $20,000, the newsletter costs you 1% annually. But if you're investing $200,000, the cost is a negligible 0.1% annually.

Once you pick a newsletter, stick with it for at least several years; even the best newsletters have periods when their rec- ommended portfolios underperform the market averages.

Following are a few top newsletters that novices should find easy to under- stand. (All are independent of the mutual fund companies they report on.)

Fidelity Insight and FundsNet Insight
($177 per year; 617–369–2500) Editor Eric Kobren offers one newsletter aimed at Fidelity mutual fund investors, and another aimed at investors who buy funds through Charles Schwab, Fidelity Discount Brokerage or Jack White. These discounters offer no advice, but they sell a wide variety of funds without charging any fees and many others with very small fees. Both letters are easy to understand and have solid performance records.

Fidelity Monitor
($96 per year; 800–397–3094) Editor Jack Bowers follows only Fidelity mutual funds. His performance has been solid. His newsletter is also a good one for investors who have 401(k) accounts with Fidelity because it offers specific advice tailored to individual 401(k) plans.

Independent Adviser for Vanguard Investors
($199 per year; 800–777–7005) Former journalist Daniel Wiener's newslet- ter offers common-sense advice in an easy-to-read format, on allocating money among Vanguard mutual funds.

No-Load Fund Investor
($129 per year; 800–252–2042) Sheldon Jacobs has written about mutual funds since the early 1970s. His newslet- ter offers portfolios for investors at differ- ent stages of life. The newsletter also offers portfolios for investors who invest only in mutual funds offered by Vanguard, T. Rowe Price or Fidelity.

Schwab or another discounter do the bookkeeping on all their accounts because it saves them time and money. You'll usually get monthly statements from the brokerage firm. Be aware that the funds the planner buys for you in a discount brokerage have expenses of their own, so whatever the planner charges you amounts to an extra layer of expenses. You'll occasionally have to pay small fees to the discount broker, as well.

CHECKING ON A BROKER

Look for many of the same qualities in a broker that you would in a financial planner or adviser. The National Association of Securities Dealers Regulation, the brokerage industry's self-regulatory organization, is the main source of information on a broker's history. By calling the NASDR, at 800–289–9999, or visiting its Web site at www.nasdr.com, you can find out about:

• **customer complaints** against a broker,

• **whether he or she has been the target of any disciplinary actions** by the NASDR or other agencies, and

• **whether he or she has lost arbitration claims** (almost all broker-ages require you to settle disputes by arbitration rather than by going to court).

State securities agencies maintain similar information. Look in the state government listings in the blue pages of your phone book under such headings as Department of Corporations, Department of Law, State Corporation Commission or Secretary of State. If you can't find the right agency, call the North American Securities Administrators Association at 202–737–0900 and ask for your state's number.

Avoid the house brands

Once you settle on a broker, you should generally stay away from the firm's "house-brand" funds. Funds managed and distributed by the brokerage firm usually have the firm's name in them. Thus, there's Merrill Lynch Capital and Salomon Smith Barney Aggressive Growth. Broker-run funds have tended to be poor performers. Moreover, a broker may be more objective in sizing up funds sold by outside firms. Some of the best fund families among broker-sold funds, include the American funds (managed by Capital Research & Management), Franklin Templeton funds and Putnam funds.

Alphabet Soup

NOT TOO MANY YEARS AGO, WHEN A BROKER OR PLANNER sold you a mutual fund, it came in only one variety: Class A shares. These shares had huge sales charges, typically 8.5%. As investors began to understand how hefty those commissions were, many stopped buying the funds. The financial-services industry reacted in two ways: It lowered its commissions to a more reasonable 5% or so, and it introduced a jumble of fee structures so bewildering it's a wonder any broker or planner—much less an investor—can keep up with them. They include:

Class A shares, which usually assess their entire sales charge when you first invest.

Class B shares, which have no initial sales charge but nick you for as much as one percentage point more than no-load funds in annual expenses. If you sell Class B shares before, say, five years are up, you pay a redemption fee, too.

Class C shares, which have no initial sales charges, leading some dishonest brokers to say they have no sales charges. Actually, C shares typically charge the same high annual expenses as B shares. Moreover, those expenses on C shares often continue for as long as you own the fund, while the annual fees on B shares often reduce to the level of the A shares after five or six years.

Confused? You don't have to be a skeptic to think that the fund industry came up with this alphabet soup precisely for the purpose of confounding investors. My advice:

If you're buying a fund for a long period—say, five years or more—go ahead and pay the front-end sales charge for the Class A shares. You'll likely end up better off, and you won't have to learn the fine points of differentiating among share classes.

Better yet, if you stick with a fee-only planner or adviser, you will invest entirely in funds that levy no sales charges. That will make life simpler, though not necessarily cheaper, because the planner will generally charge you up to 1% of assets under management annually.

Help From the Funds

AS FUND COMPANIES SEEK TO EXPAND THEIR MARKETS, MORE are going into the advice-giving business. Sometimes, fund-company advice is as expensive as what you'd pay a planner or broker. Other times, it's free. In all cases, you need to be a little wary, because fund companies usually recommend only their own funds. (Fidelity, T. Rowe Price and Vanguard also offer excellent educational materials on investing—however, you'll find most of what they offer covered in this book.)

Here's a thumbnail sketch of some of the services offered by fund companies. They change constantly, so check for details.

DREYFUS (800–782–6620)

Dreyfus will provide you access via a toll-free number to a financial planner, who will help you determine how much you need to save for various goals and provide you ongoing advice on fund selection, and financial planning issues including insurance, tax questions and estate planning. Dreyfus charges a $100 annual fee for accounts of at least $10,000, its account minimum, and no fee for accounts with more than $50,000. While many Dreyfus stock funds have been poor performers, clients of this notable program, called the Lion Account, have access to more than 1,000 no-load funds from 180 fund companies.

FIDELITY (800–544–3455)

For investors with a minimum of $200,000, Fidelity offers Portfolio Advisory Services, which will allocate your money among Fidelity and other funds and move it to different funds as conditions and your personal situation warrant. But Fidelity charges up to 1% annually for this service on top of its ordinary annual fund expenses and provides little financial planning.

SCUDDER (800–225–2470)

This program, similar to Fidelity's, is available to investors with at least $100,000, and charges a maximum of 1% annually, depending on the size of the investor's portfolio. Scudder has a few good funds but also has some weak areas, so it's probably a mistake to put all your money in its funds.

STEIN ROE (800–338–2550)

Stein Roe's Counselor plan will provide fund-selection advice— for nothing—to anyone who fills out a questionnaire. If you decide to open an account with at least $50,000, the firm will monitor your account and periodically recommend changes in your funds. It's your decision whether to implement the suggested changes. Stein Roe also offers a companion program under which the company actually makes all the changes in your portfolio, but for this service it charges a maximum annual net fee of 1%—less for accounts over $100,000. Some Stein Roe funds have been good performers. Like Scudder, however, the company lacks a full menu of consistent top performers.

USAA (800–382–8722)

Unlike other phone representatives (the people who answer the toll-free numbers when you call a mutual fund), USAA's trained representatives give clients advice. They work in clusters of seven to ten, and each group's supervisor has at least five years' experience in the investment business and usually holds a financial-planning designation, such as CFP. A state-of-the-art computer system enables phone reps to call up information from previous times you've contacted USAA. While USAA has only a few standout funds, its funds tend to be steady performers, and they charge among the lowest fees in the industry. If you want someone you can call for free advice periodically, USAA is a fine place to go, particularly if you're a beginning investor without a lot of money to invest.

VANGUARD (800–635–1511)

The mutual fund company with the lowest expenses, Vanguard charges $500 for an investment plan that includes guidance on how much you should invest and which funds to invest in (or $500 for a retirement-savings plan or an estate-planning plan) or, if you have more than $500,000 in assets, 0.5% of assets annually (with a minimum fee of $2,500) for continuing investment advice. (For slightly higher fees, Vanguard will include advice on non-Vanguard funds, too.) Vanguard has great bond and index funds, but its actively managed stock funds are a mixed bag. Still, it has a much broader array of funds than Scudder or SteinRoe. So long as you don't mind doing business solely on the phone and through the mail, Vanguard's 0.5% service offers comprehensive financial planning at about half the price you'd pay elsewhere.

Key Points

- *It takes no training to become a registered investment adviser.*
- *Friends are your best source of information on good brokers, financial planners and investment advisers.*
- *Be prepared to spend time interviewing brokers and financial planners, and to ask them blunt questions.*
- *Make sure to check disciplinary records.*
- *Load funds come in a bewildering assortment.*
- *Good fund newsletters can help.*
- *So can fund companies.*

How to Pick Good Stock Funds

his section provides the nuts and bolts of how to pick funds yourself. The first chapter contains a detailed look at how stocks and other investments have performed over the long haul—something surprisingly few investors ever see in print. It's certain to make you feel more comfortable about investing in stock funds. The other chapters in Part Three explain how to select and monitor good stock and bond funds, and how to assemble them into solid fund portfolios.

A Look at the Long Term

How stocks, bonds and cash have performed and what to expect from them in the future

HIS CHAPTER IS ONE OF THE MOST IMPORTANT IN THE book. While I presented a summary of how investors can expect stocks, bonds and cash to perform over the long term and short term in Chapter 2, this chapter examines the subject in detail. The point here is to give you a comprehensive picture of returns of different investments over time so that you can make intelligent decisions about how to deploy your money. After you've finished, you'll have all the data you need about why it makes so much sense to invest as much of your long-term money in the stock market as your gut will allow. Once you've completed this chapter, you may even want to retake · the risk test on pages 28–29. The additional knowledge may have increased your tolerance for the market's ups and downs.

Because of this chapter's significance, I've placed it at the beginning of the second half of the book—the half aimed at investors who want to delve more deeply into the whys and hows of mutual funds. Aside from a couple of cameo appearances, incidentally, the DiBenedettos have decided to bow out of these later chapters. "We've gotten all we want for now," says Nancy. I'll catch up with them in the Afterword, on page 281.

The Short and Long of Stocks

S
TOCKS CAN BE TREACHEROUS TO OWN OVER SHORT PERIODS. IN October 1987, the Dow Jones industrial average plummeted 23% in a *single day*—an even worse drop than the "Black Tuesday" 1929 stock market crash that ushered in the Great Depression. But imagine if you had been unlucky enough to buy stocks on August 25, 1987, just before the three-month, 33.5% decline in the market began. You would have been back to even within 21 months, and by August 22, 1997, you would have more than tripled your original investment. That's not bad for a ten-year span.

No one can foretell the future, but the past is clear: Despite crashes and protracted down markets—through wars, depressions, inflation and all manner of political and economic crises—since 1926 stocks in large companies have returned an annualized 11%, as measured by Standard & Poor's 500-stock index. By contrast, five-year government bonds have returned an annualized 5.4% since 1926, and cash has returned only 3.7%. By cash, I mean 90-day Treasury bills, which return roughly the same as money-market funds, ultra-short-term bond funds and bank certificates of deposit.

ACCOUNTING FOR INFLATION

Over those years, inflation has risen at an annualized 3.1%. Inflation, which measures how much more expensive things get every year (remember nickel Cokes and $3,000 new cars?), is the enemy of investors. In *Through the Looking Glass*, the Red Queen informs a distraught Alice that she has to run as fast as she can just to stay in the same place. Similarly, inflation gives you a benchmark for how fast your investments need to grow just to keep you from losing ground in terms of spending power. The *annualized returns* (see the box on the opposite page) *after inflation* since 1926 have been 7.6% for stocks, 2.5% for bonds and 0.6% for cash. Once you factor in taxes, you can actually fall behind each year by investing in "low-risk" cash.

Strikingly, over holding periods as short as five years, stocks have been far better at outpacing inflation than either bonds or cash. Since 1926, stocks have failed to beat inflation in only 21% of all five-year periods, while bonds have fallen behind inflation in 33% of those periods, and Treasury bills have failed to best inflation 39% of the time. So, even over five-year-periods, stocks are more predictable inflation fighters than either bonds or cash.

(*Note:* To make the data more reliable, I've used "rolling" five-year periods. The first period started in 1926 and ended in 1930. The next started in 1927 and ended in 1931, and so on. I've done the same thing throughout this chapter. After all, just because you're investing for ten years doesn't mean you're necessarily starting at the beginning of a decade.)

RISK AND REWARD OVER TIME

Over long periods, stocks have been, without question, the best investment. During rolling five-year periods, stocks have lost money only 10.5% of the time, and have lost more than an annualized 10% only 3% of the time—or in only two of the five-year periods since 1926. So why not invest every dollar you can in stocks, no matter what your goal? Because over short time periods, bonds are more reliable and cash is the most predictable of all. In investing, as with most other endeavors, the amount you stand to gain is roughly commensurate with the amount of risk, or volatility, you accept—at least over the short term.

WHAT THE TABLES SHOW

The "Performance Snapshots" table on page 149 shows the best, worst and annualized performance of stocks, bonds and cash

What Does "Annualized" Mean?

THROUGHOUT PARTS THREE and Four, I use the word *annualized* when discussing returns on investments. It means the same thing as "compound annual," a term sometimes used in other publications. Both terms describe how much an investment earns *per year.* For instance, if a stock doubles in five years, its annualized return is 14.9%.

But annualized returns are not quite the same as average annual returns, which you should steer clear of. Here's an example that demonstrates why: You buy a fund at $10 per share. The price rises 100%, to $20 per share, the first year you own it. The second year, it drops in price by 50%, to $10 a share. Your *annualized* return is 0%. But your *average annual* return (100% + −50% = 50%) divided by two equals 25%. Bottom line: You can't spend average annual return.

over periods of one, five, ten and 20 years. It also shows the percentage of time that stocks have failed to outperform bonds and cash. Here's what those results mean for you:

Investing for one-year periods
Over one-year periods, cash is clearly the most prudent option. Stocks have plunged as much as 43.3% in one year, while long-term corporate bonds have never lost more than 8.1%, and the worst performance for cash has been a minuscule loss of 0.02%. That's why when you're investing for a period of a year or two, as the DiBenedettos are for their new house, your money belongs in money-market funds, savings accounts or short-term bond funds. While stocks, on average, do better than bonds or cash, stocks have lost money in nearly one out of every three years.

Investing for five years or more
Over five years, however, stocks have never lost more than an annualized 12.5%, and bonds never more than an annualized 2.2%. With a five-year time horizon, it makes sense to divide your money among stocks, bonds and cash. If stocks go up, you'll get the benefit of being in the stock market, but if they go down, you'll have the bonds and cash to cushion your losses. Over five-year periods, stocks have outperformed bonds and cash 76% of the time.

Investing for ten years or more
Over periods of ten years or longer, stocks look the best. Since 1926, stocks have outperformed both bonds and cash:
- **In 84%** of the ten-year periods
- **In 98%** of 20-year periods

  Their worst ten-year return was an annualized loss of 0.9% (from 1929 to 1938).

  That's why investors with more than ten years before they need their money will want to put the bulk of it into stocks.

Average returns
The tables also show the average of the annualized returns over each time period. That's a mouthful, and forgive me for using it, but let me explain. Let's look at the five-year periods. Fund company T. Rowe Price took the annualized returns for each rolling

Performance Snapshots: Stocks Versus Bonds Versus Cash, 1926–1996

ONE YEAR	BEST ONE-YEAR RETURN	WORST ONE-YEAR RETURN	PERCENTAGE OF TIME INVESTMENT LOST MONEY	PERCENTAGE OF TIME INVESTMENT BEATEN BY STOCKS	90% OF RETURNS BETTER THAN
Stocks	54.0%	−43.3%	28.2%	—	−15.7%
Bonds	42.6	−8.1	9.9	65%	−0.7
Cash	14.7	−0.02	2.8	63	0.2

FIVE YEARS	BEST ANNUALIZED FIVE-YEAR RETURN	WORST ANNUALIZED FIVE-YEAR RETURN	PERCENTAGE OF TIME INVESTMENT LOST MONEY	PERCENTAGE OF TIME INVESTMENT BEATEN BY STOCKS	AVERAGE OF ANNUALIZED RETURNS	90% OF ANNUALIZED RETURNS BETTER THAN
Stocks	23.9%	−12.5%	10.5%	—	10.4%	−7.5%
Bonds	22.5	−2.2	0	78%	5.3	1.4
Cash	11.1	0.07	0	81	3.8	0.1

TEN YEARS	BEST ANNUALIZED RETURN	WORST ANNUALIZED RETURN	PERCENTAGE OF TIME INVESTMENT LOST MONEY	PERCENTAGE OF TIME INVESTMENT BEATEN BY STOCKS	AVERAGE OF ANNUALIZED RETURNS	90% OF ANNUALIZED RETURNS BETTER THAN
Stocks	20.1%	−0.9%	3.2%	—	10.8%	1.2%
Bonds	16.3	1.0	0	84%	5.2	1.6
Cash	9.2	0.2	0	84	3.8	0.2

20 YEARS	BEST ANNUALIZED RETURN	WORST ANNUALIZED RETURN	PERCENTAGE OF TIME INVESTMENT LOST MONEY	PERCENTAGE OF TIME INVESTMENT BEATEN BY STOCKS	AVERAGE OF ANNUALIZED RETURNS	90% OF ANNUALIZED RETURNS BETTER THAN
Stocks	16.9%	3.1%	0%	—	10.8%	6.1%
Bonds	10.6	1.3	0	98%	4.7	2.0
Cash	7.7	0.4	0	100	3.7	0.5

SOURCE: T. ROWE PRICE ASSOCIATES, IBBOTSON ASSOCIATES

five-year period from 1926 to 1996. It then *averaged* the returns for those periods over the long term to compute the answers you see in the tables. While the process is a bit complicated, the results are not. For instance, if you invested in stocks, the average of the annualized five-year returns was 10.4%. So, if you held stocks five years, on average, you would have earned 10.4% per year. By comparison, in bonds, the average of the annualized five-year returns was only 5.3%.

A measure of your risk

Finally, the tables present a useful look at risk. The last column shows the *worst return* you could expect in each investment type 90% of the time. In other words, it presents your near-worst-case scenario. Another way of looking at the last column: *90% of the time you would have done better than the percentage return it lists.* Since most people are willing to take a risk when the odds are stacked 90% in their favor, this is a meaningful number.

Don't Bet Against History

OF COURSE, THERE'S ALWAYS THE CHANCE THAT THE NEXT ten or 20 years will not be like the last 70 years. The past, after all, is not always prologue. But a longer time period should inspire even greater confidence that the past 70 years were not a historical fluke. Jeremy Siegel, a finance professor at the University of Pennsylvania's Wharton School, examined the returns of stocks, bonds and cash since 1802—the earliest date for which he could find meaningful data. (Some academics, to be fair, assert that there is *no* reliable data going back that far.) Remarkably, he found that stocks have returned an annualized 6.8% after inflation since 1802—*precisely* what they have returned since 1926. Before inflation, stocks have returned an annualized 8.1% since 1802.

In addition to examining returns for U.S. stocks, Siegel looked at stock-market returns since 1802 in Great Britain and

---

Combining Stocks, Bonds and Cash

THIS TABLE LOOKS at how you would have done with various mixtures of stocks and bonds in your investment portfolio in the 70 years between 1926 and 1996.

	ANNUALIZED RETURN	WORST ANNUAL LOSS	NUMBER OF YEARS WITH A LOSS
80% stocks, 20% bonds	9.9%	−35.7%	19
60% stocks, 40% bonds	8.9	−28.1	16
40% stocks, 40% bonds, 20% cash	7.6	−19.3	15

SOURCE: VANGUARD GROUP

The Calming Effect of Time

THIS BAR GRAPH ILLUSTRATES how little risk there is in stocks over long time periods. It uses the same numbers—the best and worst annualized returns for stocks, bonds and cash in each of four periods—as the "Performance Snapshots" table on page 149. Over one-year periods, stocks are unpredictable, but over 20-year periods they are actually more predictable, as well as more profitable than competing investments. (*Note:* Some values are so small that, given the scale of the graph, they appear as zero.)

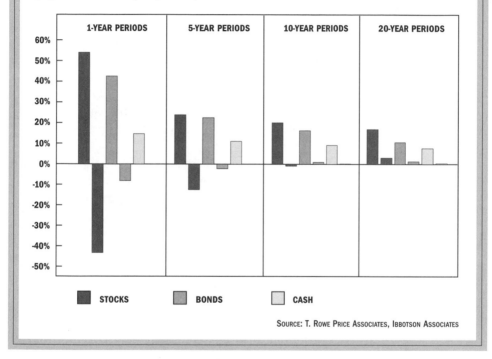

SOURCE: T. ROWE PRICE ASSOCIATES, IBBOTSON ASSOCIATES

since 1926 in Germany. Those markets produced approximately the same results as the U.S. stock market despite nearly being destroyed in World War II. In the U.S., there has been no 30-year period since 1802 in which stocks failed to outperform bonds and cash. In his book, *Stocks for the Long Run,* Siegel found that U.S. bonds historically have returned an annualized 4.7% before inflation since 1802—a little less than they have since 1926. Cash has returned an annualized 4.3% since 1802. Inflation, meanwhile, has taken a toll of 1.3% annually.

It's possible that history won't repeat itself—that stocks will lose money over the next 20 years, or fail to outperform other investments. But the odds are overwhelmingly against such an occurrence. As Sir John Templeton, the legendary investor who pioneered overseas mutual fund investing for Americans, said, "The four most dangerous words in investing are, 'This time is different.'" In this context, it means simply: Never bet against stocks over the long run.

How Bad Can It Get?

WHILE STOCKS OFFER THE BEST ROUTE TO LONG-TERM investment success, don't delude yourself about how bumpy the road to wealth can be. Understanding how the stock market behaves will make it easier to stay invested, however. "If people are emotionally prepared for a bear market, they are more apt to stay the course, which is what they should be doing when the tough days come," says John Bogle, chairman of the Vanguard funds.

Imagine for a moment that in August 1929 you decided it was the perfect time to put all your money into stocks. The market fell a staggering 86.2% between then and June 1932, when it hit bottom. Just to break even, an investor who bought at the peak in 1929 would have had to wait until July 1944, about a month after the Allied landing in Normandy on D-Day.

Unfortunately, there's been a more recent bear market in stocks (a bear market is a decline in the S&P 500 of 20% or more) that cruelly depressed prices. Starting in early 1973, the stock market lost 48% over two years. An investor who got in at the top wouldn't have broken even until late 1976, and, if you factor in inflation, not until October 1983.

The average bear market since 1926 has meant a drop in value for Standard & Poor's 500-stock index of 35.3%, and it has taken people who invested at the top two years and five months to break even. On average, there is one such bear market about every five years. Investors can also expect the stock market to decline by 10% or more twice in every three years. Most of these declines do not become bear markets but, in retrospect, represent buying opportunities.

Some of the pithiest advice on preparing for bear markets came from a stockbroker who later became a minister. He jokingly equated them with the Second Coming of Christ. He quoted from the book of Mark: "Watch therefore, for you know neither the day nor the hour."

The clear lesson of stock-market history is that stocks are the place to be for the long haul. Moreover, the market has a lot more safeguards in place than it did in 1929. The volatility of the U.S. stock market in 1929 is arguably more akin to what exists in today's emerging stock markets, such as Mexico, Thailand and Russia. Nor is there any sign at this writing that circumstances like those of 1973–74—which included high inflation, recession, an oil embargo and the resignation of a president—are on the horizon.

Key Points

- *Stocks can be volatile and dangerous to own over short periods.*
- *Over longer periods, stocks offer the best returns.*
- *Studies going back to 1802 in the U.S. and Great Britain and to 1926 in Germany support the idea that stocks return about an annualized 7% after inflation.*

Starting the Search for the Right Funds

There are funds for every purpose, though their names may not tell you so

SCOTT FITZGERALD ONCE SAID THAT A TEST OF A first-rate intelligence is the ability to keep two contradictory ideas in your head at the same time and still be able to function. While you don't have to be a genius to invest well in mutual funds, it will help to keep these two somewhat contradictory rules in mind:

• **Learn the precise name** of every mutual fund you are considering.

• **You can't count on funds' names** to tell you much about how they invest.

Rule one comes into play partly because fund companies—which have created nearly 7,000 mutual funds—sometimes get carried away and create funds that aren't much different from other funds. For example, Dreyfus has a fund called *Dreyfus Muni Bond*. The name is simple and straightforward—this fund invests in tax-exempt municipal bonds, which we'll discuss in Chapter 18. But how does this fund differ from *Dreyfus General Muni Bond*? Not by a lot. Then there's *Dreyfus Basic Muni Bond*. And *Dreyfus Premier Muni Bond*, which is sold by brokers and comes in A, B and C share classes. Think that should about cover it? Guess again. Dreyfus also sells a line of *intermediate muni bond* funds in all these same flavors (muni, general, basic and premier), as well as a similar number of *limited-term muni bond* and *insured muni bond* funds. In all, Dreyfus has almost 90 municipal bond funds—all of which have pretty similar names, but some of which do different things.

I read the last few paragraphs to the DiBenedettos after work one day, and the number of choices appalled them. Paul said that, lacking any further guidance, he would probably have chosen the Dreyfus Basic fund. "Since I'm a novice investor, I guess the basic one would be the one I would want to buy. Basic means simple, doesn't it?" Paul has a wry sense of humor; he wasn't serious. And Dreyfus's Basic line of funds isn't for beginners. "All these different names are confusing," added Nancy. "How can anyone keep them straight? The fund companies are in business to make money, so they keep coming out with new things. If you figure out how funds work, you might get ahead for a while. But it seems like you're taking one step forward and two steps backwards."

Nancy's comments are worth remembering. Mutual fund companies are not in business just to make money for you; they are in business to make money. Unfortunately, coming out with a seemingly endless procession of new funds is the best way many fund companies have hit on to drum up more business. They're frequently variations on the same theme, but occasionally fund companies come up with bizarre funds. One fund, Pauze Tombstone, focuses on companies in what its sponsor terms the "death-care" industry, running funeral homes, making caskets and providing grave markers.

Just as in buying a car or a refrigerator, it takes work to sort through the thousands of funds—and plethora of names—to find the ones that are the best values for you. Before you invest, you'd better know exactly which fund you're buying—its precise name and what it does. Otherwise, you might end up owning one you didn't want or a type of fund that doesn't lend the proper balance to your investment plan.

This chapter will help by describing the different types of funds. I've also provided some guidance on which of them belong in long- and short-term portfolios. Even if you don't remember all the types of funds enumerated in this chapter, you can always turn back to it for reference.

Remember that Part Two gave you portfolios of specific funds that match your goals. As a check of any portfolio you assemble yourself, you may want to turn back to Part Two and see what percentage of each fund type I've included in portfolios for different goals.

Once you assemble a good portfolio, fund investing is pretty low-maintenance. Despite Nancy DiBenedetto's fears, you won't have to keep up with every new mutual fund that comes to market; you'll find that most are retreads of similar funds and you can ignore them.

How Fund Followers Type the Funds

YOU'D THINK THAT A NAME WOULD AT LEAST REALLY TELL YOU what a fund does. Unfortunately, that's not always so. Consider Fidelity Select Regional Banks. Rather than stick to regional banks, this fund also buys huge national banks; in 1997 it included BankAmerica, NationsBank and Citicorp among its top ten holdings. Or Robertson Stephens Value and Growth fund, which is a pure growth fund with no value, or bargain, component. Or, T. Rowe Price Capital Appreciation, a fine fund (see page 216), typically has only about half its assets in stocks— yet capital-appreciation funds are considered the highest-octane of all stock funds. Then there's Alliance North American Government Income Trust, which in 1997 held nearly 25% of assets in Argentine government bonds. There are dozens of other examples of misnamed funds—stock funds that own few stocks, and supposedly well-diversified funds that have most of their money stuffed into one or two sectors. The bottom line: When it comes to mutual funds, you can't judge a book by its cover.

Before you buy a fund, you need to examine its semiannual report to determine what it actually does. Or consult resources such as *Morningstar Mutual Funds* or *Value Line Mutual Fund Survey*, available at many public libraries, which give full-page descriptions of most funds.

To help you see through the fog of misnamed funds, most sources of fund information—including *Morningstar, Value Line* and *Kiplinger's Personal Finance Magazine*—go beyond names when they classify funds into different groups. They scrutinize the holdings of each fund to see what it actually does, and take a careful look at how volatile each fund is relative to its peers. Then they divide funds into broad categories, also called investment objectives. Unfortunately, every fund-rating service classifies funds in slightly different ways. Be aware of this when you are consulting more than one source on funds.

Keep Your Eye on Total Return

THE NUMBER TO FOCUS on when evaluating funds is *total return*. Most funds pay dividends and capital gains to their shareholders at least once a year. Payment of those distributions shrinks the per-share price (or net asset value per share) of the fund, but doesn't change your stake in the fund—so long as you reinvest the distributions in additional shares.

Suppose the XYZ fund has a net asset value of $10 per share on January 1, and you buy 100 shares with a total value of $1,000. Over the course of a year, the share price rises to $11, and in late December, the fund pays out dividends of $1 per share and capital gains of $1 per share. Because of the $2-per-share distribution, the net asset value of the fund is now only $9. But you haven't lost money because you have your $2 per share in distributions. If you reinvest those distributions, you now own 122.2 shares at $9 per share, worth $1,100. That's a $100 increase in value from the beginning of the year, and $100 divided by $1,000 gives you a *total return* for the year of 10%.

Total return also takes into account how much a fund charges you in expenses. In short, a fund's bottom line is its total return. As shorthand, I sometimes use the word "return" to refer to total return. Total return figures in newspapers and magazines typically don't reflect sales charges, but those in prospectuses do.

Even if you are living in retirement and require income from your funds, don't pay too much attention to a fund's yield—that is, how much monthly or quarterly income it pays you. The problem with investing for yield is that you can end up with funds that don't grow enough to keep you ahead of inflation. Instead, you should buy funds likely to produce good total returns. Then spend some of the yearly distributions rather than reinvesting them—or even sell some shares of your funds to meet your needs.

I'll describe the way *Kiplinger's* classifies funds. Don't feel as though you have to memorize these categories and what they mean. Each time I discuss a fund in detail, I'll explain again what it does and where it fits into the scheme of things. Moreover, you'll likely do just fine without ever investing in most of the fund types listed.

Stock Funds

KIPLINGER'S BREAKS DOWN STOCK FUNDS INTO EIGHT investment categories, or objectives. Here are descriptions of each:

AGGRESSIVE-GROWTH FUNDS

Aggressive-growth funds seek maximum gains. Often they invest in risky stocks of small companies, and usually they pay no attention to dividend income. These funds tend to outperform the market in rising (or "bull") markets but to fall sharply in declining (or "bear") markets. They are best suited for investors with ten years or so before they'll need their money. As you get closer to your goal, you'll want to scale back on these funds.

LONG-TERM-GROWTH FUNDS

Long-term-growth funds also aim for big gains. But they tend to invest in stocks of larger, more stable companies. These funds typically mirror the market—rising about as much as Standard & Poor's 500-stock index when the stock market is on a roll. When the market falls, they also tend to fall just about the same amount. They should typically make up the biggest part of long-term portfolios.

BALANCED FUNDS

Balanced funds generally have 30% or more of their assets in bonds, no matter what the market looks like. They tend to underperform the stock market when it's rising, but will usually hold up better than all-stock funds when the market turns down. Most investors are better off creating their own "balanced" funds, by buying both pure stock funds and pure bond funds. That way *you* decide how much to invest in stocks and bonds, rather than a fund manager who doesn't know your individual situation.

GROWTH-AND-INCOME FUNDS

Growth-and-income funds tend to concentrate more on predictable dividend income than on stupendous growth. These funds usually invest in large companies and, in addition to stocks, often own bonds and other income-producing securities. They generally produce lower returns than aggressive-growth and long-term-growth funds in good times (though they outpaced their more aggressive brethren, on average, over the 15 years through April 30, 1998), but should decline less than those two categories of funds in a bear market. Growth-and-income funds are often the ballast of long-term portfolios. In shorter-term portfolios, though, they may be your largest stock-fund holding.

You can subdivide the growth-and-income category into additional types:

Plain growth-and-income funds (sometimes called equity-income) usually own few or no bonds.

Total-return funds use a variety of strategies but typically vary their percentage of bonds depending on the manager's prognosis for the markets.

Asset-allocation funds usually have a flexible division of assets in stocks and bonds. Some asset-allocation funds invest 100% in stocks in good times and nothing in stocks in bad times. Others vary their percentage of stocks only slightly.

I mention these subcategories because you may see a fund referred to in these ways. But for the most part, the growth-and-income moniker tells you what you need to know.

INTERNATIONAL FUNDS

International funds generally have all, or almost all, of their assets invested in foreign companies. These funds allow U.S. investors to take advantage of growth opportunities in other parts of the world. However, they are usually riskier than domestic funds because foreign political upheaval, looser regulatory environments and changes in the value of the dollar against foreign currencies can affect them. The chief advantage of owning international funds is that foreign markets often do not move in tandem with the U.S. market, so they reduce the volatility of your overall portfolio. They usually invest some of their money in risky emerging markets. Most long-term investors will profit by placing 20% to 25% of their money in these funds.

Subcategories of international funds are:

Emerging-markets funds, which invest in developing nations, mostly in Asia and Latin America. These funds tend to be extremely volatile but sometimes produce big gains.

Regional funds, which specialize in just one part of the globe, such as Asia or Europe.

Single-country funds, which invest in only one country. Many of these funds are closed-end funds (discussed in Chapter 22).

Most investors will do well to put 10% to 30% of their assets in a broad-based international fund but to use subcategories sparingly, if at all.

GLOBAL FUNDS

Global funds invest most of their assets overseas, but they also invest in the U. S. These funds often vary in the percentage of assets that they invest in the U.S., depending on where managers perceive the most value. Most investors will do better with pure international funds because you can more reliably and easily track how much of your money is invested abroad. Global funds are sometimes called *worldwide* funds.

SECTOR FUNDS

Sector funds invest in a single industry, such as automobiles or software, or in a broader economic sector, such as transportation or technology. These funds tend to be extremely volatile, and you can often find some of them atop the market leaders' lists for the preceding 12 months. Alas, you can usually find some sector funds on the laggards' list for the same 12 months. Predicting which sectors will do well is nearly impossible, so take these funds in small doses or abstain from them altogether. One exception to this rule is *real estate* funds, which provide a high-level of dividend income and tend to be much less risky than other kinds of sector funds.

UTILITY FUNDS

Another exception to the rule, utility funds are really a subset of sector funds. *Kiplinger's* groups utility funds separately because there are a lot of them and they've traditionally been more conservative than other sector funds. They generally aim to pay big dividends and to incur little risk. But the utility industry has become much more competitive in recent years, and it's likely to become even more cutthroat in the future. That has reduced the dividend yields of these funds and made them somewhat more volatile. A utility fund, however, is still likely to be safer than other sector funds.

PRECIOUS-METALS FUNDS

Precious-metals funds invest in stocks of gold-mining companies. Some also own stock in silver-mining companies, as well as in gold and silver themselves. Many financial planners in the 1980s considered these so-called "hard assets" to be ideal hedges against inflation. Planners often recommended that investors hold 5% or so of their stock money in these funds, to cushion against declining markets. But since the mid 1980s these funds haven't acted well as an inflation hedge. They've even done badly in times of global political upheaval, such as the 1990 Gulf War.

Bond Funds

A S A GROUP, BOND FUNDS ARE LESS RISKY, AND LESS REWARDING, than stocks. Think about it. If you had bought shares in Microsoft years ago, your money could have grown a hundredfold or more. On the other hand, if you had had the misfortune to own shares of one of the many Microsoft wannabes, you may have made little or no money—or even lost it all. But if you had bought bonds from any company, regardless of how rosy its future, the best you could have hoped for is the return of your money with interest. Unless the company went bankrupt, you'd be repaid—but your potential for gain would have been limited. During periods of rising inflation and interest rates, such as the 1970s, bonds actually paid you back less *after inflation* than you had invested in the first place. Since the early 1980s, however, long-term bonds have been unusually profitable—as interest rates have dropped, thus driving up bonds' prices.

You can ordinarily count on bond funds to reduce risk in your portfolio and provide steady income. They are an essential part of shorter-term portfolios and portfolios for people living in retirement. Most investors will do well to put most of their bond money into high-grade bond funds and a smaller amount into high-yield bond funds (see below), because owning the two types tends to minimize your portfolio's overall volatility. Even with fairly a short time horizon until you'll need your money, you'll want to own different types of bond funds. It's only when you're within two or three years of your goal that you'll want to stick largely to short-term bonds.

Kiplinger's divides the bond universe into the following investment objectives:

HIGH-GRADE CORPORATE FUNDS

High-grade corporate funds emphasize safety by owning mostly bonds that bond-rating agencies have rated as "investment grade." (That means Standard & Poor's ratings of BBB–, A, AA or AAA, or Moody's Investors Service ratings of Baa, A, Aa or Aaa.) There's little likelihood that the issuers of these bonds will default (fail to make payments on time), so investors will want to put most of their bond money into high-grade bonds—either corporates or municipals depending on their tax brackets. The risk in high-grade bonds comes from rising interest rates. All bonds lose value when rates rise (see page 21 in Chapter 2 for an explanation of why), but lower-quality bonds rise and fall more with the fortunes of the issuing company, so rising rates tend to affect them less.

HIGH-YIELD CORPORATE FUNDS

High-yield corporate funds are also called "junk" bond funds because they invest in lower-quality bonds. These bonds tend to pay high rates of interest because they are low-rated or unrated and are issued by corporations that have a real risk of defaulting or going bankrupt. When the economy is growing, the companies that issue junk bonds tend to prosper and junk-bond funds likewise do well. But when the economy falls into recession, some junk-bond issuers default, and junk-bond funds do badly. These funds are almost as risky as stock funds. At the same time, in small to midsize helpings they can increase the yield in a portfolio without raising your overall risk, because junk bonds often rise and fall in value at different times than high-quality bonds.

HIGH-GRADE MUNICIPAL FUNDS

High-grade municipal funds own mostly tax-free bonds classified as investment-grade. States, municipalities and other tax-exempt agencies issue tax-free bonds. Like their taxable cousins, muni funds tend to be sensitive to interest-rate swings. They are usually a better bet than taxable bond funds for investors in the 28% federal tax bracket or higher who are investing in an account that's subject to income taxes. While municipal bond funds are free from federal taxes, they are usually not exempt from state and local income taxes.

HIGH-YIELD MUNICIPAL FUNDS

High-yield municipals invest in lower-quality muni bonds. They offer higher yields but also carry more risk than high-grade munis. While defaults have been rare in recent years, these funds yield only a bit more than safer funds.

SINGLE-STATE MUNICIPAL FUNDS

Single-state municipals invest in the municipal bonds of a single U.S. state or territory. Their advantage to investors is that they are free not only from federal income taxes but also from the state (and often local) taxes of the state in which they are issued. Single-state munis often make sense for high-income investors who live in states with an income-tax rate of 6% or more. But tread carefully here; not all states treat income from their own state bonds in such a favorable way. If you're a resident of Iowa, Illinois, Kansas, Oklahoma or Wisconsin, only some in-state bond issues are exempt from state taxes. Owning shares of a single-state municipal bond fund from one of these states may have limited benefit, depending on the bonds in the fund's portfolio. Moreover, single-state muni funds generally charge higher expenses and are riskier than other muni funds. People in low-tax or no-tax states, such as Florida and Texas, should avoid them.

GOVERNMENT FUNDS

Government bond funds are the safest in terms of credit quality, because they invest mostly in securities issued by the U.S. Treasury or other government-related agencies. These bonds are not without risk, however. Their prices will fluctuate with changes in interest rates. Investors will generally do better with high-yield corporate bonds than with government bonds.

MORTGAGE FUNDS

Mortgage bond funds own mortgage-backed securities, most of which are issued or insured by the government or government-related agencies such as Ginnie Mae (the Government National Mortgage Association), Fannie Mae (the Federal National Mortgage Association), and Freddie Mac (the Federal Home Loan Mortgage Association). While Ginnie Mae only insures mortgages, Fannie and Freddie Mac bundle hundreds of mortgages together and sell them to dealers who, in turn, sell them to mutual funds and other large investors.

Mortgage bonds do best in times of relatively stable interest rates. When rates rise, their prices decline just as do the prices of most other bonds. When rates drop a lot, however, homeowners refinance their mortgages at the lower rates, so the yields from these funds falls. Despite their disadvantages, mortgage-security funds make a great addition to your portfolio if you are seeking high income. Moreover, they tend to zig when other funds are zagging, smoothing your portfolio's volatility.

Mortgage securities can be relatively straightforward, or among the most complicated investments available. Investments in complex mortgage-backed bonds triggered several bond fund disasters during the 1990s. It's best to keep it simple here: Rather than trying to get a bit of extra yield, stick with funds that invest in ordinary Ginnie Maes and Fannie Maes. We'll get into more detail on specific funds in Chapter 18.

GLOBAL BOND FUNDS

Global bond funds invest all or most of their assets in bonds of foreign countries. These bond funds are quite volatile, because changes in currency valuations influence them as much as interest rates. In very small amounts, though, a global fund can be a decent addition to a large bond portfolio.

Key Points
- *Learn a fund's precise name before investing.*
- *Fund names are sometimes misleading.*
- *Funds are divided into numerous categories and subcategories.*

Investing With Style

Make sure part of your portfolio is always "in"

hen you think of style, do you think of designer dresses or spiked hair? Do you think of people who have a certain panache, who light up a room when they enter it? Well, it might surprise you to learn that mutual funds have style, too. "You've got to be kidding," says Paul DiBenedetto. "Well, you've got my attention now." Just as with fashion, funds' styles of investing are quite distinct. Understanding how they vary is important, and while the concepts in this chapter are the most difficult in the book, once you grasp them you'll be a much better investor.

As important as it is to know a fund's objective, which we discussed in the last chapter, that tells you only what the fund aims to accomplish. It doesn't tell you how the fund attempts to achieve its goal. A fund's style describes the method by which a fund seeks to meet its objective. Let's pursue our fashion analogy just a little further. Say two young women go to a party hoping to meet attractive young men. Their objective is the same. But one may wear a Versace gown and diamonds, while the other sports a mini-skirt and nose ring. Their styles are quite different.

Determining a stock fund's style depends on the answers to two questions:
- **Is it a fund that invests in stocks of large companies** or stocks of small companies?
- **Is it a growth-style fund** (looking for fast-growing companies) or a value-style fund (seeking bargain stocks)?

Investors who don't understand style often end up buying a portfolio of currently top-performing funds without realizing that all of them use the same investment approach. Then, when that style goes out of favor, the funds lose their sparkle, and the investor ends up replacing them with new funds—all of which again follow a common style. By contrast, when you understand fund styles, you can build portfolios of funds with different styles that work in harmony. When one style goes out of favor and another one comes in, your overall portfolio may barely notice the difference; in other words, your portfolio's volatility will be much lower. Just as important, you'll be able to compare funds with their real peers—other funds with the same objectives and styles—so that you don't end up buying an average or below-par fund simply because its investment style is currently working.

If you're a beginner without a lot of money to invest, you probably won't want to go to all the work of tearing apart each top-performing fund's innards to determine whether it's a large-company fund or a small-company fund, a growth-style fund or a value-style fund. You'll find you can do okay by selecting for your portfolio:

• **one aggressive-growth fund,** which is likely to contain smallish, growth-style stocks;

• **one long-term-growth fund,** which is likely to contain medium-size or large stocks;

What's a Stock's Market Value?

A STOCK'S MARKET value is the value that shareholders collectively place on a company's stock. It's computed by multiplying the stock's share price by the total number of shares the company has issued. For instance, in mid 1998 General Electric traded at about $83 a share, and there were 3,335 million shares of GE outstanding. Multiply those two numbers and you get GE's market value, which is about $277 billion. (General Electric just happens to have the highest market value of any U.S. stock.)

A stock's market value is use-ful for mutual fund investors chiefly because it gives you an idea of whether a fund is investing in small, medium or large stocks. A stock's market value doesn't necessarily tell you anything about the company's earnings or sales, or the value of its physical plant and other assets. In other words, market value is not necessarily what the company would be worth if it were sold. In the late 1990s, for instance, many stocks of Internet companies, such as Yahoo and Excite, have had huge market values, but scant earnings or assets.

• **one growth-and-income fund,** which will probably contain large, value-oriented stocks; and
• **one international fund.**

Then, as you become more proficient in sorting out funds, you'll want to refine your methods. For the purposes of this book, I've tried to make things easy. Chapter 17, "Great Stock Funds," tells you the investment style of each fund, allowing you to easily pick top funds from each category.

If you do well enough on your basic investments, you may want to use some of your earnings to spice up your wardrobe. Then you can truly say that you are in style.

Is the Fund Large-Company or Small-Company?

L ET'S START LEARNING FUND INVESTMENT STYLES BY LOOKING at just two funds. *Franklin Balance Sheet* and *Harbor Capital Appreciation* are both considered long-term-growth funds because they seek to increase your capital without regard to dividend income. But the two funds employ very different investing styles:

The average stock that Franklin Balance Sheet buys has a market value (see the box on page 166) of just under $300 million. Some of its largest holdings recently were Aztar, Niagra Mohawk Power and Ryland Group. Haven't heard of any of these companies? Stocks with market values of less than $300 million represent smaller companies, many of which are obscure.

Now let's look at Harbor Capital Appreciation. Its average stock has a market value of $33.7 billion—or about 112 times the value of the Franklin fund's average stock. Top holdings at this writing included such household names as Disney, Home Depot and Microsoft.

To put it simply, Franklin Balance Sheet invests mostly in stocks of small companies, while Harbor Capital Appreciation prospects among big companies.

WHAT'S IN AND WHAT'S OUT?

That wouldn't be especially noteworthy to investors except that the stock market goes through fads that are just as extreme (and sometimes as nonsensical) as those in the world of fashion. It's not unusual for small stocks to be hot for two or three years, as they were in the late 1970s and early 1990s, while big stocks are as out-of-favor as polyester leisure suits. Then things change. In 1995, 1996 and 1997, for instance, investors couldn't get enough of large stocks. Behemoths like Coca Cola, Procter & Gamble and Citicorp, with growing global franchises, were the darlings of investors and money managers, while smaller stocks were wallflowers. Investing in large stocks almost guaranteed that a fund manager would do well in those three years, while even the most talented managers of funds specializing in small companies fell behind.

COMPARING APPLES WITH APPLES

Why does this matter? For two reasons:

You need to make a valid comparison

First, if you compared Harbor Capital Appreciation's performance with Franklin Balance Sheet's for the three years of 1995, 1996 and 1997, knowing only their objective (long-term-growth), you'd decide that Harbor Capital Appreciation was a far better fund than Franklin Balance Sheet. Harbor Capital Appreciation rose an annualized 29.5% over the three years, while Franklin Balance Sheet rose 24.4% in the same three years. But Standard & Poor's 500-stock index, the benchmark large-company stock average against which to judge Harbor Capital Appreciation's performance, rose 31.1% from 1995 through 1997, while the Russell 2000, a small-company-stock average against which to judge Franklin Balance Sheet's performance, rose only 22.3% during those three years. What you can conclude is that, by comparison with their benchmarks, Harbor Capital Appreciation actually did a bit worse than Franklin Balance Sheet during those three years.

Definitions of precisely what constitutes a small, medium or large stock often differ—confusing even the most conscientious investors.

Only by comparing a stock fund against a suitable index or against stock funds employing similar styles can you come to an intelligent conclusion about how well the fund has performed. Just as you wouldn't learn anything about the abilities of two football players by comparing a lineman's total touchdowns against those of a quarterback, you can't learn much about a fund's performance unless you compare it with its peers.

You can reduce your portfolio's volatility

There's another reason it's important to know what size stocks a fund invests in. That's because the goal of a good portfolio is to attain maximum returns with minimum fluctuations in the value of your holdings. Now, remember how small stocks stalled in the mid 1990s. If you had held a portfolio that consisted only of funds investing in small stocks, the value of your holdings wouldn't have grown nearly as much as that of the overall stock market. You would have done better by owning some large stocks as well.

Over the long haul, however, small stocks are almost certain to catch up with large stocks. As I noted earlier in the book, since 1926 small stocks have outperformed large stocks by roughly two percentage points per year. But to minimize your portfolio's volatility—which is especially important if your time horizon isn't very long—you'll do best owning some funds that invest in small stocks and others that invest in large stocks.

DIFFICULTIES IN COMPARING FUNDS

Definitions of precisely what constitutes a small, medium or large stock often differ—and, unfortunately, that can be confusing to even the most conscientious investors. The BARRA Style Analyzer (a computer tool *Kiplinger's* occasionally uses to determine which funds invest in small, medium or large stocks), defines small stocks as those with a market value of $300 million or less. BARRA calls stocks between $300 million and $1 billion medium-size stocks and those over $1 billion large stocks.

But another popular information source, *Morningstar Mutual Funds*, uses very different definitions. It calls stocks with market values up to $1 billion small stocks, stocks between $1 billion and $5 billion medium-size, and only stocks over $5 billion large-size. In an effort to refine its descriptions, *Morningstar* in 1997 added a "micro" category for funds that hold stocks with average market values of up to $250 million and a "giant" category for stocks over $20 billion.

BARRA and *Morningstar* use different methods to determine how big a fund's stocks *really* are. Funds must release a list of their holdings only every six months, and these listings are often out of date the day they are released. That can make it difficult to get current information on precisely what a fund is up to. Most funds, however, are fairly consistent in what kinds of stocks they own, so this usually isn't a major problem.

BARRA analyzes the fund's day-to-day price changes. If big stocks outperformed small stocks on a given day, and a particular fund did very well on that day, the BARRA software would consider that evidence that the fund owns big stocks. By analyzing daily price changes over several years (noting which kinds of stocks did well on which days), BARRA can come up with a good idea of exactly what size stocks are in a fund. BARRA analyzes mutual funds, in essence, by saying: If it walks like a duck, it probably is a duck.

> **Analyzing funds' styles: There is no perfect way to capture what a fund does statistically and place it into a neat little box.**

Morningstar looks at actual portfolio holdings of each fund. At first blush, that seems a superior method. After all, actual holdings give you an accurate picture of what size stocks really are in the fund. But as I noted above, lists of funds' holdings can be woefully out of the date.

Alas, analyzing funds' styles forces you to conclude that there is no perfect way to capture what a fund does statistically and place it into a neat little box. Efforts by BARRA and *Morningstar*—as well as *Value Line Mutual Fund Survey,* which uses methods similar to *Morningstar's*—are crude, albeit essential, attempts to identify which funds are roughly comparable.

So what is an investor to do? One good solution is to stick to a single data source, especially when you are first analyzing funds. That will help you avoid confusion. Another is to look at *Morningstar* or *Value Line* and find the average market value for each stock in the portfolio. While this figure is dated, it at least gives you a hard number.

Growth Versus Value

THERE'S GROWTH (FUNDS) & THERE'S GROWTH (-STYLE FUNDS)

Understanding whether a fund invests in large-company stocks or small-company stocks is half the battle in determining its investment style. The second half of the struggle is concluding whether the fund invests in growth stocks or value stocks. Harbor Capital Appreciation and Franklin Balance Sheet differ in this regard just as they differ in the size of the stocks they buy.

Harbor Capital Appreciation hunts for companies with growing earnings. (A company's earnings are its profits after taxes and other expenses have been deducted. The relevant number for investors is earnings per share—that is, earnings divided by the number of outstanding shares of common stock.) As a result, Harbor Capital Appreciation's investment *style* is labeled "growth." What's confusing here is that the fund's objective, is long-term-growth, and growth in that context has an entirely different meaning. If you remember from the previous chapter, a fund with an objective of long-term growth seeks capital gains rather than dividends, and typically, but not always, invests in stocks of midsize to large companies. I say typically because the fund research services also classify Franklin Balance Sheet, which buys small companies, as having long-term-growth as its objective. *Be careful to differentiate between a fund with "growth" as an objective and a "growth-style" fund—which is one that specializes in stocks with growing earnings. The two terms mean different things.*

So what is an investor to do? One good solution is to stick to a single data source, especially when you are first analyzing funds.

Some growth-style funds hunt for stocks with steadily rising earnings; others, like Harbor Capital Appreciation, look for companies with rapidly growing or accelerating earnings. These companies usually are Wall Street's glamour stocks, stocks that investors are willing to pay high prices for (expressed as a multiple of their earnings).

Harbor Capital Appreciation's average stock traded at 37 times the previous 12 months' earnings in mid 1998. (During the same period, the average S&P-500 stock traded at 28 times earnings.)

Franklin Balance Sheet buys a totally different type of stock than Harbor Capital Appreciation does. It looks for so-called "value" stocks—stocks that Wall Street has so pummeled or ignored that they sell at bargain prices relative to their earnings, sales or assets—that is, relative to what an informed buyer might be willing to pay for the whole company. These stocks typically reach their depressed prices because earnings have been disappointing, investors have no faith in the company's management, or some other perceived failing. So Franklin Balance Sheet is a "value-style" fund. Value stocks tend to be less volatile than growth stocks because their share price already reflects much of the bad news; they usually don't have as far to fall as growth stocks. Franklin Balance Sheet's average stock sold at 18 times earnings in late 1997 (about half what Harbor Capital Appreciation's average stock sold for).

One example of a growth stock is software giant Microsoft, which more than quadrupled in price from 1994 through 1997. The stock was hot because investors believed Microsoft would continue to see fast-growing earnings as it increased its dominance over other software makers amid mushrooming demand for computer-related products. But Microsoft was not cheap by early 1998. Its share price of $154 amounted to more than 50 times what the company had earned per share in the preceding 12 months (meaning the stock traded at a price-earnings ratio of more than 50), while the S&P 500 traded at 24 times earnings (or

Two Ways to Value Stocks

PRICE-EARNINGS RATIOS and price-to-book-value ratios are the two most common measures used to ascertain the value of a stock. While the terms will surely sound confusing to new investors, they are simple to understand if you take a minute to learn them.

A PRICE-EARNINGS RATIO is determined by dividing a stock's earnings per share into its share price. So, if a company earned $2 per share over the previous 12 months and it now sells for $40 a share, the stock has a P/E ratio of $40 divided by $2, or 20. All other things being equal, the higher a stock's price-earnings ratio, the more expensive it is and the faster investors anticipate its earnings will grow in the future. Essentially, a price-earnings ratio represents the number of dollars investors are willing to pay for each dollar of a company's profits.

BOOK VALUE is how much is left after all assets and liabilities of a company are

taken into account. Say a stock has total assets (things such as the value of its buildings, products in its inventory, its cash on hand, and what customers owe) of $100 million, and total liabilities (things such as bills due to suppliers and loans it must repay) of $80 million. Book value is $100 million minus $80 million, or $20 million. If the company has a million shares outstanding, each share has a book value of $20 ($20 million divided by one million shares). And if the stock sells at $40 a share, that's two times its book value. As with price-earnings ratios, the higher a stock's price-to-book ratio, the more expensive it is and the faster investors expect its earnings will increase. It can also mean, however, that a company doesn't have much physical plant.

P/E ratios of stocks are listed daily in newspaper stock tables, and price-to-book ratios are available in most other stock- and fund-information sources.

had a P/E ratio of 24). Stocks trading at high P/E ratios are vulnerable to even the smallest whiff of bad news. One bad quarterly earnings report, and Wall Street takes the stock out and shoots it. Declines of 15% and 20% in a single hour are not uncommon for high-flying growth stocks. For instance, Qualcomm, a telecommunications firm, experienced such a plunge in early 1998. Many growth stocks, however, offer the promise of increasing earnings without too much regard to the ebbs and flows of the economy.

HOW VALUE IS DEFINED

Fortunately, there is more agreement among the experts over what a value stock is and what a growth stock is than over the size of stocks. *Morningstar* and *Value Line* look at the price-earnings ratios and the price-to-book ratios of all the stocks in a fund. Rather than looking at portfolios, BARRA again analyzes price movements of a fund to determine whether its stocks have high or low P/E ratios and book values. BARRA, *Morningstar* and *Value Line* then compare a fund's weighted price-earnings ratio and weighted price-to-book ratio with those of an index, such as the S&P 500 (weighting accounts for the proportion of each stock in a fund's portfolio). Those funds owning stocks with low price-earnings ratios and low price-to-book ratios are considered value funds, while those with high price-earnings and price-to-book ratios are considered growth funds. Funds somewhere in the middle are considered to "blend" growth and value styles.

The Four Food Groups of Funds

F RANKLIN BALANCE SHEET HUNTS FOR SMALL UNDERVALUED stocks. Other funds specialize in small growth stocks. Harbor Capital Appreciation buys large growth stocks, while other funds invest in large value stocks. These four variations are the main styles of investing. Although it takes work to determine which funds are truly peers, the result is well worth the effort. Comparing the funds in each of these four groups against their peers is the best way to identify outstanding funds. Academic studies show that by comparing funds that are similar you have a better chance of predicting which funds will outperform others in the future.

Furthermore, to have a truly diversified portfolio, it's best to have some representation from each of these four styles. Then, if one or two of these styles are out of favor, your whole portfolio won't fall apart on you. Diversifying is the only way you can increase your potential return while minimizing your portfolio's volatility—the amount it bounces around from month to month.

You can also think of these fund styles as personality types. **Small-company growth funds** tend to be tightly wound, high-energy creatures, soaring in good times and crashing to Earth in bad times.

Large-company growth funds are still mighty peppy.

Small-company value funds are typically more sedate.

Large-company value funds are the most somnolent of all stock funds—moving slowly compared with the market when stock averages are careening to new highs or plunging sharply.

Fund Mini Styles

TO MORE ACCURATELY compare funds, some analysts go beyond the four styles explained in detail in this chapter. Most of these subcategories lie on the cusp of two of the broader styles. Commonly used mini styles include:
• *blend,* a cross between growth and value
• *growth at a reasonable price,* growth funds that also consider value criteria
• *relative value,* which buy stocks that are cheap relative to other stocks in the same industry sector, even if they aren't cheap in comparison to the whole market.
• *earnings momentum,* a substratum of growth funds, which specialize in stocks with accelerating earnings and rising share prices.

Some analysts also identify:
• *mid-cap (for "capitalization," or market value),* which fall between small-company and large-company funds, and
• *micro-cap,* which invest in companies that have smaller market values than those in small-company funds.

You usually don't need to use these fine points to effectively evaluate funds, because the narrower style slices don't generally behave all that much differently from the broader ones. But you should be aware of them for the rare times that mini styles do diverge significantly. For instance, small-company momentum-style funds were in a terrible slump from mid 1996 through early 1998, while most other small-company growth-style funds didn't suffer as much.

Like Fund, Like Manager, Like Investor?

IT'S STRETCHING THE TRUTH TO SAY THAT MOST FUND managers reflect their fund's investment styles. But there are enough examples of managers who match the personalities of their funds to make it seem more than mere coincidence. The prototypical growth fund manager is impatient, and keeps his eyes glued to a computer screen and his ears attached to several telephones. Foster Friess, manager of Brandywine, a growth-style fund, has only one chair in his office—so he holds all meetings with everyone else standing up. That tends to keep meetings short. Friess doesn't even like his employees talking to one another—on the phone or in person. He says e-mail and faxes are far more efficient for quickly exchanging information, even for, say, inviting a colleague to lunch.

Meanwhile, value managers, though they may put in as many hours studying stocks as their growth counterparts, tend to trade less frequently. They can be slower-moving, thriftier types. The late Max Heine, founder of the Franklin Mutual Series funds (now part of the Franklin fund group) and a multimillionaire, was known for taking the subway to work, wearing the same suit every day and, once he got older, always insisting on senior-citizen discounts.

Investors may find themselves drawn to one style or another. Technology-laden, small-company growth funds may attract those who crave excitement. Conservative investors, on the other hand, are often more at ease with large-company value funds. To a certain extent, it's fine to overweight your portfolio with funds you feel comfortable with. But you'll profit more as an investor if you also fight your instincts to a degree—and, say, buy some shares in a volatile growth fund even if its thrills and spills unnerve you at times.

SHIFTING STYLES

It's wise to own funds that represent all four styles of investing. But some investors—and many pension-fund managers—take that maxim so seriously that they won't consider buying a fund that strays even slightly from its investment style. That can be a mistake. Some of the craftiest fund managers shift styles as they perceive changes in the market. James Craig, manager of Janus fund, for instance, buys some value stocks and some growth stocks. When he thinks the economy will be weak, he'll generally buy more growth stocks with dependable earnings. On the other hand, if he sees a strong economy—one that will help earnings of even beaten-down companies—he's more apt to buy value stocks. Craig has managed to pull off this shift in styles with aplomb. So have Kenneth Heebner, manager of CGM Focus, and Will Danoff of Fidelity Contrafund.

Switching from a growth style to a value style can be a tricky business, however, and many managers don't do it well. Also, the rise in their funds' assets forces most successful fund managers to shift style from smaller to larger companies. Some execute the transition flawlessly, while others fall flat on their faces.

It's best to be a little skeptical of those funds that aren't consistent. *Morningstar Mutual Funds* shows a fund's style, as well as the style it has followed in previous years, so you can tell whether the fund has been consistent. BARRA also shows a fund's historic style. But don't let intelligent skepticism become knee-jerk rejection—as we just noted, some great managers seem to be able to sense when it's time to change styles. You'll read about a couple of them in Chapter 17, "Great Stock Funds."

Key Points
- *A fund's style tells you what kinds of stocks it specializes in.*
- *Telling small-company funds from large-company funds is difficult, partly because the experts disagree on their definitions.*
- *Growth funds buy stocks with growing earnings.*
- *Value funds buy cheap, undervalued stocks.*
- *A portfolio with funds that use different styles will be less volatile than a portfolio that owns stocks of only one style.*

How to Pick Winning Stock Funds

Performance, risks, management, method and costs

ICK UP MOST FINANCIAL PUBLICATIONS AND YOU'LL SEE a list of the top-performing stock funds for the past 12 months. If only you could figure out, in advance, which funds would fill those pages 12 months from now! Like many people, you probably receive junk mail promising you sure-fire methods for picking those funds. Fact is, picking next year's top funds is as hard as hitting the trifecta at the race track.

But that's no reason to despair. You can identify funds with good odds of outperforming their peers. By comparing funds that are similar in both their investment objective and their style, you can identify which ones have a good chance to be top performers. I emphasize a *good chance* here, because picking funds is three parts number crunching and one part instinct.

Focus on the Long Term

THIS CHAPTER SPOTLIGHTS THE SIGNPOSTS OF EXCELLENCE TO look for when sizing up funds. While past performance is no guarantee of future success, it's the best indicator we have. Just make sure to compare funds against their peers. As you've learned already, comparing a large-company growth fund against a small-company value fund is pointless. As noted in the previous chapter, academic studies have found that stock funds that have done well in past years *against their peers* tend to continue to outperform.

When evaluating past performance, statisticians tell us, the longer period you can consider, the better. Performance of a fund over three months means virtually nothing. *American Heritage*, among the worst-performing funds around, put up terrific numbers in the first quarter of 1997. In fact, American Heritage was the number-one aggressive-growth fund in 1997. But even one-year performance has little long-term predictive value. *(Note:* Momentum investing relies on past fund performance over short periods to predict future *short-term* performance; I discuss it in Chapter 10, "13 Investment Pitfalls and How to Avoid Them.") Performance over three years has more meaning, and performance over five years is, perhaps, the best single number to employ.

From a purely statistical standpoint, it would be better to consider ten or 20 years. But very few funds have been run by the same managers for that long, and, even if they have, often the nature of the fund has changed radically during that period.

Keeping Up With the Indexes

TO TELL HOW a fund is doing compared with the indexes, you may want to go beyond looking at the S&P 500 large-company index and the Russell 2000 small-company index. Several companies—most notably BARRA, Russell and Wilshire—maintain value and growth indexes, as well as large-company and small-company indexes. You can find information on performance of those indexes in most of the fund sources mentioned in the preceding chapter (see page 169; see also page 202 in Chapter 17). You can also find BARRA indexes on the Internet at www.barra.com, Russell at www.russell.com, and Wilshire at www.wilshire.com

Many newspapers publish averages of various composites of stock funds: small-company value, large-company growth, and so on. If your newspaper doesn't contain composites, use the Vanguard index

funds as benchmarks.

Vanguard Index Small Cap Stock mirrors the Russell 2000 index,

Vanguard Index Value tracks the S&P 600 BARRA Value, which tracks value stocks of all sizes, and

Vanguard Index Growth reflects the S&P 600 Barra Growth, which tracks growth stocks of all sizes.

Vanguard Index 500 fund is also a good source of total-return data of the S&P 500 (unlike many data sources, which neglect dividends when reporting the S&P 500's performance).

Vanguard Total International tracks the Morgan Stanley Capital International's combined Europe, Australasia, Far East (EAFE) and Emerging Markets Index. It's a good proxy for international funds.

Vanguard Index Extended Market tracks the Wilshire 4500 Index, which represents all stocks except those in the S&P 500.

By all means, though, examine ten- and 20-year performance, if a fund has had the same manager that long, as well as five- and three-year performance. Some long-term top performers, such as *Dodge & Cox Stock* (started in 1965), *Acorn* (begun in 1970) and *Davis New York Venture* (started in 1969) are still great funds. The more useable data you have, the more likely a fund's top-notch performance wasn't a fluke.

But don't stop with long-term total returns. Consistency is also important. Examine how a fund has done *each year* of the period you're looking at relative to its peers or against an appropriate benchmark (such as Standard & Poor's 500-stock index for large-company funds or the Russell 2000 for small-company mutual funds).

Performance isn't everything. How risky is a fund relative to its peers or an appropriate stock-market average?

If a fund's performance is consistently above average, it is likely be a winning fund. For instance, Dodge & Cox Stock has finished in the top 10% among growth-and-income funds only once since 1992. But it has always finished in the top 40%. And the fund's performance over the five years ending in 1997 was in the top 4% among its peers.

Conversely, if a fund beat the pants off its competitors for a year or two, only to slump badly in other years, you'll want to steer clear of it. For instance, *Excelsior Small Cap A* finished in the top 20% against aggressive-growth funds in 1993 and 1994. But the fund finished in the bottom 30% against its peers in 1995, and the bottom 10% in 1996. This is probably a fund to avoid—unless you can satisfactorily account for the substandard years and gain a measure of faith in its long-term potential.

Look at Risk

PERFORMANCE ISN'T EVERYTHING IN PICKING A FUND. YOU'LL want to determine how risky a fund is relative to its peers or an appropriate stock-market average. Think of risk as the chance that you won't achieve the return you expect or that you'll lose money. For instance, large-company stocks have returned an average of more than 10% annually, but that doesn't mean you can expect to earn 10%-plus in large-company stocks next year. The stock market is volatile over the short term, rising 30% one year, then falling 20% the next. It's only over periods of ten and 20 years that returns smooth out and stocks become (or, at least, have been in the past) fairly predictable investments.

Similarly, when you are evaluating funds, you want to know how much they tend to fall when the overall market tumbles. The simplest way to estimate this is to compare a fund's performance during the last two market downturns with that of its peers or with an appropriate benchmark. In 1997, Standard & Poor's 500-stock index lost 10.8% from October 7 to October 27. But if you were unlucky enough to have invested in *Oberweis Emerging Growth*, your fund would have plunged 17.4% during that one-month span. By contrast, *T. Rowe Price Capital Appreciation* lost just 4% in that period.

A MEASURE OF THE FUTURE

An even better way to determine how a fund will do during a downturn is to look at its *standard deviation*. Standard deviation measures a fund's volatility—how much it tends to bounce around from month to month. By knowing a fund's standard deviation compared with that of its peers or a market average, you can estimate how it will fare relative to a benchmark when the market plunges.

T. Rowe Price Capital Appreciation fund has a three-year monthly standard deviation (standard deviations can be measured over different periods) of 1.57, which is less than half the 3.39 three-year-monthly standard deviation of Standard &

Risk Measures

STANDARD DEVIATION is a rather weighty-sounding mathematical term. Trust me, you really don't need to know how it is computed. Just remember that it measures to what degree returns of a fund vary during some period of time. That may be month to month or year by year, depending on how the number is expressed; it doesn't matter much what time period you use, so long as you are consistent. While many data sources provide standard deviation, if you stick to one data source, you'll be sure of getting consistent information. The higher a fund's standard deviation, the more the fund's net asset value is likely to plunge during a down market. Other measures of risk that you may have heard of, such as beta, measure a fund's volatility compared with a stock index. They're not nearly as useful as standard deviation.

Poor's 500-stock index. In the 1997 selloff, the T. Rowe Price fund lost less than half what the S&P did.

Oberweis Emerging Growth has a standard deviation of 8.4, twice that of the Russell 2000, a small-company stock index. And, in fact, Oberweis Emerging Growth lost close to twice what the Russell 2000 did.

Because of its low standard deviation, odds are that in the next bear market the T. Rowe Price fund will lose a little less than half what the S&P does, while Oberweis will likely lose about twice as much as the S&P 500. When stock prices have been rising virtually unchecked, it's particularly important to monitor a fund's volatility. That will give you a better feel for how the fund will likely do in more normal times, when bear markets more frequently follow bull markets.

Is It Still the Same Fund?

L ONG-TERM PERFORMANCE AND RISK ARE THE MOST IMPORTANT numbers you need to know about a fund compared with its peers. But don't stop there. There are several other items you need to consider before settling on a fund. Skip one and you may find you've bought a lemon. Following are things to keep your eyes peeled for.

A CHANGE OF MANAGER

Fund companies spend millions of dollars every year on advertisements aimed at persuading consumers that they offer the best funds. But only a small percentage of those advertisements ever name the fund company's managers. Fund managers earn fat salaries, and other companies constantly court the good ones. No fund company wants to tout its manager in advertisements only to have him or her leave for another firm.

A lot of things go into the success—or failure—of a mutual fund. The culture of a fund company matters a lot. The quality of its research analysts, the working conditions, how well managers work with one another and with research analysts are all important. But at the end of the day, when you invest your money in a fund, you're hiring a manager. When Brett Favre leaves the Green Bay Packers, the next player to quarterback the team isn't likely to be as good at throwing footballs. By the same token, if Favre were traded to another team, he would take his skills with him.

So when a manager leaves a fund, think of the fund as a new, untested animal. Most of its past record will be of little value in judging how it will do going forward. In evaluating a fund's performance, you'll usually want to look at only its record under the current manager or managers. If a manager hasn't been at a fund for at least five years, call the new fund family to ask for the manager's pedigree—which fund he or she ran previously and the results he or she produced. For the greatest likelihood of success, you'll want a manager whose previous fund used a similar investing style and contained as much money as the new one. As I've noted, running bigger funds undoes some managers. Be a little skeptical of a record chalked up as a manager of private money. These numbers are not as reliable as mutual fund performance records.

> **When a manager leaves a fund, think of the fund as a new animal. Most of its past record will be of little value in judging the future.**

Some funds are "team managed," making it more difficult to tell which manager is really calling the shots. In that case, you should be less willing to invest in a fund. But some firms, such as the American funds, managed by Capital Research & Management, as well as Dodge and Cox funds, have chalked up superb long-term records with team-managed funds. Similarly, some firms, especially Fidelity, have a habit of rotating managers about as often as the Yankees change managers. Fidelity and T. Rowe Price generally hire good people to run their funds, so the new manager's previous record (or lack of one) may be of less importance at these firms.

What should you look for in a fund manager?

Start by looking for experience. Some new managers are great, but let other investors test these newcomers. Until a manager has at least three years, and preferably five years, under his or her belt, be skeptical.

You also want a manager who has a disciplined approach to investing. Managers who can clearly articulate their approach to picking and selling stocks, and who have demonstrated an ability to stick with that method through thick and thin, tend to have the best long-term records.

Finally, just as in other endeavors, the best managers tend to love their work. You're not necessarily looking for a workaholic manager, but you want one with a passion for investing.

Unfortunately, most of these personal qualities are not on view to individual investors. As a journalist, I spend a good deal of time talking with managers, trying to determine which ones have the right stuff. I've attempted to put that knowledge to use in selecting the funds in Part Four. However, by reading interviews with managers in newspapers and *Kiplinger's* and other personal-finance and business magazines, you can gain insight into a manager's approach. And some managers, particularly at smaller funds, are willing to take calls from prospective investors who want to quiz them on their approach.

A CHANGE IN INVESTMENT METHOD

A change in managers isn't the only way a fund can be fundamentally altered. Sometimes managers change their investment methods, so the fund that you're considering buying isn't using the same approach as it did when it chalked up a good record.

Managers most frequently run off the rails by losing faith in their own methods. This typically happens during a long period when the stock market is not favoring their investment style. Rather than stick to it, trusting that eventually their style will come back into vogue, they lose their nerve and begin following whatever style seems to be working right then. This kind of capitulation, alas, often happens just as the market is finally making its long-awaited turn to the management style the manager had practiced in the first place.

Inexperience may also cause a manager to change methods. Veteran managers often relate stories of their own early mistakes in this regard. And poorly run fund companies put pressure on managers to boost short-term performance, even to the point of firing them if results don't improve, even if their investing style is currently out of vogue.

> **Managers most frequently run off the rails by losing faith in their own methods, typically when their investment style is out of the market's favor.**

TOO MUCH OF A GOOD THING

Perhaps the most common way funds fail is that they become victims of their own success. They put up such good numbers that more and more money flows in. Pretty soon they can't buy the same stocks they used to—particularly if they built their record by specializing in fast-growing, small-company stocks. Funds that invest in such stocks tend to trade frequently, and it's a lot easier for a small fund than a big fund to buy or sell a stock without disturbing its price. I'll get into more detail about fund size, and how it can hinder performance, in the next chapter.

In general, however, be wary of small-company growth funds that have more than, say, $1 billion in assets. Don't count just the assets in the fund you are studying, but all the money run by that manager—whether in other funds or in private accounts. A call to the fund's toll-free number should quickly tell you how much money a manager has under his or her purview.

Add Up the Costs

WHILE PREDICTING FUTURE PERFORMANCE OF A FUND IS NO sure thing, you can be pretty certain of one thing: how much a fund will charge you in expenses every year. The higher a fund's expense ratio, the less is left for you. All things being equal, the more expensive a fund, the less likely it is to perform well. That's because it has to work that much harder to overcome its expense ratio and still produce a good return. Moreover, a fund that charges a high expense ratio demonstrates its lack of respect for you as an investor. You want your fund's manager and research analysts to earn a good living, but you don't want the company to fleece you.

The average stock fund annually charges about 1.46%— or about one-third of your long-term, after-inflation, after-tax gain.

In a bull market, when stocks are soaring, it's easy to overlook the importance of expenses. Don't make that mistake. The average stock fund charges expenses of 1.46% annually. Assume that stocks will continue to return an average of 11% a year—as they have since 1926. Inflation has averaged 3.1% annually, and federal and state income taxes take about another 3% annually in a taxable account. That leaves you with only 4.9% after inflation and taxes. So the expense ratio of the typical fund is equal to almost one-third of your long-term, after-inflation, after-tax gain.

Excessive trading also drives up your costs. The fund's expense ratio doesn't reflect these trading costs, although funds must disclose in their annual reports to shareholders how much, on average, they have paid per share in brokerage commissions.

The more a fund trades, the more it pays in commissions. In addition to brokerage commissions, trading adds further costs, because the firms your fund trades with boost the prices of the stocks they sell so that they can earn profits.

The average stock fund has a turnover ratio of 70%, which means about 70% of the assets invested in stocks turn over every year. It doesn't necessarily mean 70% of the stocks in the portfolio change. For example, it's possible that 35% of the assets could turn over twice. A much smaller percentage could turn over more than once. In general, be wary of fund turnovers that creep much over 100%—although there are exceptions here; some gifted managers trade more rapidly and still come out ahead of their peers.

New sources of information on personal finance are springing up everywhere.

Don't be penny-wise and pound-foolish, however. Good funds often require lots of resources to be run well; some really good funds charge a little more than might appear reasonable at first blush, particularly if they are funds without much money invested in them. Such funds have fewer shareholders to split their costs.

How high an expense ratio is too high? The average varies by category. The following averages don't include one class of fees, known as 12-b1 fees, which are used to compensate brokers and pay other marketing expenses, not to run the fund:

STOCK FUNDS	EXPENSE RATIO
Growth-and-income	1.32%
Long-term-growth	1.46
Aggressive-growth	1.55
Precious metals	1.79
Sector	1.84
International	1.86
Global	1.91

Where to Look It Up

With the booming bull market in recent years and Americans' growing love affair with mutual funds, new sources of information on personal finance are springing up everywhere from bookstores to magazine racks to newspapers to the Internet. Moreover, publications that previously didn't cover personal finance are hiring writers to do so. The hard job is to separate the wheat from the chaff. Following are some suggested sources of information.

MORNINGSTAR MUTUAL FUNDS AND VALUE LINE MUTUAL FUND SURVEY

Both of these resources offer a wealth of material. While they are expensive, they often run introductory specials. A single copy or short-term subscription may be all that you need, since most of the information doesn't become outdated quickly. These publications are also available at many public libraries. A *Morningstar* or *Value Line* page will give you almost all the information you need to size up a fund. Trouble is, many beginners find these pages about as comprehensible as quantum physics. If you stick with it awhile, you'll find the information begins to make sense.

MAGAZINES

Kiplinger's Personal Finance Magazine, Business Week, Forbes and *Money* magazines all publish annual mutual fund issues, mostly in late summer, that provide data on thousands of funds. *Kiplinger's* also publishes an annual mutual fund guide (available on newsstands in February) that provides key fund data and advice.

SOFTWARE

Several computer programs supply data useful for analyzing funds. Here are two:

Alexander Steele's Mutual Fund Expert ($29.95; 800–379–0679) offers the most speed and variety in screening funds.

Morningstar's Principia ($195 per year with quarterly updates; 800–735–0700) and Value Line's *No Load Analyzer* ($95 per year with quarterly updates; $29 for two-month trial subscription; 800–535–8760) are a little harder to navigate but offer much more data.

ONLINE RESOURCES

These are just a few of the best sites:

Morningstar's Web site (www.Morningstar.net) contains a lot of helpful articles about fund investing.

www.fundalarm.com keeps you up-to-date on funds you might consider selling.

www.fundspot.com gives you a directory of mutual funds' Web

When to Sell a Fund

How to tell when it's time to cut bait

Y MUTUAL FUND STANDARDS, ROBERT BACARELLA'S Monetta fund was a midget, ending 1990 with a mere $6 million in assets. But while most stock averages fell in 1990, Monetta achieved a total return of 11.4%. As Bacarella remembers it, "All of a sudden one day our phones started ringing."

Bacarella had formerly spent weekends visiting suburban Chicago malls to check out retailing companies as prospective stock purchases. Now he began working 12 to 15 hours on Saturdays and Sundays, stuffing envelopes with prospectuses for investors. Joining him were his parents, his wife and his three children—the kids got a penny an envelope. Each weekend, the family was able to prepare about a thousand mailings. But the phone calls came so quickly that the mailings disappeared by noon on Monday.

By the end of 1992, Monetta's assets had snowballed to more than $400 million. By then, Bacarella had long since hired an outside firm to field requests for information. But the fund's performance collapsed under the avalanche of new money. Bacarella added personnel and tried several new investment strategies, but it took him five years to regain his investment footing. The fund trailed Standard & Poor's 500-stock index every year from 1992 through 1996. Over those five years the fund returned a meager annualized 5.3%. Monetta suffered from an all-too-common phenomenon in mutual fundom: It turned red-hot for a year or two, money flooded in the door, and performance chilled. Holders of a fund like Monetta should ask themselves why they continue to own it.

Despite your best efforts, count on making a few mistakes in your fund picks. One of the most common: buying a highflier like Monetta just before it nose-dives. The important thing is to recognize your mistakes and sell them before they become disasters.

Once you've assembled your portfolio, you should review it at least annually. If things go wrong at a fund, you'll want to know why before you consider replacing it. Don't be too hasty about selling funds, though. More investors make the mistake of selling funds whose styles are temporarily out of favor (see Chapters 14 and 15) than of holding on to losers too long.

Why Investors Sell Too Soon

FIGURING WHETHER TO KEEP A FUND IS LIKE SELECTING A NEW fund: it's most important to keep your eye on the fund's performance relative to its peers. If total return compared to that of similar funds deteriorates over two or three months, don't even give it a second thought. The best funds can have terrible three-month periods. If performance lags for a year, it's time to begin watching more closely, but probably not to sell. Usually you should sell only if a fund underperforms over an extended period—say, two or three years.

USING THE WRONG YARDSTICK

A common mistake investors make is to compare a fund against the wrong index or the wrong group of funds. *Mutual Shares*, among the most successful growth-and-income funds of the past 20 years, had poor returns relative to the market for three straight years. In 1989, it returned 14.9%, less than half the gain of Standard & Poor's 500-stock index. The following year, Mutual Shares *lost* 9.8%—more than three times the loss of the S&P 500. And in 1991, Mutual Shares again lagged the S&P, this time by nine percentage points. But investors who sold missed out on the fund's resurgence in the subsequent years. From 1992 through 1997, the fund gained an annualized 2.2 percentage points *more* than the S&P.

How could you have known that this fund was worth holding on to? You couldn't have, without knowing more about fund manager Michael Price and his investment style. If you hadn't known that Price is a value investor, one who looks for stocks selling at depressed prices, you might have sold his fund without knowing that there was nothing wrong with him—it was just that his style of investing lay becalmed for three miserable years.

Other renowned value investors—such as John Neff, who formerly ran *Vanguard Windsor*; Charles Royce, manager of *Royce Pennsylvania Mutual* fund; and Preston Athey, who runs *T. Rowe Price Small Cap Value* fund—also had wretched slumps then. So by comparison with its peers in the market, Mutual Shares wasn't doing badly. (As an investor in the fund, you also would have known that Price made a big investment mistake he was unlikely to repeat. His three funds participated in the buyout of Macy's, which subsequently entered bankruptcy. Price argues that the funds came out about even in this huge investment, but this means the assets were dead in the water for awhile.)

THE MANAGER'S LONG-TERM RECORD

The other reason to hang on to Mutual Shares through its long drought was Price's long and successful record. He had been with the fund since 1976. If a relatively new manager stumbles for two or three years—or occasionally even one year—you'll want to pull the plug. On the other hand, if you have a manager with a proven long-term record, give him or her longer to pull out of a slump.

Warning Signs to Heed

USUALLY, IF A FUND'S PERFORMANCE IS COLLAPSING, A BIT OF detective work will tell you why. Often it turns out to be one of the following reasons, which can be signals that it's time to consider ditching a fund, even if performance has not yet begun to slump:

A CHANGE IN MANAGERS

When a manager changes, you may own what amounts to an untried fund, and you should question whether it remains worthy of your money. Sometimes you can assuage your doubts.
• Did the new manager run another fund previously?
• If so, what was its record relative to its peers?
• Did the new manager assist the departing manager?
• If so, for how long and in what capacity?

How Assets Weigh Down a Fund

THE FOLLOWING GRAPH shows how a popular fund, Fidelity Equity-Income II, stumbled under the weight of burgeoning assets. In the graph, the benchmark S&P 500 index is shown as a flat line to better illustrate the performance of the fund relative to the S&P. Equity-Income II was piloted by Brian Posner from April 1992 (when the fund had just $737 million in assets) through the end of 1996. As the graph shows, the fund's returns declined against the S&P almost every year as assets grew to more than $15.2 billion. The drop-off in returns came even though Equity-Income II is a large-company value fund—a style of fund that can often handle increased assets. Bettina Doulton, who replaced Posner at the end of 1996, was unable to turn things around in 1997.

Annual Return (%) Compared with S&P	'92	'93	'94	'95	'96	'97
Fund's Assets at Year-End (in billions of dollars)	$2.2	$5	$7.7	$12	$15.2	$17

Such was the case when John Neff left Vanguard Windsor fund. His successor as manager, Charles Freeman, had been the top analyst on the fund for more than 25 years, and he had mastered Neff's methods well—as the fund's subsequent returns have demonstrated.

TOO MANY ASSETS: WHEN IT'S A PROBLEM, WHEN IT'S NOT

In the case of Monetta, the warning sign that the fund was facing trouble was a rapidly growing asset base. It's one thing to manage a couple of million dollars in a fund. It's quite another to manage hundreds of millions or billions of dollars. Small fund companies that lack the infrastructure to handle huge growth are especially vulnerable to catastrophe when assets balloon. A bigger company that can throw more seasoned analysts in to help a fast-growing fund and allow the manager to devote full-time efforts to picking stocks (rather than stuffing envelopes or hiring analysts) is much more likely to handle growth effectively. Don't be too quick to pull the trigger on a fund that's grown, though. It's usually best to watch for a year or two in which the fund has lagged its peers.

Small-company growth vs. value funds

Sometimes a fund can thrive even as assets mushroom. But that won't be true in a fund that buys small-company growth stocks. Cast a wary eye at a fund whose assets are much over $1 billion.

Value funds—which usually trade less frequently than growth funds, and typically sell stocks that many investors want to buy and buy stocks that many investors want to sell—can usually handle much more in assets. A small-company value fund should be able to handle $2 billion in assets—and sometimes more. *Acorn* fund, a small-company value fund, is still doing well despite assets of more than $3 billion. (One reason: Manager Ralph Wanger was prescient enough to close Acorn to new investors for several years while he trained additional analysts and adjusted to his fund's newfound popularity.)

Too many stocks to handle

Time after time, funds start off with hot performance, only to cool as they gain in popularity. To cope with exploding size, fund managers typically start buying stocks of bigger, more well-established companies because big funds can't easily profit from investing in small companies (to learn why, see the box on page 193). A manager who specialized in small stocks might start buy-

---

New Funds With Proven Managers

OCCASIONALLY, THE MANAGER of a fund that has outgrown its ability to turn in top numbers will leave to run a smaller fund. When that happens, investors can often do very well. Such was the case when Brian Posner jumped ship from Fidelity, where he had run the $15 billion Equity Income II fund with great returns that gradually dropped off as the fund grew. He took over Warburg Pincus Growth & Income, which had less than $1 billion. An opportunity to invest with a manager like Posner at the helm of a smaller fund doesn't come along too often, but it's worth grabbing when you spot it.

Trading a Stock Without Getting Killed

UNLIKE AN INDIVIDUAL investor who buys, say, 100 shares of a stock, fund managers often buy hundreds of thousands of shares of a stock. That's tricky to pull off, and it's why fund companies employ traders, whom they pay handsome salaries to trade stocks without roiling the markets.

The problem is that when a manager wants to buy a large quantity of a stock, its price will tend to go higher—because too few investors want to sell at the lower price. The manager creates extra demand, which drives the price up. If a fund specializes in small-company stocks, which tend not to trade in great volumes, buying even a couple of thousand shares will send the price higher *before* the manager has finished buying.

Traders at small-company funds, or at funds that have huge amounts of money invested in them, will try to buy stock slowly, sometimes over months, to avoid disturbing the price. Then, when the fund manager wants to sell, the same agonizing process is repeated in reverse. That's why smaller funds have an edge. They can be more nimble, buying and selling smaller quantities of stock more quickly to execute the ideas of their manager.

ing medium-size stocks, for example. The problem is two-fold: the manager might not be as talented at picking bigger stocks and the nature of the fund changes.

Another way managers deal with swelling assets is to own more stocks. Instead of owning, say, his or her 40 or 50 favorite stocks, a manager may buy 200 or 300 stocks. This can also hurt performance, because a manager's favorite stocks typically do better than those in which he or she lacks the same level of conviction. "Why would I want to buy my 81st–most attractive stock?" wonders L. Roy Papp, who limits the Papp funds to 30 or fewer stocks each.

Difficulties finding small, proven funds

Good funds that have grown too big are a huge problem in fund investing. "Let there be no doubt that I could manage $100 million better than $50 billion," Fidelity Magellan fund manager Jeffrey Vinik said before leaving the fund in 1996 to manage a smaller, private investment fund available only to wealthy investors. But there's often a Catch-22 at work when you're hunting for small, proven funds. In general, you want to avoid unseasoned funds. But by the time a fund has a good five-year record, it's often bigger than you'd like—or it's closed to any new investors.

What large-company funds can do

In contrast to small-company funds, large-company growth funds seem to be able to keep up with their peers as assets grow to about $10 billion, and sometimes more—so long as the fund company is willing to hire enough analysts to research stocks. Backed by Fidelity's huge research staff, *Fidelity Contrafund* beat most of its competitors even as assets soared past $25 billion. Large-company stocks are much easier to buy and sell without disturbing the stock's price. And large-company value funds can sometimes outperform their rivals even after assets reach $20 billion or more.

An opportunity in soon-to-close funds

The best-run funds will close their doors to new investors before size becomes a problem. For that reason, it sometimes pays to buy a small stake in a promising small-company fund if you think it might close soon, even if you aren't totally convinced that the fund will be a great one. Often, there are fewer good, open small-company funds than there are closed ones. Funds like *T. Rowe Price Small-Company Value, Heartland Value, Franklin Balance Sheet, Longleaf Partners Small Cap, Oakmark Small Cap and Skyline Special Equities* are all closed to new investors.

Other Times to Sell

NOT ALL THE REASONS TO SELL A FUND HAVE TO DO WITH A fund's failings. Here are three other equally important reasons:

A BETTER FUND

There's no more appropriate time to sell a fund than when you identify a superior one. If you match the two funds up carefully and the advantages are clearly with the new fund, it's probably time to trade.

A BAD FIT

Sometimes you buy a fund only to realize later that it's not what you needed. Say you own *AIM Aggressive Growth, PBHG Growth,* and American Century *Twentieth Century Vista*. All invest in stocks whose earnings (and share prices) are accelerating. You'd do better selling one or two of these funds and putting the proceeds into a fund that can better balance out your portfolio. At other times, you'll find you simply made a mistake in buying a fund. Go ahead and sell it.

YOUR SITUATION CHANGES

Go-go growth funds are perfect for a big chunk of your money when you're in your twenties, thirties and forties, and can occupy a small portion of your portfolio in later years. In general, though, the closer you get to needing your money, the more conservative you need to be with the funds you own. Don't hang on to a high-octane growth fund simply because it's done well for you in the past.

Key Points

- *Be careful about selling a fund too quickly. Generally, look for poor performance over two or three years before selling.*
- *A change in managers may be a signal to sell.*
- *Funds that grow too big often stumble.*
- *Sell if your situation changes or if you made a mistake buying the fund in the first place.*

Winning Mutual Funds

his section describes some of the best stock funds among the thousands on the market. These funds aren't, by any means, a recommended "buy" list. Using what you've learned in Part Three, you're well equipped to pick good funds on your own. But the funds described in Part Four give you a starting point—and they can be a finishing place, too, if you want to build or augment your portfolio from among them. In addition, Part Four explains how to pick bond funds, money-market funds and niche funds, and describes some top funds in each of those categories. The final chapter discusses socially responsible funds and highlights some top performers.

Great Stock Funds

Profiles of 34 funds with helpful data

CHRISTINE BAXTER AND RON BARON BOTH MANAGE top-performing funds that invest in rapidly growing small companies. But while Baron spends two out of every three weeks on the road visiting companies, Baxter does most of her work from behind a computer terminal in suburban Philadelphia. The lesson here is that there is no one right way to run a mutual fund. There are good managers like Baxter, who use a largely numbers-driven approach to pick stocks, and there are good managers like Baron, who wouldn't dream of buying a stock without talking to the company's management, as well as its competitors, suppliers and anyone else he can think of.

The point here is that even if the numbers and categories indicate that two funds are twins, the odds are that they are very different beneath the surface. In the end, each fund is defined by the distinct investment methods of the person or people who run it. That's why this chapter does more than simply offer the names and statistics of top-flight funds. It also provides descriptions of how each fund works toward its goal.

That makes these fund profiles useful even if you decide to pick other funds, because they offer you signposts of quality to look for in evaluating any fund. By the same token, if you assemble your portfolio from among the funds described in this chapter, you'll have a better idea, from reading the profiles, of why you selected each fund. That knowledge will help you determine when to stick with a fund and when to sell it. The more you understand about why you bought specific funds, the more stalwart an investor you will be. That's important because, sometime, your commitment to investing will be tested by adversity.

What This Chapter Will Tell You

IN THIS CHAPTER, I PROFILE 34 GREAT STOCK FUNDS. (I EXCLUDED top-notch funds that are closed to new investors including *Barr Rosenberg Small Cap, FPA Capital, Harbor International, Fidelity Low-Priced Stock, PBHG Limited, Sequoia, Skyline Special Equities, T. Rowe Price New Horizons* and *Vanguard Windsor.*) I've included a diversified group of funds, so that you'll have no trouble putting together a balanced portfolio from them, if you choose.

It's important to remember, too, that even the best funds, over the long haul, are usually only a little better than the average fund with the same investment objective and style. In general, a fund's performance is determined primarily by the waters in which it fishes. That's why it's so important to put together a diversified portfolio of funds representing different objectives and styles of mutual fund investing (see Chapter 1 for more on this). And because performance is difficult to forecast, it's essential to examine expense ratios and risk—which are more predictable than total return.

THE FUND'S OBJECTIVE

I've divided the funds into general categories by objective (aggressive-growth, long-term-growth, growth-and-income, balanced and international) and defined each objective at the beginning of the appropriate section of funds.

THE FUND'S STYLE

I've also indicated the investment style of each fund. This tells whether a fund specializes in stocks of small, medium or large companies, and whether it specializes in growth stocks, undervalued stocks or a blend of the two styles. I've used *Morningstar Mutual Funds'* definitions of what constitutes growth and value stocks, as well as small, medium and large stocks. See Chapter 14 for more details on fund styles.

AND MORE

For each fund, I also give:
Annualized returns: They cover the three, five and ten years ending March 31, 1998 (if the fund has been in existence that long). These show how the fund has held up over sufficiently long periods.

Annual expense ratio: the percentage of your investment that the fund company charges each year to run the fund. It does not include any sales fees you might pay, but the only fund in this list with a load is Templeton Developing Markets.

Annual portfolio turnover: how often the fund manager trades stocks. A portfolio turnover of 50% means the manager trades half the assets in the fund annually. Low-turnover funds are sometimes superior, because they incur fewer brokerage commissions and other costs of trading stocks. Though not reflected in fund expense ratios, such costs are passed along to investors in the form of lower total returns.

Best benchmark: See the accompanying box for more on this.

Volatility: how much a fund's return varies from month to month compared with all other stock funds. Volatility is a superb predictor of how funds will hold up in market declines. A score of 1 means that the fund is less volatile than 90% of all stock funds. A score of 10 means a fund is in the top 10% for volatility among all stock funds. These rankings are derived from funds' standard deviations (see page 180).

Same manager since...: how long at least one of the managers has been at the helm. If a fund has more than one manager and one started later than the other, that information is included in parentheses.

Total assets: how much money is invested in the fund. Funds whose assets mushroom sometimes lose their touch, particularly if they specialize in small stocks.

Median stock-market value: market value of the median stock in the fund. (The median stock is the stock halfway between the largest and the smallest in value.) A stock's market value is computed by multiplying the share price times the number of shares outstanding. The median market value indicates whether a fund buys small, medium-size or large stocks. While experts may disagree, for this chapter I define small stocks as those with a market value of less than $1 billion, medium-size—$1 billion to $5 billion, and large—more than $5 billion. As assets of some small-company funds have increased, their median market values have grown a bit beyond these parameters. Nevertheless, I am still classifying them as small-company funds.

Minimum initial investment: the minimum purchase the fund requires to open an account. The second number is for IRAs.

Best Benchmarks

A BENCHMARK IS the index that can be best used to measure how well a fund is doing. This table allows you to compare funds in this chapter with their appropriate benchmark to see how they have performed. For most purposes, you'll do fine comparing large-company stock funds with the S&P 500, medium-size-company funds with the S&P Midcap 400, small-company funds with the Russell 2000, and international and emerging-market funds with the Morgan Stanley indexes.

However, in case you want to delve deeper, I've also provided, whenever possible throughout this chapter, the more specific Wilshire indexes for each fund.

In each case, the table provides the index name, its description and annualized returns for the past one, three, five and ten years through March 31, 1998. It also shows their volatility ranking, when available, derived from their standard deviation (for more on standard deviation, see page 180).

| | | ANNUALIZED RETURNS | | | |
INDEX	DESCRIPTION	3-YEAR	5-YEAR	10-YEAR	VOLATILITY
S&P 500	an index of stocks of mostly large U.S. companies	32.79%	22.38%	18.92%	5
S&P Midcap 400	an index of stocks of medium-size U.S. companies	28.41	19.49	19.24	6
Wilshire 4500	an index of all U.S. companies except for those 500 included in the S&P 500	26.82	18.65	16.15	
Russell 2000	an index of stocks of small U.S. companies	24.42	17.67	14.86	7
Wilshire Large Company Growth	an index of large U.S. companies with growing earnings	35.40	23.09	20.35	
Wilshire Large Company Value	an index of undervalued large U.S. companies	30.81	19.68	17.54	
Wilshire Mid-Cap Company Growth	an index of medium-size U.S. companies with growing earnings	23.89	19.11	16.55	
Wilshire Mid-Cap Company Value	an index of medium-size undervalued U.S. companies	28.23	17.71	17.48	
Wilshire Small Company Growth	an index of small U.S. companies with growing earnings	23.01	18.81	15.43	
Wilshire Small Company Value	an index of small undervalued U.S. companies	26.92	17.06	16.99	
Morgan Stanley Capital International Emerging Markets Index	an index of small, highly volatile developing markets around the world	−1.58	4.56	9.51	
Morgan Stanley Capital International Europe Australa Asia and Far East Index	a broad index of foreign stocks in developed markets	10.89	12.24	6.51	5

Phone number: the toll-free number to call for a prospectus, semi-annual report and fund application—and to ask questions. Make sure to ask whether any of the key numbers reported in this chapter have changed since publication.

Web site: the fund's online address if it exists. Web sites contain a variety of information about funds. Most of them also allow you to print out a fund application.

Aggressive-Growth Funds

MOST OF THESE FUNDS SWING FOR THE FENCES WITH fast-growing companies or small companies. They out-perform in bull markets and get clobbered in bear markets. Use them sparingly unless you have fortitude and a long time horizon. However, some small-company value funds, such as Westcore Small-Cap Opportunity, that are classified as aggressive-growth funds aren't all that volatile.

BARON ASSET

Ron Baron looks for stocks in what he calls "sunrise industries"—sectors he thinks will grow because of major societal trends. For instance, with the average age of Americans creeping up, Baron is bullish on companies like Charles Schwab, which he says benefits from middle-aged people investing for retirement, and Manor Care, a nursing-home company. While Baron wants fast-growing companies, he isn't willing to buy them at stratospheric prices relative to their earnings because such stocks are always vulnerable to a tumble. That makes his fund less risky than many small-company growth funds, yet his returns have sparkled.

INVESTMENT STYLE:	small-company growth
THREE-YEAR RETURN:	30.35%
FIVE-YEAR RETURN:	25.02%
TEN-YEAR RETURN:	19.46%
ANNUAL EXPENSE RATIO:	1.30%
ANNUAL PORTFOLIO TURNOVER:	13%
BEST BENCHMARK:	Russell 2000, Wilshire Small-Company Growth
VOLATILITY:	8
SAME MANAGER SINCE:	1987
TOTAL ASSETS:	$4.5 billion

MEDIAN MARKET VALUE: $1.3 billion
MINIMUM INITIAL INVESTMENT: $2,000, $2,000 for IRAs
PHONE NUMBER: 800–992–2766
WEB SITE: www.baronfunds.com

SPECIAL RISKS. The big question mark is whether Baron can continue to put up good numbers as assets swell. Already he is buying bigger stocks, many of them medium-size, rather than small. Recently there was about $5 billion in this fund and Baron Growth & Income, which he also runs. I would be ready to sell if performance is under par for, say, two years.

BERGER NEW GENERATION

William Keithler looks for small, fast-growing companies, many of them technology and health issues. His average company in 1997 was expected to increase earnings at 40% and was trading at a lofty 33 times earnings. "I look for earnings growth; that's what drives stocks," he says. High price-earnings multiples make this fund riskier than most funds, but it also means that in good years it can shoot the lights out. Keithler has piloted New Generation (which returned 24.2% in 1997 and 6.8% through May of 1998) and Berger Small Company Growth (up an annualized 23.7% in the past three years) since inception, and chalked up similarly strong numbers before that at Invesco Emerging Growth.

INVESTMENT STYLE: small-company growth
THREE-YEAR RETURN: NA
FIVE-YEAR RETURN: NA
TEN-YEAR RETURN: NA
ANNUAL EXPENSE RATIO: 1.87%
ANNUAL PORTFOLIO TURNOVER: 184%
BEST BENCHMARK: Russell 2000,
Wilshire Small Company Growth
VOLATILITY: 10
SAME MANAGER SINCE: inception in 1996
TOTAL ASSETS: $142.5 million
MEDIAN MARKET VALUE: $926 million
MINIMUM INITIAL INVESTMENT: $2,000, $2,000
PHONE NUMBER: 800–333–1001
WEB SITE: www.bergerfunds.com

SPECIAL RISKS. Look out below when the market falls. The fund lost 13.6% in the brief sell-off from February 18 through April 11,

1997. Plus, the expense ratio is a potential drag.

PBHG EMERGING GROWTH

When a company's quarterly earnings come in a penny or two per share below what Wall Street expected and the stock's price is instantly cut in half, do you ever wonder who these quick-on-the-trigger sellers are? Meet Christine Baxter, lead manager of PBHG Emerging Growth. Her fund, begun in 1993, buys small, fast-growing companies with accelerating earnings—and sells them in a heartbeat if their profits begin slowing down. Almost half the fund is usually in pint-size technology companies. While the fund is relatively new and Baxter is the daughter of the firm's co-founder, PBHG's numbers-driven methods have been proven over the years—and seem to work best with small growth stocks in small funds.

INVESTMENT STYLE:	small-company growth
THREE-YEAR RETURN:	20.22%
FIVE-YEAR RETURN:	NA
TEN-YEAR RETURN:	NA
ANNUAL EXPENSE RATIO:	1.28%
ANNUAL PORTFOLIO TURNOVER:	48%
BEST BENCHMARK:	Russell 2000, Wilshire Small Company Growth
VOLATILITY:	10
SAME MANAGER SINCE:	1993
TOTAL ASSETS:	$1.4 billion
MEDIAN MARKET VALUE:	$650 million
MINIMUM INITIAL INVESTMENT:	$2,500, $2,000
PHONE NUMBER:	800–433–0051
WEB SITE:	www.pbhgfunds.com

SPECIAL RISKS. So-called momentum investing either is succeeding or it isn't. And when small companies with accelerating earnings growth are unpopular, such funds stink. Emerging Growth plunged 31% between May 24, 1996, and April 11, 1997. Assets are also on the high side.

SKYLINE SMALL CAP VALUE PLUS

Ken Kailin, the manager of this small-company-value fund, doesn't get the respect he deserves. And that's just fine for prospective investors. The fund, which he has run since it opened in

1993, has been in the shadow of Skyline Special Equities, which is closed to new investors. Because the fund was formerly named Skyline Special Equities II, many investors thought the two funds were clones, so they ignored Special Equities II. With a new name, and index-beating returns since inception (Kailin started as an analyst with the firm a decade ago) that should change. This fund tends to beat the Russell 2000 except when the index is going straight up. In flat years, or years when the small-company market goes up moderately, Small Cap Value has been a winner. Kailin starts by looking for stocks with low price-earnings ratios relative to his benchmark. Then he hunts for stocks whose earnings are growing steadily. He owns only 50 of these solid, small-company stocks, selling them when they meet their price targets. His disciplined approach, which includes visiting with all his companies, has paid off. The fund is also relatively low risk.

INVESTMENT STYLE:	small-company value
THREE-YEAR RETURN:	28.54%
FIVE-YEAR RETURN:	18.61%
TEN-YEAR RETURN:	NA
ANNUAL EXPENSE RATIO:	1.53%
ANNUAL PORTFOLIO TURNOVER:	145%
BEST BENCHMARK:	Russell 2000, Wilshire Small Company Value
VOLATILITY:	6
SAME MANAGER SINCE:	1993
TOTAL ASSETS:	$189.2 million
MEDIAN MARKET VALUE:	$1.1 billion
MINIMUM INITIAL INVESTMENT:	$1,000, $1,000
PHONE NUMBER:	800–458–5222

SPECIAL RISKS. The biggest negative to this fund is that it may grow rapidly as investors discover it. But there's a silver lining even in that: Kailin promises to close the fund when it gets to somewhere between $500 million and $800 million in assets. That will ensure the fund will be able to profit from investing in small companies.

T. ROWE PRICE SMALL CAP STOCK

Manager Greg McCrickard looks for stocks with growing earnings that are also selling at reasonable valuations. This hybrid investment approach, called growth at a reasonable price, has kept volatility lower than in some other small-company funds, but still allows Small Cap Stock to participate in rising markets. When funds like PBHG are dumping fallen stocks, McCrickard is sometimes one of those scooping them up. The fund is well diversified by industry.

INVESTMENT STYLE:	small-company growth
THREE-YEAR RETURN:	29.22%
FIVE-YEAR RETURN:	21.17%
TEN-YEAR RETURN:	15.81%
ANNUAL EXPENSE RATIO:	1.07%
ANNUAL PORTFOLIO TURNOVER:	31%
BEST BENCHMARK:	Russell 2000, Wilshire Small Company Growth
VOLATILITY:	5
SAME MANAGER SINCE:	1992
TOTAL ASSETS:	$955.1 million
MEDIAN MARKET VALUE:	$576 million
MINIMUM INITIAL INVESTMENT:	$2,500, $1,000
PHONE NUMBER:	800–638–5660
WEB SITE:	www.troweprice.com

SPECIAL RISKS. Small-company funds tend to be more risky than funds that buy larger stocks—though this one's volatility has been below average.

ROYCE PREMIER

Charles Royce began managing money in 1972 and knows what it's like to live through a ripsnorting bear market—the one that hit in 1973–74. That has influenced his thinking. "We have a very risk-averse style," Royce says. He hunts for stocks selling at low prices by traditional value measures: low price-earnings ratios, low price-to-book ratios and low debt. Then he and his analysts quiz management on how they plan to turn these cheaply valued companies around. Premier contains Royce's 50 or so sturdiest picks—the stocks least likely to get mauled in a market downturn. So, although the fund invests in small stocks, it is conservative enough for any portfolio.

INVESTMENT STYLE:	small-company value
THREE-YEAR RETURN:	20.10%
FIVE-YEAR RETURN:	16.23%
TEN-YEAR RETURN:	NA

ANNUAL EXPENSE RATIO: 1.25%
ANNUAL PORTFOLIO TURNOVER: 34%
BEST BENCHMARK: Russell 2000,
Wilshire Small Company Value
VOLATILITY: 2
SAME MANAGER SINCE: inception in 1991
TOTAL ASSETS: $555.8 million
MEDIAN MARKET VALUE: $624 million
MINIMUM INITIAL INVESTMENT: $2,000, $500
PHONE NUMBER: 800–221–4268

SPECIAL RISKS. Royce is managing roughly $2 billion in more than a half-dozen funds, a lot for a small-company manager. His funds tend to lag in bull markets.

WESTCORE SMALL-CAP OPPORTUNITY

Investing in small, undervalued companies, manager Varilyn Schock, who has run Small-Cap since its inception in late 1993, looks for companies that are "mispriced" but have improving business outlooks. She uses a proprietary system that ranks companies by such measures as the ratios of price to earnings, book value and cash flow, then identifies the cheapest 10% of stocks in ten economic sectors. These candidates for inclusion get a going-over by Schock and her analysts, who study such matters as a company's products, management and regulatory issues.

INVESTMENT STYLE: small-company value
THREE-YEAR RETURN: 29.59%
FIVE-YEAR RETURN: NA
TEN-YEAR RETURN: NA
ANNUAL EXPENSE RATIO: 1.30%
ANNUAL PORTFOLIO TURNOVER: 78%
BEST BENCHMARK: Russell 2000,
Wilshire Small Company Value
VOLATILITY: 5
SAME MANAGER SINCE: inception in 1993
TOTAL ASSETS: $53.5 million
MEDIAN MARKET VALUE: $670 million
MINIMUM INITIAL INVESTMENT: $1,000, $250
PHONE NUMBER: 800–392–2673
WEB SITE: www.westcore.com

SPECIAL RISKS. Although Schock has been managing money since

sites, as well as a compilation of good articles on fund investing from all over the Web.

www.mutualfundchannel.com provides information on thousands of mutual funds.

THE MUTUAL FUND'S PROSPECTUS AND REPORTS

Before investing, you'll want to take a look at a fund's prospectus. These used to be impenetrable documents written by lawyers, but the Securities and Exchange Commission has ordered them to be written in "plain English." Read the section on the fund's investment objectives and policies, which tells you what types of securities it may invest in. Also make sure to read the sections that describe the fund's risks and expenses.

A fund's annual and semiannual reports are equally valuable. Here you will get a snapshot of the fund's holdings. Scan them to get a sense of what securities the fund invests in. Also look at which industry sectors a stock fund is emphasizing. If the prospectus says a fund invests in blue-chip stocks and you don't recognize any of the names of the stocks in the annual report, that should set off an alarm. Call the fund to find out what's going on—before you invest.

Key Points

- *Compare stock funds against their peers.*
- *Long-term returns are the most important numbers to examine.*
- *Short-term performance means little; consistent long-term performance means a lot.*
- *Look carefully at funds' volatility.*
- *Look at the managers' past records.*
- *Low costs are important.*
- *Many good sources of fund data are available.*

1987, this fund is relatively new and unproven. Also unclear is how the fund will do when it gains more assets. Schock and her analysts don't usually visit companies, which many money managers of small-company funds consider a must.

Long-Term-Growth Funds

STOCKS OF LARGE AND MIDSIZE COMPANIES DOMINATE THESE funds. They tend to be about as volatile as Standard & Poor's 500-stock index or the Dow Jones industrial average. They are the bread and butter of most portfolios.

BARR ROSENBERG DOUBLE ALPHA MARKET

The brainchild of money manager and former finance professor Barr Rosenberg, Double Alpha Market is an extremely complicated vehicle. Opened in early 1998, it starts by investing in Standard & Poor's 500-stock index futures. That guarantees the fund will deliver roughly the same performance as the S&P 500. Next, Rosenberg—or, rather, a computer program he and his colleagues have built over the years—pores over some 6,000 U.S. companies, looking for undervalued stocks, and stocks that exceed analysts' projected earnings estimates. The most favorable stocks are bought; the least favorable stocks are *shorted*. Shorting involves borrowing stock from one investor and selling it to a second investor, with the hope that you'll be able to buy the stock back from the second investor at a lower price. It's a bet that the price of the stock will go down.

Rosenberg's investments in stocks and shorts are equally balanced, so that his stock-selection skill, not fluctuations of the market, determines how well this portion of the portfolio will perform. In private accounts run since 1989, this part of the strategy has delivered an annualized 13.4% return with little volatility. By adding the return (or loss) from the S&P futures to the return (or loss) from the stock investments and shorts, investors may be able to do better than the S&P, perhaps by quite a bit, with little if any extra volatility. A much lower-risk fund (but one that should earn lower returns), called Market Neutral, uses a similar strategy but omits the investments in S&P futures.

INVESTMENT STYLE: large company value

ANNUAL EXPENSE RATIO:	2.35%
ANNUAL PORTFOLIO TURNOVER:	NA
BEST BENCHMARK:	S&P 500
VOLATILITY:	10
SAME MANAGER SINCE:	1998
TOTAL ASSETS:	$5 million
MEDIAN MARKET VALUE:	NA
MINIMUM INITIAL INVESTMENT:	$2,500, $2,000 for IRAs
PHONE NUMBER:	800–447–3332
WEB SITE:	www.riem.com

SPECIAL RISKS. Even for a "rocket scientist" like Rosenberg, this fund contains a lot of moving parts. The fund is untried, and it simply may not work. Both Double Alpha and Market Neutral also generate lots of short-term gains, which make these funds best suited for retirement accounts. Since the fund is so new, they hadn't yet reported an annual portfolio turnover rate nor a median market value of the stocks in the portfolio as we went to press.

BRANDYWINE

Manager Foster Friess's fund has never lost money over a full calendar year, and has beaten its peers most years. Friess seeks fast-growing stocks, many of them technology issues. Management of the big fund is divided into seven teams, each with responsibility for a portion of its assets. Under Friess's rules, before any stock can be bought, another must be sold, which often leads to rapid trading. The fund's $25,000 minimum keeps many investors away.

INVESTMENT STYLE:	medium-size-company growth
THREE-YEAR RETURN:	21.85%
FIVE-YEAR RETURN:	18.72%
TEN-YEAR RETURN:	19.65%
ANNUAL EXPENSE RATIO:	1.04%
ANNUAL PORTFOLIO TURNOVER:	192%
BEST BENCHMARK:	S&P Midcap 400, Wilshire Mid-Cap Company Growth
VOLATILITY:	9
SAME MANAGER SINCE:	1985
TOTAL ASSETS:	$8 billion
MEDIAN MARKET VALUE:	$2.8 billion
MINIMUM INITIAL INVESTMENT:	$25,000, $25,000

PHONE NUMBER: 800–656–3017
WEB SITE: www.brandywinefunds.com

SPECIAL RISKS. Asset growth has forced Brandywine to buy bigger stocks. Plus, Friess occasionally makes big moves out of the market and into cash, subjecting investors to his market-timing calls.

CGM FOCUS

Kenneth Heebner has one of the best long-term records of any manager. Unfortunately, CGM Capital Development, which he has managed since 1977, has been closed to new investors for years. (The fund returned an annualized 18.6% over the past 15 years.) But in 1997, Heebner launched CGM Focus, which he runs similarly to Capital Development. The new fund, like the old one, sticks to 30 or fewer stocks. In both funds, Heebner offers a wild ride. He aggressively switches from one sector to another when he sees opportunity. He can be a frenetic trader. While his overall record is superior, his bad years are also spectacular. In 1994, for instance, Heebner bet on a strong economy that would propel his concentrated bet on steel and other industrial materials. He was wrong, and the fund's total return was –22.9%, the worst in its category. "You can really look like an idiot," Heebner notes. Unlike CGM Capital Development, CGM Focus can sell stocks short, which further increases its risk (see definition of short-selling on page 125).

INVESTMENT STYLE:	medium-size company blend of growth and value
THREE-YEAR RETURN:	NA
FIVE-YEAR RETURN:	NA
TEN-YEAR RETURN:	NA
ANNUAL EXPENSE RATIO:	NA
ANNUAL PORTFOLIO TURNOVER:	NA
BEST BENCHMARK:	S&P Midcap 400, Wilshire 4500
VOLATILITY:	10
SAME MANAGER SINCE:	inception in 1997
TOTAL ASSETS:	NA
MEDIAN MARKET VALUE:	$2.5 billion
MINIMUM INITIAL INVESTMENT:	$2,500, $1,000
PHONE NUMBER:	800–345–4048
WEB SITE:	www.cgmfunds.com

CLIPPER

Lead manager James Gipson is an independent thinker who is not afraid to bet against the conventional wisdom on Wall Street. His fund holds only about 20 stocks—big companies with valuable franchises and the muscle to keep growing. Plus, he buys these stocks only when they're selling at depressed prices. About half the fund is in financial-services companies. Gipson is especially fond of Freddie Mac (Federal Home Loan Mortgage Corporation) and Fannie Mae (Federal National Mortgage Association), which process home mortgages. Other big holdings include Wal-Mart and Philip Morris. When the market looks richly priced, Gipson and co-manager Michael Sandler let cash build up and wait for their next opportunities.

INVESTMENT STYLE:	large-company value
THREE-YEAR RETURN:	29.33%
FIVE-YEAR RETURN:	20.33%
TEN-YEAR RETURN:	17.47%
ANNUAL EXPENSE RATIO:	1.08%
ANNUAL PORTFOLIO TURNOVER:	31%
BEST BENCHMARK:	S&P 500, Wilshire Large Company Value
VOLATILITY:	3
SAME MANAGER SINCE:	inception in 1984
TOTAL ASSETS:	$973.2 million
MEDIAN MARKET VALUE:	$41.3 billion
MINIMUM INITIAL INVESTMENT:	$5,000, $1,000
PHONE NUMBER:	800–776–5033
WEB SITE:	www.clipperfund.com

SPECIAL RISKS. Because Clipper holds so few stocks and often has a lot of cash, performance won't always be in line with the market. It tends to lag the averages in bull markets and outperform in bear markets and flat markets. So patience is sometimes required.

HARBOR CAPITAL APPRECIATION

Spiros Segalas has built an enviable record at this fund by buying fast-growing, large-company stocks, many of them technology issues. "We emphasize appreciation," Segalas says. For him, that means annual 15%-plus earnings growth for the companies he buys. It also means not being afraid to buy richly priced stocks, because such fast-growers don't come cheap. In 1997, his average holding sold at 30 times the previous 12 months' earnings. The fund owns some of the same stocks as Brandywine, but Segalas runs the fund by himself. In addition to a much smaller minimum initial investment than Brandywine ($2,000), Harbor Capital Appreciation boasts a low 0.70% expense ratio.

INVESTMENT STYLE:	large-company growth
THREE-YEAR RETURN:	31.46%
FIVE-YEAR RETURN:	23.69%
TEN-YEAR RETURN:	20.49%
ANNUAL EXPENSE RATIO:	0.70%
ANNUAL PORTFOLIO TURNOVER:	73%
BEST BENCHMARK:	S&P 500, Wilshire Large Company Growth
VOLATILITY:	9
SAME MANAGER SINCE:	1990
TOTAL ASSETS:	$3 billion
MEDIAN MARKET VALUE:	$31 billion
PHONE NUMBER:	800–422–1050

SPECIAL RISKS. This is a volatile fund that can be expected to significantly trail the averages in bear markets.

MASTERS' SELECT EQUITY

What happens when the publisher of a first-rate, highly sophisticated fund newsletter, *No-Load Fund Analyst* ($225 annually; 510–254–9017, carries out a strategy that looks great on paper? Ken Gregory has thought for years that managers tend to have more confidence in their favorite ten or 15 stocks than in their smaller holdings. Yet a typical fund contains about 150 stocks. Gregory went to six top managers who use different investment styles and asked them to pick five to 15 of their favorite stocks. The contributing fund managers are Foster Friess of Brandywine, Spiros Segalas of Harbor Capital Appreciation, O. Mason Hawkins of Longleaf Partners, Shelby M.C. Davis of Selected American Shares, Jean-Marie Eveillard of SoGen International and Dick Weiss of Strong Opportunity. Each is responsible for a percentage of the fund. Gregory promises to close the fund by the time it reaches $750 million, perhaps sooner, so this fund might be worth taking a small stake in—in case it turns out to be a winner.

INVESTMENT STYLE:	large-company growth

THREE-YEAR RETURN:	NA
FIVE-YEAR RETURN:	NA
TEN-YEAR RETURN:	NA
ANNUAL EXPENSE RATIO:	NA
ANNUAL PORTFOLIO TURNOVER:	NA
BEST BENCHMARK:	S&P 500, Wilshire Large Company Growth
VOLATILITY:	8
SAME MANAGER SINCE:	1996 inception
TOTAL ASSETS:	$372.1 million
MEDIAN MARKET VALUE:	$7.3 billion
MINIMUM INITIAL INVESTMENT:	$5,000, $1,000
PHONE NUMBER :	800–960–0188

SPECIAL RISKS. While the fund had a great 1997, returning 29.1%, it's too early to tell whether Gregory's brainstorm will really be a success.

MONTAG & CALDWELL GROWTH

Manager Ronald Canakaris and a team of eight other portfolio managers focus on large companies that are growing at a rate of at least 10% a year. When they find attractive candidates, they estimate future earnings over the next ten years—though they never assume long-term growth greater than 20%—and use that to calculate a company's "intrinsic value." A stock must be priced below that value to be a "buy" candidate. Canakaris invests primarily in blue-chip growth stocks—household names such as Coca-Cola, Intel and Procter & Gamble. The fund is fairly new, but manager Ronald Canakaris has compiled an impressive record running Enterprise Growth, a nearly identical broker-sold fund, since 1980. In the big-stock-oriented markets of 1996, 1997 and 1998, Montag & Caldwell Growth has done quite well.

INVESTMENT STYLE:	large-company growth
THREE-YEAR RETURN:	36.17%
FIVE-YEAR RETURN:	NA
TEN-YEAR RETURN:	NA
ANNUAL EXPENSE RATIO:	1.28%
ANNUAL PORTFOLIO TURNOVER:	26%
BEST BENCHMARK:	S&P 500, Wilshire Large Company Growth
VOLATILITY:	7

SAME MANAGER SINCE: 1994
TOTAL ASSETS: $782.7 million
MEDIAN MARKET VALUE: $45 billion
MINIMUM INITIAL INVESTMENT: $2,500, $500
PHONE NUMBER: 800–992–8151
WEB SITE: www.alleghanyfunds.
chicago-trust.com

SPECIAL RISKS. When the market turns away from the big-company stocks that Canakaris likes, this fund won't perform nearly as well.

Oakmark and Oakmark Select

Oakmark fund manager Robert Sanborn lives and invests by the value code. "I was a Filene's Basement kind of kid growing up in Boston," he says. "I like bargains in anything." Like all Oakmark managers, Sanborn looks for companies selling at a discount to their underlying value, which he defines as "what a rational businessperson would pay to own the whole enterprise." Sanborn keeps a large percentage of assets in a small number of his favorite stocks. Oakmark Select, an aggressive-growth fund started in 1996, uses the same methods, but is more concentrated still: Manager Bill Nygren tries to limit himself to 15 or fewer stocks.

INVESTMENT STYLE: Oakmark: large company value
(Oakmark Select: medium-size
company value)
THREE-YEAR RETURN: 27.76% (NA)
FIVE-YEAR RETURN: 23.25% (NA)
TEN-YEAR RETURN: NA (NA)
ANNUAL EXPENSE RATIO: 1.08% (1.12%)
ANNUAL PORTFOLIO TURNOVER: NA (NA)
BEST BENCHMARK: S&P 500,
Wilshire Large Company Value
(S&P Midcap 400, Wilshire
Mid Cap Company Value)
VOLATILITY: 3 (9)
SAME MANAGER SINCE: 1991 (1996)
TOTAL ASSETS: $7.7 billion ($1.1 billion)
MEDIAN MARKET VALUE: $15.8 billion ($2.5 billion)
MINIMUM INITIAL INVESTMENT: $1,000, $1,000 ($1,000, $1,000)
PHONE NUMBER: 800–625–6275
WEB SITE: www.oakmark.com

SPECIAL RISKS. Being concentrated makes a fund less likely to perform the way the market averages do. Growing assets reduced Oakmark from an exceptional fund to merely a very good one. It remains to be seen whether the same fate awaits Oakmark Select.

T. ROWE PRICE CAPITAL APPRECIATION

Manager Richard Howard has an aversion to losing money. "I went through the 1973–74 bear market, and I was an oil analyst when oils got body-slammed in the 1980s," Howard says. As a result, he looks for the safest possible ways to invest. With just over half the volatility of Standard & Poor's 500-stock index, his fund has yielded solid returns. About half the fund is in stocks; most of the remainder is in high-yielding bonds. In his stock investments, Howard diversifies widely among industry groups, further reducing risk.

INVESTMENT STYLE:	large-company value
THREE-YEAR RETURN:	18.67%
FIVE-YEAR RETURN:	15.32%
TEN-YEAR RETURN:	14.33%
ANNUAL EXPENSE RATIO:	0.76%
ANNUAL PORTFOLIO TURNOVER:	44%
BEST BENCHMARK:	no single appropriate benchmark
VOLATILITY:	1
SAME MANAGER SINCE:	1989
TOTAL ASSETS:	$1 billion
MEDIAN MARKET VALUE:	$5.6 billion
MINIMUM INITIAL INVESTMENT:	$2,500, $1,000
PHONE NUMBER :	800–638–5660
WEB SITE:	www.troweprice.com

SPECIAL RISKS. This fund will lag the averages in bull markets.

T. ROWE PRICE MID-CAP GROWTH

Brian Berghuis, who has run this fund since inception, invests in growing, midsize companies that have competitive advantages, low debt and shareholder-friendly managements. Medium-size companies, which Berghuis defines as between $300 million and $4 billion in market value at the time of purchase, tend to produce a lot of the extra return of small stocks with less risk. He also diversifies among industry sectors. To temper risk further, he invests in some companies growing as little as 12% a year. Berghuis avoids "highfliers"—stocks that are selling at inflated prices relative to their earnings—for fear he'll get caught holding a stock whose price goes into a freefall.

INVESTMENT STYLE:	medium-size company growth
THREE-YEAR RETURN:	30.76%
FIVE-YEAR RETURN:	24%
TEN-YEAR RETURN:	NA
ANNUAL EXPENSE RATIO:	0.95%
ANNUAL PORTFOLIO TURNOVER:	43%
BEST BENCHMARK:	S&P Midcap 400, Wilshire 4500
VOLATILITY:	6
SAME MANAGER SINCE:	inception in 1992
TOTAL ASSETS:	$2.1 billion
MEDIAN MARKET VALUE:	$2.6 billion
MINIMUM INITIAL INVESTMENT:	$2,500, $1,000
PHONE NUMBER:	800–638–5660
WEB SITE:	www.troweprice.com

SPECIAL RISKS. This fund won't produce the outsize returns of supercharged small-company funds in any one year.

THIRD AVENUE VALUE *AND* THIRD AVENUE SMALL CAP

Manager Martin Whitman is known as a "vulture" investor who likes to swoop down on distressed securities and gobble them up. When he sees a good value, he's not afraid to put 5% of the assets of Third Avenue Value into it. "Diversification is a poor substitute for knowledge," Whitman says. A lot of beaten-down stocks are depressed for good reasons, so he places a big emphasis on research to uncover issues with strong upward potential. The fund's volatility is far below the norm for this group. The fund owns stocks and bonds.

The Small Cap fund, begun in 1997 is an aggressive growth fund. It buys even smaller stocks and holds no bonds. Given its smaller size, Small Cap may be a better bet, but it will probably be more volatile.

INVESTMENT STYLE:	Value: small-company value (Small Cap: small-company value)
THREE-YEAR RETURN:	25.49% (NA)
FIVE-YEAR RETURN:	17.77% (NA)
TEN-YEAR RETURN:	NA (NA)

ANNUAL EXPENSE RATIO: 1.13% (1.65%)
ANNUAL PORTFOLIO TURNOVER: 10% (NA)
BEST BENCHMARK: S&P Midcap 400,
Wilshire Mid-Cap Company Value
(Russell 2000, Wilshire
Small Company Value)
VOLATILITY: 3 (8)
SAME MANAGER SINCE: inception in 1990 (1997)
TOTAL ASSETS: $1.9 billion ($143.5 million)
MEDIAN MARKET VALUE: $1.1 billion ($295 million)
MINIMUM INITIAL INVESTMENT: $1,000, $500 ($1,000, $500)
PHONE NUMBER: 800–443–1021
WEB SITE: www.mjwhitman.com

SPECIAL RISKS. Whitman was born in 1925. While there's no evidence his energy or enthusiasm is flagging, these funds will be big question marks when he leaves. The new Small Cap fund lists Curtis Jensen as co-manager. Jensen may be a great stock picker, but he lacks Whitman's record.

YACKTMAN

Don Yacktman likens the stocks he buys to beach balls pushed under water—they won't stay down long. Yacktman looks for high-return businesses run by first-class managers. "Then what we want to do is wait for those stocks to get battered and buy them when they're out of favor," he says. Yacktman fund has only been around since 1992, and it had a bad first year because he "stocked" it with companies in the doghouse. But Yacktman ran Selected American Shares for a decade before starting his own fund and had above-average results. His method of buying growing companies that have a high rate of return on assets and depressed share prices also minimizes risk. (*Yacktman Focused,* run similarly but holding only Yacktman's ten to 15 favorite stocks, is a way to get the same management in concentrated form. Focused should bounce around more from month to month, but over the long pull it will likely produce better returns.)

INVESTMENT STYLE: medium-size company blend
of growth and value
THREE-YEAR RETURN: 24.33%
FIVE-YEAR RETURN: 17.30%
TEN-YEAR RETURN: NA

ANNUAL EXPENSE RATIO: 0.86%
ANNUAL PORTFOLIO TURNOVER: 69%
BEST BENCHMARK: S&P Midcap 400, Wilshire 4500
VOLATILITY: 2
SAME MANAGER SINCE: 1992
TOTAL ASSETS: $1 billion
MEDIAN MARKET VALUE: $2.2 billion
MINIMUM INITIAL INVESTMENT: $2,500, $500
PHONE NUMBER: 800–525–8258
WEB SITE: www.yacktman.com

SPECIAL RISKS. Yacktman can be expected to have an occasional year or so when he underperforms because he owns only about 30 stocks and tends to avoid technology, energy and utilities. When his stocks and sectors are out of favor, he'll lag the market. Also, he doesn't invest with a consistent style; when attractive large companies are in short supply, he'll shift to smaller companies.

Growth-and-Income Funds

THESE LOWER-RISK FUNDS USUALLY INVEST IN LARGE companies and often produce some income as well. They serve as the anchor to many portfolios. You'll want to increase your holdings in growth-and-income funds and scale back your holdings in aggressive-growth, international and long-term growth funds as you get nearer to needing your money.

BABSON VALUE

Roland "Nick" Whitridge is a by-the-numbers investor. This veteran holds little or no cash and buys equal positions of 40 high-yielding stocks that are out of favor and cheap on the basis of earnings and book value. He uses a computer to do most of the screening, then hands over the best candidates for Jones & Babson analysts to report back on. "I try to identify companies that are statistically cheap but that have something happening on the earnings side to give us hope they are coming out of their trough," Whitridge says. The process results in a portfolio loaded with financial stocks—recently 30% of assets—and such out-of-favor names as Apple Computer and Kmart. Portfolio turnover is as little as 6% some years.

INVESTMENT STYLE: large-company value

THREE-YEAR RETURN:	28.44%
FIVE-YEAR RETURN:	22.81%
TEN-YEAR RETURN:	17.28%
ANNUAL EXPENSE RATIO:	0.97%
ANNUAL PORTFOLIO TURNOVER:	17%
BEST BENCHMARK:	S&P 500, Wilshire Large Company Value
VOLATILITY:	4
SAME MANAGER SINCE:	1984
TOTAL ASSETS:	$1.7 billion
MEDIAN MARKET VALUE:	$11.2 billion
MINIMUM INITIAL INVESTMENT:	$1,000, $250 for IRAs
PHONE NUMBER:	800–422–2766
WEB SITE:	www.jbfunds.com

SPECIAL RISKS. Whitridge tends to hold stocks longer than most value investors, refusing to sell them until they lose their upward price momentum. That makes his fund a little less value-oriented than some. But it is results that count.

BERWYN INCOME

It's hard to find a lower-risk fund than this that still produces stock-like returns. Only half as volatile as Standard & Poor's 500-stock index, Berwyn Income is a high-yielding stew that contains less than 25% common stocks. The remaining assets are divided among bonds and other high-yielding securities. Manager Ed Killen invests in obscure, beaten-down stocks, and the fund yields almost 7%. "We hunt for out-of-favor companies with little downside risk," he says. Killen took over from his older brother, Bob, in 1994. Both are still principals in the money-management firm.

INVESTMENT STYLE:	small-company value
THREE-YEAR RETURN:	15.25%
FIVE-YEAR RETURN:	12.19%
TEN-YEAR RETURN:	12.76%
ANNUAL EXPENSE RATIO:	0.68%
ANNUAL PORTFOLIO TURNOVER:	38%
BEST BENCHMARK:	no single appropriate benchmark for this fund
VOLATILITY:	1
SAME MANAGER SINCE:	1994
TOTAL ASSETS:	$184.4 million

MEDIAN MARKET VALUE: $1.3 billion
MINIMUM INITIAL INVESTMENT: $10,000, $1,000
PHONE NUMBER: 800–992–6757

SPECIAL RISKS. Don't expect market-beating returns in a low-risk fund like this. Since many of its bonds are below investment quality, the fund might be hurt in an economic downturn.

DODGE & COX STOCK

There's nothing sexy about Dodge & Cox: It's an old-fashioned, large-company stock fund managed by an eight-member committee. Started in 1965, this low-cost, dependable fund beats the averages among all U.S. stock funds by a wide margin for virtually every time period. It seeks out-of-favor bargains. The fund's holdings are well diversified and include many household names: American Express, Citicorp, General Motors. Once the fund settles on a stock, it tends to hold on nearly forever. For instance, it has owned IBM for more than a decade—watching the stock first skyrocket, then tumble, then more than double in price again. A team of analysts researches stocks for the investment committee.

INVESTMENT STYLE: large-company value
THREE-YEAR RETURN: 27.95%
FIVE-YEAR RETURN: 21.55%
TEN-YEAR RETURN: 17.51%
ANNUAL EXPENSE RATIO: 0.59%
ANNUAL PORTFOLIO TURNOVER: 10%
BEST BENCHMARK: S&P 500,
Wilshire Large Company Value
VOLATILITY: 4
SAME MANAGER SINCE: 1974
TOTAL ASSETS: $4.5 billion
MEDIAN MARKET VALUE: $11.6 billion
MINIMUM INITIAL INVESTMENT: $2,500, $1,000
PHONE NUMBER: 800–621–3979

SPECIAL RISKS. This fund won't deviate greatly from the returns of Standard & Poor's 500-stock index.

FIDELITY

Because Fidelity moves its managers around faster than you can blink, it's sometimes hard to track their performance. But Beth

Terrana, who has run this fund since 1993, has one of the best long-term records among Fidelity managers. What's more, she's perhaps Fidelity's best-kept secret: Despite her proven abilities, the flagship Fidelity fund contains less than $8 billion, making it nimble enough to dart in and out of the huge stocks that the fast-trading Terrana favors. Terrana looks for downtrodden stocks she thinks are ripe for a turnaround, as well as those with hidden earnings potential. She is flexible, sometimes emphasizing growth-style stocks but more often buying value issues.

INVESTMENT STYLE:	large-company blend of growth and value
THREE-YEAR RETURN:	30.48%
FIVE-YEAR RETURN:	22.04%
TEN-YEAR RETURN:	17.98%
ANNUAL EXPENSE RATIO:	0.59%
ANNUAL PORTFOLIO TURNOVER:	107%
BEST BENCHMARK:	S&P 500
VOLATILITY:	5
SAME MANAGER SINCE:	1993
TOTAL ASSETS:	$7.9 billion
MEDIAN MARKET VALUE:	$32.6 billion
MINIMUM INITIAL INVESTMENT:	$2,500, $500
PHONE NUMBER:	800–544–8888
WEB SITE:	www.fidelity.com

SPECIAL RISKS. Terrana produced disappointing numbers in 1995 and 1996.

T. ROWE PRICE EQUITY INCOME

Brian Rogers, who has been at the helm since the fund's inception in 1985, concentrates on stocks with high dividends relative to their own history and to the overall market. Then he researches each company. He winds up with a fund of large, cheap stocks. "We like to buy someone else's underperformers and try to benefit from a subsequent shift in investor perception," says Rogers. In addition to being a top performer, the fund exhibits extremely low volatility. (*T. Rowe Price Value,* also run by Rogers, shows a more aggressive, and riskier, version of the same investment style).

INVESTMENT STYLE:	large-company value
THREE-YEAR RETURN:	27.68%
FIVE-YEAR RETURN:	20.55%

TEN-YEAR RETURN: 16.58%
ANNUAL EXPENSE RATIO: 0.79%
ANNUAL PORTFOLIO TURNOVER: 24%
BEST BENCHMARK: S&P 500,
Wilshire Large Company Value
VOLATILITY: 2
SAME MANAGER SINCE: 1985
TOTAL ASSETS: $13.7 billion
MEDIAN MARKET VALUE: $13.9 billion
MINIMUM INITIAL INVESTMENT: $2,500, $1,000
PHONE NUMBER: 800–638–5660
WEB SITE: www.troweprice.com

SPECIAL RISKS. This fund is big, with assets of nearly $14 billion.

SELECTED AMERICAN SHARES

In 1997, Shelby Davis turned this top-performing fund over to his co-manager and son, Chris Davis. But investors needn't fear a change in strategy. Davis remains chief investment officer and says, "I intend to be around a good long time." Shelby Davis, who also managed broker-sold New York Venture from 1969 until 1997 with consistently superior results, says he "looks for growth at a reasonable price." He dislikes buying stocks whose price-earnings ratios are higher than their expected rates of profit growth. For example, he wouldn't buy a stock expected to grow at 15% a year that was selling at 17 times earnings. About half the fund is in financial stocks. The Davises think that Americans, concerned about retirement, will save more, boosting the fortunes of companies that provide financial sevices. They also believe many financial companies remain undervalued.

INVESTMENT STYLE: large-company value
THREE-YEAR RETURN: 34.77%
FIVE-YEAR RETURN: 22.25%
TEN-YEAR RETURN: 18.58%
ANNUAL EXPENSE RATIO: 1.03%
ANNUAL PORTFOLIO TURNOVER: 29%
BEST BENCHMARK: S&P 500,
Wilshire Large Company Value
VOLATILITY: 6
SAME MANAGER SINCE: 1997
TOTAL ASSETS: $2.2 billion

MEDIAN MARKET VALUE: $30.8 billion
MINIMUM INITIAL INVESTMENT: $1,000, $250
PHONE NUMBER: 800–243–1575
WEB SITE: www.selectedfunds.com

SPECIAL RISKS. While Chris Davis seems as savvy as his father, the real test will be in his results—particularly as his father slowly moves off center stage. As is always true in funds concentrated in an industry sector, the overweighting in financial stocks also poses potential risks somewhere down the line.

VANGUARD INDEX 500

Gus Sauter doesn't try to beat Standard & Poor's 500-stock index. In effect, he *is* the index. His goal is to come as close as possible to matching it. And after the fund's tiny 0.2% annual

An Easy Way to Beat Index Funds?

WHILE THE FUND industry is littered with failed "enhanced" index funds that attempted to add just a smidgen to the return of Standard & Poor's 500-stock index, two well-respected bond houses may have come up with a way to pull off that tricky maneuver. Either of these funds is a fine alternative for investors considering an S&P index fund.

PIMCO Stocks Plus (800–426–0107) and **Smith Breeden Equity Plus** (800–221–3138) buy S&P 500-stock futures, investment vehicles that mimic the performance of the S&P 500. Investing in futures requires a deposit of only about 5% of each fund's assets. PIMCO and Smith Breeden invest the other 95% in relatively short-term bonds, but bonds that yield slightly more than the shortest-term Treasury bills—which are used to fix the price of the S&P futures. PIMCO invests in a mix of corporate, government and mortgage bonds that mature in an average of one year or less. Steven Treadway, chairman of PIMCO funds, says

he expects the fund to beat the S&P three of every four years and to match or slightly underperform the S&P the fourth year. John Sprow, manager of Smith Breeden Equity Plus, says he uses low-risk mortgage-backed securities for extra yield. Both funds beat the S&P for the three years ending with 1997.

Because these funds generate mostly short-term capital gains, which may be taxed at a higher rate than long-term gains, they make the most sense in tax-sheltered accounts. The Smith Breeden fund has a $1,000 minimum initial investment ($250 minimum for IRAs and gifts to minors) and annual expenses of 0.88%. PIMCO offers one version of Stocks Plus for small investors ($2,500 minimum; $1,000 minimum for IRAS and gifts to minors), 3% sales charge and 1.05% expense ratio) and another version for larger investors available through discount broker Jack White & Co. (800–323–3263), with a $2,000 minimum, 4.5% load, and 0.7% expense ratio.

expenses, he has pretty much been on the button every year. This is the fund (and the index) all active fund managers love to hate. Often they are paid incentive bonuses if they beat the average, and, if they fail to match the average for too long, they may be fired. When you're considering one of the actively managed funds in this chapter, this is a good fund to measure it against. It's also a fine way for any investor to get exposure to large-company U.S. stocks.

INVESTMENT STYLE:	large-company blend of growth and value
THREE-YEAR RETURN:	32.68%
FIVE-YEAR RETURN:	22.25%
TEN-YEAR RETURN:	18.73%
ANNUAL EXPENSE RATIO:	0.20%
ANNUAL PORTFOLIO TURNOVER:	5%
BEST BENCHMARK:	S&P 500
VOLATILITY:	5
SAME MANAGER SINCE:	1987
TOTAL ASSETS:	$55.3 billion
MEDIAN MARKET VALUE:	$41.3 billion
MINIMUM INITIAL INVESTMENT:	$3,000, $1,000
PHONE NUMBER:	800–662–7447
WEB SITE:	www.vanguard.com

SPECIAL RISKS. When big companies are out of favor, this fund will not impress you as much. Moreover, it holds virtually no cash to shield it from bear markets.

Balanced Funds

L OOK FOR SOME BONDS AND OTHER HIGH-YIELDING SECURITIES in these funds, as well as stocks. These are the lowest-risk stock funds and belong primarily in low-risk portfolios. They also make sense for investors who have only a short time period before they'll need their money, since they are unlikely to fall precipitously.

GREENSPRING
Greenspring buys a lot of the same types of depressed stocks as Berwyn Income (listed above under Growth-and-Income), but

manager Charles Carlson holds about 60% of assets in stocks—meaning this fund is likely to do a little better than Berwyn Income in bull markets and fare a little worse in bear markets. It's about three-fifths as volatile as Standard & Poor's 500-stock index, but has achieved decent returns. Greenspring owns a lot of banks and high-yield real estate investment trusts. "This fund is for conservative investors who want to own stocks and still be able to sleep at night," Carlson says.

INVESTMENT STYLE:	small-company value
THREE-YEAR RETURN:	21.41%
FIVE-YEAR RETURN:	15.54%
TEN-YEAR RETURN:	13.40%
ANNUAL EXPENSE RATIO:	1.04%
ANNUAL PORTFOLIO TURNOVER:	61%
BEST BENCHMARK:	no single appropriate benchmark
VOLATILITY:	1
SAME MANAGER SINCE:	1987
TOTAL ASSETS:	$197 million
MEDIAN MARKET VALUE:	$460 million
MINIMUM INITIAL INVESTMENT:	$2,000, $1,000 for IRAs
PHONE NUMBER:	800–366–3863

SPECIAL RISKS. Greenspring trails the averages in bull markets.

International Funds

T HESE FUNDS INVEST ABROAD. MOST PORTFOLIOS SHOULD contain at least one international fund, although there are often additional risks from currency fluctuations and political uncertainty in investing overseas. Confining yourself to U.S. stock funds limits you to a little more than half the world's stocks. Also, foreign stock markets tend to hit peaks and troughs at different times than the U.S. market, although this is tending to be less the case as stock markets globalize. Investors getting closer to needing their money will want to trim their exposure to international funds.

ARTISAN INTERNATIONAL

San Francisco–based Mark Yockey has achieved good numbers with this fund and had similarly strong results running United International Growth from 1990–1996. Yockey likes companies with rising earnings, but he won't pay exorbitant prices for them. He and his two analysts spend about one-fifth of their time identifying countries to invest in, and the rest examining companies in those nations, frequently in person. "We look for the best-run, fastest-growing, cheapest companies," he says. While most of the fund is in developed countries, primarily in Europe, about 25% may be invested in emerging markets. The fund returned only 3.5% in 1997, but it produced a 29% return through May 31, 1998.

INVESTMENT STYLE:	medium-size-company value
THREE-YEAR RETURN:	NA
FIVE-YEAR RETURN:	NA
TEN-YEAR RETURN:	NA
ANNUAL EXPENSE RATIO:	1.61%
ANNUAL PORTFOLIO TURNOVER:	104%
BEST BENCHMARK:	Morgan Stanley Europe Australasia and Far East
VOLATILITY:	6
SAME MANAGER SINCE:	1995
TOTAL ASSETS:	$339.7 million
MEDIAN MARKET VALUE:	$3.1 billion
MINIMUM INITIAL INVESTMENT:	$1,000, $1,000 for IRAs
PHONE NUMBER:	800–344–1770

SPECIAL RISKS. When Artisan has a big stake in emerging markets, with their attendant volatility, the fund will be more volatile than some other foreign funds.

HARBOR INTERNATIONAL GROWTH

Howard Moss and Blair Boyer believe that if you like a stock you should buy a lot of it. So even though they are managing a total of about $4 billion in this fund and in private accounts, they own only about 30 stocks. "It's a lot easier to choose your 30 favorite companies than your 100 or 200 favorite companies," Moss says. They look for big, well-managed firms that are growing rapidly yet selling at reasonable prices. They also usually keep about 20% of assets in volatile emerging markets. Rather than predicting which countries will excel, they put together the fund stock by stock. "All we do is visit companies and read research on them," Moss says. While this fund is fairly new, Moss managed institutional money successfully for more than a decade before its inception.

INVESTMENT STYLE:	large-company blend of growth and value
THREE-YEAR RETURN:	27.04%
FIVE-YEAR RETURN:	NA
TEN-YEAR RETURN:	NA
ANNUAL EXPENSE RATIO:	1.02%
ANNUAL PORTFOLIO TURNOVER:	76%
BEST BENCHMARK:	Morgan Stanley Europe Australasia and Far East
VOLATILITY:	7
SAME MANAGER SINCE:	1993
TOTAL ASSETS:	$943.8 million
MEDIAN MARKET VALUE:	$10 billion
MINIMUM INITIAL INVESTMENT:	$2,000, $500
PHONE NUMBER:	800–422–1050

SPECIAL RISKS. The small number of stocks and the big slug in emerging markets makes this a volatile fund.

OAKMARK INTERNATIONAL

David Herro scours the globe for undervalued companies ripe for a turnaround. "We are value investors," says Herro. "We try to determine the intrinsic value of a business." After determining that a company's stock is selling for significantly less than its value, Herro and his five analysts try to assess whether the corporate brass is shareholder-friendly and savvy enough to build up the company through efficient use of revenues. Swedish car and truck maker Volvo, a longtime Herro favorite, had diversified into many unrelated businesses—from drugs to brewing to brokerages. When management began selling off those businesses and refocusing on its core franchise, Herro started buying. About one-third of the fund is typically in emerging markets.

INVESTMENT STYLE:	medium-size company value
THREE-YEAR RETURN:	19.24%
FIVE-YEAR RETURN:	14.10%
TEN-YEAR RETURN:	NA
ANNUAL EXPENSE RATIO:	1.26%
ANNUAL PORTFOLIO TURNOVER:	NA
BEST BENCHMARK:	Morgan Stanley Europe Australasia and Far East
VOLATILITY:	6

SAME MANAGER SINCE:	1992
TOTAL ASSETS:	$1.2 billion
MEDIAN MARKET VALUE:	$1.4 billion
MINIMUM INITIAL INVESTMENT:	$1,000, $1,000
PHONE NUMBER:	800–625–6275
WEB SITE:	www.oakmark.com

SPECIAL RISKS. This fund has had some ups and downs. Perhaps Herro's biggest mistake was staying bullish on Mexico in 1994 as that country's stock market and currency took a nosedive.

TEMPLETON DEVELOPING MARKETS I

This is the only load fund in the book, because none of its no-load competitors in emerging-market funds come close to matching the long-term record of manager Mark Mobius. Not only will you pay a 5.75% sales fee to get into this fund, but expenses are high. In spite of the cost, if you want to invest part of your portfolio in an emerging-market fund, this one, managed by Yul Brynner look-alike Mobius, has the best and longest record of any emerging-markets fund. This fund is the top-ranking emerging markets fund over the past five years, and has been consistent: It has finished below average among emerging markets funds only once during the past five years.

Mobius helped pioneer emerging-markets investing when he launched Templeton Emerging Markets, a closed-end fund, in 1987 (see Chapter 22 for more on Mobius and closed-end funds). The closed-end fund has returned an annualized 23.4% over the past ten years—an annualized five percentage points more than the S&P 500.

Mobius relies mainly on a team of country-based analysts to pick stocks for the funds, but he still tries to personally meet the management of each company the funds invest in. His people place an unwavering emphasis on undervalued companies and ignore most political and economic risks in the companies' home countries. Mobius believes that companies that have put up with bad governments develop the toughness they need to prosper if their governments ever turn around.

INVESTMENT STYLE:	medium-size company value
THREE-YEAR RETURN:	7.26%
FIVE-YEAR RETURN:	10.75%
TEN-YEAR RETURN:	NA

ANNUAL EXPENSE RATIO:	2.03%
SALES FEE:	5.65%
ANNUAL PORTFOLIO TURNOVER:	12%
BEST BENCHMARK:	Morgan Stanley Emerging Markets
VOLATILITY:	8
SAME MANAGER SINCE:	1991
TOTAL ASSETS:	$3.5 billion
MEDIAN MARKET VALUE:	$2 billion
MINIMUM INITIAL INVESTMENT:	$100, $100
PHONE NUMBER:	800–292–9293
WEB SITE:	www.franklin-templeton.com

SPECIAL RISKS. Emerging-markets stocks are among the riskiest investments. Moreover, Mobius today is less the stock picker and more the manager of those who pick the stocks for him. Mobius also was either wrong, or very early, on Southeast Asia, rushing in to buy stocks in late 1997, long before they had hit bottom. Moreover, with $6.8 billion under management in this fund and his institutional and closed-end funds, Mobius and his people are trying to invest a lot in these illiquid markets.

Tweedy Browne Global Value

John Spears and brothers Christopher and William Browne are dyed-in-the-wool value investors, who delight in finding small and midsize companies stuffed with cash or other valuable assets that other managers might overlook. (A company with far more assets than its stock-market value is usually a terrific buy.) They have been managing money in their unhurried, almost professorial style since 1958 and have $19 million of their own money in this fund. Unique among the foreign funds listed here, Tweedy Browne hedges against all of its foreign currency exposure, so that a rise or fall in the dollar against other currencies has little effect on the portfolio's value. "We are stock pickers, not currency speculators," explains Spears. While currency gyrations tend to even out over time, currencies can be nearly as volatile as stocks over the short run. Thus, this fund is less volatile than most foreign funds.

INVESTMENT STYLE:	medium-size company value
THREE-YEAR RETURN:	25.03%
FIVE-YEAR RETURN:	NA

TEN-YEAR RETURN:	NA
ANNUAL EXPENSE RATIO:	1.58%
ANNUAL PORTFOLIO TURNOVER:	20%
BEST BENCHMARK:	Morgan Stanley Europe Australasia and Far East
VOLATILITY:	1
SAME MANAGER SINCE:	1993
TOTAL ASSETS:	$2 billion
MEDIAN MARKET VALUE:	$2.8 billion
MINIMUM INITIAL INVESTMENT:	$2,500, $500
PHONE NUMBER:	800–432–4789

SPECIAL RISKS. Unlike the other foreign funds in this section, Tweedy Browne is a global fund and typically invests 10% to 15% of its money in the U.S. (For more on global funds, see page 159.) Be aware of that when allocating your assets so that you don't end up with less invested in overseas stocks than you intended. Also, this is a conservative fund that won't keep pace with more aggressive funds in bull markets.

Key Points

- *Make sure to compare a fund with its relevant benchmarks.*
- *Volatility is a superb predictor of how a fund will perform in a bear market.*
- *Even the best funds are usually only a bit better than average over the long run.*

How to Pick Top Bond and Money-Market Funds

Low expenses are the key

VER WISH YOU COULD STAY AT THE RITZ CARLTON AND pay Days Inn prices? If so, you'll love buying bond funds. Being a cheapskate pays off in spades: You'll not only wind up with less expensive funds, but you'll usually get better-performing and lower-risk funds, too. Why? Because high expenses drag down bond funds' returns, and their managers must take greater chances if they hope to do well.

Expenses, of course, figure into the total returns of all kinds of funds. But a good stock-fund manager can overcome the handicap of high expenses by skillful stock-picking. Not so with bond funds. A bond is a bond is a bond, and it's hard for a bond-fund manager to get an edge. As John Markese, president of the American Association of Individual Investors, puts it: "You're playing for a quarter of a point here, a sixteenth of a point there." Bond managers count their gains and losses in basis points—hundredths of a percentage point. Expense ratios, which often vary by one-half of one percentage point or more among bond funds, can overwhelm whatever value adroit management can add to a bond fund.

To test this premise, I lumped together all high-quality corporate-bond funds, mortgage-bond funds and government-bond funds, and then divided them into two categories: those with below-average expense ratios and those with above average-expense ratios. (The average was 1.03%.) As a group, the cheaper funds over the past one, three and five years had:

- **higher total returns** than their more expensive brethren
- **higher dividend yields**
- **shorter maturities** in their portfolios (making them less sensitive to interest-rate fluctuations)
- **less month-to-month volatility.**

So, not only are these funds better-performing, they are also less risky. The same characteristics hold true when you look separately at the expense ratios of municipal-bond funds and high-yield, or junk-bond funds.

THE VANGUARD DIRT-CHEAP ADVANTAGE

What's more, dirt-cheap beats merely cheap. It turns out that funds in the cheaper half of cheap funds did better on all counts than their merely cheap counterparts. Many of the dirt-cheap bond funds (those that charge 0.71% or less of fund assets per year) are run by Vanguard. Vanguard is the lowest-cost provider of mutual funds. It's technically owned by its shareholders and doesn't try to turn a profit. As a result, it's hard to beat Vanguard when it comes to bonds, particularly municipal bonds.

Signposts of Quality

EXPENSES ARE AN IDEAL STARTING POINT FOR PICKING BOND funds. For most bond funds, the expense ratio should be no more than about 0.8%—just this side of dirt-cheap. Be especially frugal when looking at municipal-bond funds, which have lower yields than taxable funds. Conversely, you can tolerate higher expenses for junk-bond funds (or funds that contain a fair amount of junk), which can be nearly as different from one another as stock funds are. Here are other things to consider when you're shopping for a bond fund (all of which are listed for each fund discussed later in this chapter):

Total return. Don't fixate on the size of your monthly income check to the detriment of all else. The better number to know about a bond fund is its total return—the income yield plus (or minus) capital appreciation. Yield can be juiced up, but sometimes only by guaranteeing future declines in a fund's value. Total return is the bottom line.

Weighted average maturity. Make sure you compare apples with apples: Compare long-term funds with other long-term funds and short-term funds with other short-term funds. The most useful number to know is a fund's weighted average maturity, which essentially tells you how long the average bond holding in the fund has until its maturity date. A bond's maturity date is the date on which the issuing company or government is due to pay off all it owes on a bond. This date is set before bonds are sold—although often issuers are allowed to redeem bonds early. (A fund's maturity is "weighted," meaning bonds that make up a larger portion of the portfolio count for more than bonds that are a smaller part of the fund.) The higher a fund's weighted average maturity, the more long-term the fund is, and the more it will fluctuate in value as interest rates change. Other things being equal, long-term bond funds—those with high weighted average maturities—tend to be riskier than short-term bond funds.

Credit quality. A high-quality (or investment-grade) bond fund should hold mostly bonds rated BBB– or better by Standard & Poor's. The lower a bond's credit quality, the greater the risk that it will decline in value during periods of economic weakness, and the greater the risk that its issuer will default on interest payments. At the same time, low-credit-quality bonds tend to have higher yields and to be less sensitive to interest-rate changes. A fund's credit quality—the average quality of the bonds it holds—is also important when assessing its performance. Make sure to compare high-quality funds with other high-quality funds and low-quality funds with other low-quality funds.

Manager tenure. As with stock funds, a good past record isn't as meaningful if there's a new manager, so favor funds with experienced managers. Some top bond houses, such as Loomis Sayles, PIMCO and Vanguard, tend to hire top managers even for their new funds.

Volatility. It's important to know how much a fund's performance bounces around from month to month. The lower a fund's volatility, the better it should hold up when rates rise (remember, bond yields always move in the opposite direction of bond prices—when bond prices fall, yields rise, and vice versa). A volatility score of 1 means that a bond fund is less volatile than 90% of all taxable bond funds, a score of 2 means it's less volatile than 80% of all taxable bond funds, and so forth.

Consistency. Even more so than with stock funds, you don't want a bond fund that tops the charts one year only to fall to the bottom the next. Bonds are the ballast of your portfolio. You want to hire a sure-handed skipper to manage your low-risk money.

Sales fees. It's difficult to justify paying a sales load for a bond fund. If you use a full-service broker and plan to hold your bonds for a long time, you'll likely do better buying and holding individual bonds if you have at least $50,000 to invest (see box on page 243). Among bond funds with loads, Bond Fund of America and FPA New Income are solid performers.

Bond Funds by Category

I'VE DIVIDED BOND FUNDS INTO SEVERAL BROAD CATEGORIES. Note that I haven't included all the varieties listed in Chapter 13. That's because many of the best bond funds tend to buy bonds from a number of different areas of the bond market, rather than confining themselves to one segment. Here are the categories I've included:

HIGH-GRADE CORPORATE BOND FUNDS

These mutual funds invest mainly in bonds of companies with high credit quality.

Harbor Bond

Through adept interest-rate calls and an unwillingness to go too far out on a limb, manager William Gross has built a consistently superior record over the past two decades. Harbor Bond reflects those skills and conservatism. Over the past five years, it has delivered returns in the top 20% among its peers. Gross holds a lot of government bonds and mortgage-backed securities, and spices the portfolio with a few lower-quality bonds and foreign bonds.

THREE-YEAR RETURN:	10%
FIVE-YEAR RETURN:	7.50%
TEN-YEAR RETURN:	9.72%
ANNUAL EXPENSE RATIO:	0.67%
WEIGHTED AVERAGE MATURITY:	8.9 years
AVERAGE CREDIT QUALITY:	AA

VOLATILITY: 7
SAME MANAGER SINCE: 1987
MINIMUM INITIAL INVESTMENT: $2,000, $500 for IRAs
PHONE NUMBER: 800–422–1050

Loomis Sayles Bond

Sometimes called "the best bond picker in America," Dan Fuss has been managing bonds since the 1960s and still favors a slide rule over a computer for many calculations. His fund is a lot riskier than Harbor Bond, because Fuss buys longer-term bonds and tends to keep about a third of this fund in junk bonds. He ventures abroad, often finding attractive bonds in such locales as New Zealand. "We do a lot of strange things," Fuss says. Fortunately for shareholders, few of them fail. Even in periods of rising rates, such as 1994, Loomis Sayles has managed to hold up relatively well. (New investors can only buy this fund through discount brokers. See Chapter 8 for more on discounters.)

THREE-YEAR RETURN: 17.3%
FIVE-YEAR RETURN: 13.2%
TEN-YEAR RETURN: NA
ANNUAL EXPENSE RATIO: 1.00%
WEIGHTED AVERAGE MATURITY: 20.2 years
AVERAGE CREDIT QUALITY: A
VOLATILITY: 10
SAME MANAGER SINCE: 1991
MINIMUM INITIAL INVESTMENT: $250,000 (but much less through various discount brokers such as Fidelity, Charles Schwab, and Waterhouse), NA
PHONE NUMBER: 800–633–3330
WEB SITE: www.loomissayles.com

T. Rowe Price Spectrum Income

This fund of funds charges investors nothing beyond the costs of the underlying T. Rowe Price funds it invests in. It spreads its bets among seven other funds, including a high-quality corporate bond fund, a junk-bond fund, a money-market fund, a mortgage-backed fund, a foreign-bond fund, and even a high-yielding stock fund. The mix is adjusted periodically. The point of using different funds, says manager Peter Van Dyke, is that "some are doing well when others are not." The method has worked: Spectrum Income has produced good returns with relatively low risk.

THREE-YEAR RETURN:	11.77%
FIVE-YEAR RETURN:	9.4%
TEN-YEAR RETURN:	NA
ANNUAL EXPENSE RATIO:	0%
WEIGHTED AVERAGE MATURITY:	9.5 years
AVERAGE CREDIT QUALITY:	A
VOLATILITY:	5
SAME MANAGER SINCE:	1990
MINIMUM INITIAL INVESTMENT:	$2,500, $1,000
PHONE NUMBER:	800–638–5660
WEB SITE:	www.troweprice.com

HIGH-YIELD CORPORATE BOND FUNDS

So-called junk-bond funds invest mostly in lower-quality bonds. While these funds can be nearly as volatile as some stock funds, in small helpings they not only provide high income but also help diversify your portfolio. You might consider putting about 25% of your bond money into junk-bond funds.

Loomis Sayles High Yield

This is a relatively new fund, but based on Dan Fuss's record managing Loomis Sayles Bond, I have no problem suggesting it. Fuss has a great record, and he has been picking undervalued junk bonds for decades. He approaches bond investing the way many stock managers approach their craft: by hunting for undervalued securities. Like his other fund, you must buy it through a discount broker. And like other junk-bond funds, this one is more vulnerable to a recession than to higher interest rates.

THREE-YEAR RETURN:	NA
FIVE-YEAR RETURN:	NA
ANNUAL EXPENSE RATIO:	1.00%
WEIGHTED AVERAGE MATURITY:	15.6 years
AVERAGE CREDIT QUALITY:	BB
VOLATILITY:	10
SAME MANAGER SINCE:	1997
MINIMUM INITIAL INVESTMENT:	$250,000, NA

PHONE NUMBER: 800–633–3330
WEB SITE: www.loomissayles.com

Northeast Investors Trust

Ernest Monrad has been investing in junk bonds since the 1960s, and his son Bruce joined him in 1993. Experience must count for something: This has been one of the best-performing junk-bond funds. The fund is not for the faint of heart, though. The Monrads often shop at the bottom of the junk-quality barrel, and they use leverage (borrowed money) to buy more bonds when they are bullish on junk bonds. They also hold some high-yielding stocks to flesh out their portfolio. In short: This is a risky bond fund, but one whose gambles have paid off handsomely.

THREE-YEAR RETURN:	16.47%
FIVE-YEAR RETURN:	14.46%
TEN-YEAR RETURN:	11.90
15-YEAR RETURN:	12.36
ANNUAL EXPENSE RATIO:	0.64%
WEIGHTED AVERAGE MATURITY:	7.2 years
AVERAGE CREDIT QUALITY:	B
VOLATILITY:	6
SAME MANAGER SINCE:	1960 (1993 for Bruce)
MINIMUM INITIAL INVESTMENT:	$1,000, $500
PHONE NUMBER:	800–225–6704

MORTGAGE FUNDS

These funds invest in pools of home mortgages. They are less predictable than other bond funds, because they lag when rates fall (and homeowners refinance at lower rates), as well as when rates rise. But they also pay higher yields. The key is not to over-do mortgage-backed funds (about 25% of your bond portfolio is enough) and to stick to funds that keep it simple. The biggest problems in bondland in recent years have come from managers playing with risky mortgage securities.

Vanguard GNMA

This fund gives you just what the label says: government-guaranteed mortgages backed by Ginnie Mae (the Government National Mortgage Association). Manager Paul Kaplan has worked on the fund since its inception in 1980 and took sole control in 1994. He doesn't stick his neck out very far on the direction of interest rates, but he buys high-yielding securities because he knows many shareholders depend on the fund's income. "I pay attention to yield," Kaplan says. The fund has produced top returns without undue volatility.

THREE-YEAR RETURN:	9.30%
FIVE-YEAR RETURN:	6.96%
TEN-YEAR RETURN:	9.00
ANNUAL EXPENSE RATIO:	0.27%
WEIGHTED AVERAGE MATURITY:	7.6 years
AVERAGE CREDIT QUALITY:	AAA
VOLATILITY:	4
SAME MANAGER SINCE:	1994
MINIMUM INITIAL INVESTMENT:	$3,000, $1,000
PHONE NUMBER:	800–635–1511
WEB SITE:	www.vanguard.com

SHORT-TERM BOND FUNDS

Funds with short weighted average maturities, say three years or less, can be a great place to stash money you plan to spend in a couple of years. You get higher income than you would in a money-market fund, and you incur little risk of loss if rates rise.

Strong Advantage *and* Strong Short-Term Bond

Both these funds use the same method to obtain relatively high yields with low volatility. The only difference is their weighted average maturities. Ultra-short-term Advantage, run by Jeffrey Koch, keeps average maturity at a mere 0.7 years, while Short-Term Bond, run by Bradley Tank, keeps average maturity at around 2.5 years. To make up for their relatively high expense ratios, both these funds pick up extra yield by placing 20% or more of assets in junk bonds. In a weakening economy, some bonds might face a risk of default.

THREE-YEAR RETURN:	6.87% (8.34% for Short-Term)
FIVE-YEAR RETURN:	6.25% (6.12%)
TEN-YEAR RETURN:	NA (7.45%)
ANNUAL EXPENSE RATIO:	0.8% (0.9%)
WEIGHTED AVERAGE MATURITY:	.7 years (2.5 years)
AVERAGE CREDIT QUALITY:	BBB (A)
VOLATILITY:	1 (2)

SAME MANAGER SINCE: 1991 (1990)
MINIMUM INITIAL INVESTMENT: $2,500, $2,500 ($2,500, $1,000)
PHONE NUMBER: 800–368–1030
WEB SITE: www.strongfunds.com

USAA Short-Term Bond

This fund buys high-quality, short-term bonds, exposing investors to far less risk than either of the Strong funds. As with many USAA funds, expenses are higher than Vanguard's but lower than just about anybody else's. Add to that USAA's record for steady fund management—rarely topping the charts, but never providing unpleasant surprises—and you have a recipe for a good, solid short-term fund that will deliver more income than a money-market fund (this fund actually holds about one-third of assets in cash) with very little extra risk.

THREE-YEAR RETURN: 7.83%
FIVE-YEAR RETURN: NA
TEN-YEAR RETURN: NA
ANNUAL EXPENSE RATIO: 0.5%
WEIGHTED AVERAGE MATURITY: 2.3 years
AVERAGE CREDIT QUALITY: A
VOLATILITY: 2
SAME MANAGER SINCE: 1993
MINIMUM INITIAL INVESTMENT: $3,000, $250
PHONE NUMBER: 800–382–8722

Vanguard Short-Term Corporate

Like most Vanguard funds, this one is straightforward. Robert Auwaerter has produced results similar to Strong Short-Term Bond's. Indeed, the weighted average maturity is similar, at 3 years. But this fund doesn't buy any junk bonds, and expenses are just 0.25%. You won't get quite the kick that you get from the Strong funds, but the risks are much lower.

THREE-YEAR RETURN: 7.27%
FIVE-YEAR RETURN: 5.90%
TEN-YEAR RETURN: 7.75%
15-YEAR RETURN: 8.71
ANNUAL EXPENSE RATIO: 0.25%
WEIGHTED AVERAGE MATURITY: 3 years
AVERAGE CREDIT QUALITY: A

VOLATILITY: 2
SAME MANAGER SINCE: 1993
MINIMUM INITIAL INVESTMENT: $3,000, $1,000
PHONE NUMBER: 800–635–1511
WEB SITE: www.vanguard.com

MONEY-MARKET FUNDS

These funds hold bonds with less than six months until they mature. While their yields vary, they seek to maintain a stable share price of $1. That makes them an ideal place to park short-term savings—money you don't need in a bank checking account, but that you wouldn't want to put in a risky investment. Most money-market funds offer check-writing privileges.

Because money-market funds invest in only the shortest-term bonds, and because federal rules require them to invest almost all their assets in high-quality bonds, expenses are paramount in picking a money fund. Fund sponsors know this, so sometimes they hold "sales"—waiving expenses on a money-market fund while they build up assets and a good track record, and then slowly reinstating expenses. If you're prepared to move your money to another fund when a sale ends at a money-market fund, pick one that is waiving expenses. But if you write a lot of checks on money-markets, you'll need to be careful not to bounce a check while you're transferring your money.

Low expenses. The simpler way to shop for a money-market fund is to look for one that charges consistently low expenses and stick with it. Two good ones are *USAA Money Market* (800–531–8722) which charges 0.45%, and *Vanguard Money Market Prime* (800–635–1511), which charges 0.32%.

Miscellaneous service charges. When you pick a money fund, check whether its sponsor assesses pesky little charges for, say, writing a check or more than a certain number of checks, or your balance falling below a certain amount, or even for making deposits or withdrawals. Also find out the minimum for which you can write a check on your money-market account, and whether the fund returns your checks or copies of them. Dreyfus Basic Money Market, for instance, requires a minimum balance of $10,000, and has a minimum check amount of $1,000. It also charges a $2 fee for every check if your balance is below $50,000 (other Dreyfus money-market funds have lower requirements).

Money-Market Math

To figure your taxable-equivalent yield on a muni money-market (or any muni fund) so you can compare it with the taxable yields of other funds, divide the yield by one minus your tax bracket. For instance, a 3% yield on a muni money-market, divided by 1 minus 31% (or .69), equals a 4.35% taxable-equivalent yield. That means a taxpayer in the 31% bracket would have to earn more than 4.34% on a taxable money-market to do better than in a 3% tax-exempt money-market.

Deep pockets. In the unlikely event that a money-market holds bonds that go into default, it helps to have your money invested with a well-capitalized company, such as Dreyfus, Fidelity, T. Rowe Price or Strong. Such companies have the financial strength to eat the loss, rather than forcing you to. If you're very concerned about your share price ever falling below a dollar, which is what could happen if a borrower defaults on some of a money-market's bonds, you can invest in a slightly lower-yielding Treasury-only money-market, such as Vanguard Treasury Money Market, which is virtually risk-free.

MUNICIPAL BOND FUNDS

These are exempt from federal income taxes and usually are good deals for anyone in the 28% tax bracket or higher. Funds that hold muni bonds issued in a single state are also exempt from that state's taxes, but generally charge higher expenses and limit your diversification. There's really no need to look beyond Vanguard for tax-exempt funds. Besides charging the lowest costs, around 0.2% annually, Vanguard has Ian MacKinnon. He has served capably as lead manager of these funds since 1981, ensuring that they buy high-quality bonds and don't make overly aggressive interest rate bets. The results, year in and year out, are among the best of any muni funds.

Vanguard Muni Intermediate Term makes a good center-of-the-plate bond fund. It has a weighted average maturity of about seven years, which means it won't get killed when rates rise, yet it produces generous income.

For the more aggressive part of your portfolio, consider *Vanguard Muni Long Term* or *Vanguard Muni High Yield*, both with average maturities of more than 10 years. (High Yield is not a junk-bond fund; its average credit quality is AA.)

For short-term money, *Vanguard Muni Limited Term*, with an average maturity of 3.3 years, and *Vanguard Muni Short Term*, with an average maturity of just 1.2 years, are good choices.

Another bond fund worth considering is *Excelsior Long-*

Bonds or Bond Funds?

IN TWO CIRCUMSTANCES, it's cheaper and sometimes better (though more work) to buy individual bonds rather than bond funds:
• if you're buying Treasury securities
• if you're investing more than $50,000 in municipal bonds and plan to hold them to maturity.

Individual municipal bonds
Buy individual munis only if you're fairly certain you'll hold them until maturity. Working with a discount or full-service broker, put together a "laddered" portfolio—one with staggered maturities, which will help insulate you against interest-rate fluctuations. You might, say, buy one bond maturing in roughly four years, one in eight years, one in 12 years and one in 16 years. Then, when the four-year bond matures, replace it with another 16-year bond, which returns your portfolio to the same maturities it had originally.

Purchase only low-risk, AA or AAA-rated bonds, and, to keep things simple, stick to general-obligation bonds, which are guaranteed by the taxing power of a city, county or state. Or buy insured bonds, which automatically are rated AAA. If possible, avoid bonds that can be called (redeemed early by their issuer).

Comparison shop among brokers for the best prices on specific bonds. With some bargaining you should be able to

keep your commissions to no more than 1.5% of the bonds' price. You can sell these bonds before they mature, but if you do, your expenses will likely wind up higher than if you'd simply bought a muni fund. By purchasing high-quality individual munis and holding them to maturity, you'll probably earn as much as you would in a bond fund and keep your risks lower.

Treasury securities
Treasury securities are as safe as the U.S. government, so there's no need for the diversification or professional management you get in a mutual fund. You can buy Treasuries through a broker for about $50, or you can avoid commissions by buying them directly from the Bureau of the Public Debt (Division of Customer Services, Washington, DC 20239; 202–874–4000) or from any of the 36 Federal Reserve banks and branches across the country. (The regional banks and branches, listed in the blue government pages of your phone book, are usually easier to deal with than the Bureau of the Public Debt.) Buying Treasuries directly from the government almost always costs less than buying a government-bond fund. If you need to sell a Treasury before maturity, moreover, the government charges just $34.

Term Tax Exempt (800–446–1012). A top-performing fund—albeit one with high risks because of its recent 19.9-year weighted average maturity and its manager's attempts to guess the direction of interest rates—Excelsior returned 9.46% in 1997 and has returned 8.94% over the last three years and 8% over the past five years. Annual expenses are 0.74%. Manager Ken McAlley buys longer-term bonds when he thinks rates will fall; he buys shorter-term bonds and even raises the percentage of assets in cash when he thinks rates will rise. "The major risk to bond investors is rising interest rates," he notes. "If you're not aware of that, you're asleep at the watch."

On the other end of the risk spectrum, *Sit Tax-Free Income* (800–332–5580) is also worth a look. This fund is for the risk-averse investor looking for tax-free income. Its weighted average maturity is generally between 14 and 19 years, but that overstates its volatility because manager Michael Brilley hunts for high-yielding bonds with low sensitivity to changes in interest rates. Not surprisingly, the fund has held up well in bear markets. It returned 9.83% in 1997, 8.40% over the past three years and 7.23% over the past five years. Annual expenses are 0.79%. "We buy high-income, stable-value securities," Brilley says. "When you do that, you don't have to worry about interest-rate forecasting."

Key Points
- *Expenses are crucial in choosing bond funds and money-market funds.*
- *Vanguard's low expenses are hard to beat, but there are other good bond funds.*
- *While a fund's long-term record is important, so is its volatility, weighted average maturity and average credit quality.*
- *Compare bond funds with their peers.*
- *Some investors will do better with individual bonds than they will with bond funds.*

Sector Funds and Other Niche Funds

Some are conservative; handle the others with care

ICK THE RIGHT SECTOR FUND AND YOU CAN BECOME very rich, very quickly. The ten top-performing sector funds more than tripled in value over the five years ending with 1997. Over ten years, the ten top funds each rose by more than 400%, and the top fund, Fidelity Select Regional Banks, rose a staggering 584%. But the moral here is clear: Live by the sword, die by the sword. The worst-performing sector fund, Steadman Technology & Growth, lost 89% of its value over those ten years. Just to get even in the next five years, it would have to increase in value by more than 800%. That probably won't happen, however, because the Steadman fund is likely to be merged out of existence, something that fund sponsors often do with particularly poor performers.

The fact is that picking the top sector for the next three months, one year or five years is a lot harder than picking top-performing diversified funds. Furthermore, the typical sector fund is almost twice as volatile as Standard & Poor's 500-stock index.

Not surprisingly, most financial advisers contend that the boom-and-bust behavior of sector funds makes them inappropriate for all but the most risk-tolerant investors. "I never use them," declares Jane King, president of Fairfield Financial Advisors, in Wellesley, Mass. "They are the antithesis of everything you should be doing with a mutual fund: protecting a client's assets through diversity, managing risk and investing for the long term. They encourage people to jump in and out."

Other critics point out that relatively inexperienced managers often run sector funds. Fidelity tends to use its three dozen sector funds as a training ground for young, inexperienced managers before it promotes them to its mainstream funds. Fidelity's sector managers, moreover, spend the overwhelming majority of their time analyzing stocks for the managers of the bigger diversified funds. One sector manager told me it took her about ten minutes each day to run her sector fund.

What's true of sector funds is also true of foreign funds that invest in a single country or region. The more highly focused a fund is in one area, the more likely it is to meet with catastrophe. For example, the average emerging-markets fund, which can usually invest in any country outside the major industrialized nations, lost −3.2% in 1997. The average Asian emerging-markets fund was down −28.83%. And the single-country Matthews Korea Fund lost −64.75%.

Moreover, sector funds arguably undermine one of the most important purposes of a mutual fund: to have an expert decide how to deploy your assets among various stocks and sectors. Invest in a sector fund and you are, in effect, tying your manager's hands.

Exceptions to the Rule

B UT NOT EVERY TYPE OF SECTOR FUND IS ERRATIC. REAL estate funds and utility funds are less volatile than most aggressive funds and have been a haven for conservative, income-oriented investors. Natural-resources funds, while more volatile, might have a place in a portfolio as a hedge against inflation—although most investors will be better off letting managers of diversified funds decide when to invest in oil and gas and other natural resources.

As we pointed out in Chapter 13, "Starting the Search for the Right Fund," utility stocks were until recently a great place for income-oriented investors, including many elderly people, to earn generous yields and not have to contend with the volatility of the overall stock market. Times have changed. With competition starting to shake up utilities, these stocks have become less steady. Some utilities will be winners in the coming shakeout, and some will be losers. Picking among them is not easy, and utility funds are no longer the place to put the bulk of your money if you're a conservative investor seeking income. Most such investors will get all the exposure they need to utility funds through growth-and-income funds.

Funds that invest in real estate investment trusts (REITs)—which themselves invest in commercial real estate, including apartments, hotels, office buildings and shopping centers—have recently emerged as a good way to diversify a portfolio. (REITs are much safer and easier to get out of than the money-losing real estate limited partnerships that many investors got stuck in during the early 1980s.) REIT funds are the equal of utility funds as a relatively conservative way to earn high yields, because they must pass almost all their profits on to shareholders. Furthermore, REITs provide some cushion against inflation in a strengthening economy, because rents will presumably rise under such conditions. "This is not a vehicle for finding red-hot stocks," cautions Barry Greenfield, manager of Fidelity Real Estate. "I simply want this fund to do better than bonds, better than utility funds and better than certain kinds of balanced funds." (Balanced funds own both stocks and bonds.) REITs are a fine place to put 5% or 10% of a balanced portfolio of stocks and bonds. Here are two of the most attractive funds.

CGM REALTY

Kenneth Heebner is one of the wiliest sector pickers among stock managers, and he's convinced REITs are poised to outperform for years to come. "I think there's tremendous opportunity," says Heebner, who since 1977 has run CGM Capital Development, one of the top-performing stock funds. He points to the unwillingness of many insurance companies, until recently a big source of capital for real estate, to invest directly with developers since their losses in the early 1990s. As a result, he says, "the best real estate developers in this country have been forced to sell shares of their companies to the public." For a REIT fund, CGM Realty is aggressive, shifting from sector to sector as Heebner spots value, which makes the fund's small size a plus.

THREE-YEAR RETURN:	28.70%
FIVE-YEAR RETURN:	NA
TEN-YEAR RETURN:	NA
ANNUAL EXPENSE RATIO:	1.00%

ANNUAL PORTFOLIO TURNOVER: 57%
VOLATILITY: 6
SAME MANAGER SINCE: 1994
TOTAL ASSETS: $430 million
MEDIAN MARKET VALUE: $699 million
MINIMUM INITIAL INVESTMENT: $2,500, $1,000 for IRAs
PHONE NUMBER: 800–345–4048
WEB SITE: www.cgmfunds.com

COHEN & STEERS REALTY SHARES

One of the oldest real estate funds, the Cohen & Steers fund has been in operation since 1991, and the firm has been investing in real estate since 1986. Managers Martin Cohen and Robert Steers pursue well-managed REITs with strong balance sheets. "We invest in REITs with the greatest potential for growth, not the highest yield," says Steers. The fund employs a team of analysts who scour the country for the best REITs. The only negative to this fund is its size, $3.2 billion in assets. The entire REIT market is relatively small, making it difficult for Cohen & Steers to trade as easily as it did in previous years. The fund has a $10,000 minimum initial purchase, but is available for less through discount brokers.

THREE-YEAR RETURN: 23.46%
FIVE-YEAR RETURN: 14.42%
TEN-YEAR RETURN: NA
ANNUAL EXPENSE RATIO: 1.08%
ANNUAL PORTFOLIO TURNOVER: 33%
VOLATILITY: 6
SAME MANAGER SINCE: 1991
TOTAL ASSETS: $3.2 billion
MEDIAN MARKET VALUE: $1.4 billion
MINIMUM INITIAL INVESTMENT: $10,000, NA
PHONE NUMBER: 800–437–9912
WEB SITE: www.cohenandsteers.com

Riskier Opportunities

REITS ARE WELL-SUITED FOR CONSERVATIVE PORTFOLIOS. Aggressive investors with longer time horizons may want to spice up their portfolios with hotter sector funds. A case can be made that some sector funds offer rewards that more than offset the risks. "They do add a little zip," says Michael Martin, president of Financial Advantage Inc., in Ellicott City, Md. Several economic sectors have broad, long-term appeal to investors, and within those sectors there are funds that regularly stand out from the rest.

But use caution: Venture into sector funds only if you first have a diversified group of funds. For example, you wouldn't want a technology fund to be the largest or only aggressive-growth fund in your portfolio. Specialized funds are like Tabasco: Add too much and you ruin the dish. The same goes for some of the specialized closed-end funds we'll discuss in Chapter 22.

Following are two volatile sector funds that can add some pizazz to your portfolio. Keep these to less than 5% of your overall stock fund investments and you'll likely avoid indigestion.

T. Rowe Price Science & Technology

Charles Morris's fund covers such a broad area that it can barely be called a sector fund. The fund is into biotechnology, computers, communications, and environmental and data services. "What we're really doing is running a fairly sector-concentrated growth fund," Morris says. Still, there are times, most notably 1997, when the market provides no escape for a fund invested in these high-growth areas. The fund suffered its next-to-worst year since inception in 1997, gaining only 1.7%. Its worst year was 1990, when it had a one-year loss of –1.3%. This fund is about one-third more volatile than the average aggressive-growth fund, but over the long haul, it has also been more rewarding.

THREE-YEAR RETURN:	23.92%
FIVE-YEAR RETURN:	24.85%
TEN-YEAR RETURN:	23.53%
ANNUAL EXPENSE RATIO:	0.94%
ANNUAL PORTFOLIO TURNOVER:	134%
VOLATILITY:	10
SAME MANAGER SINCE:	1991
TOTAL ASSETS:	$3.9 billion
MEDIAN MARKET VALUE:	$4.8 billion
MINIMUM INITIAL INVESTMENT:	$2,500, $1,000
PHONE NUMBER:	800–638–5660
WEB SITE:	www.troweprice.com

VANGUARD SPECIALIZED HEALTH CARE

With an aging population, it's hard to argue that the U.S. and other nations aren't going to keep spending more on health care, although a lot of that future potential already is reflected in the price of health care stocks. This fund should profit if the health care sector does. But don't expect Edward Owens's fund to lead the pack in years when health stocks are on a rampage, such as 1995. His value-oriented style pays off when the market is more placid. He buys stocks of large companies and emphasizes sectors that aren't popular with other investors and, as a result, are selling at attractive valuations. That makes this fund one of the least volatile among health-sector funds, yet it has finished in either first place or second place for total return over the past three,

Other Kinds of Funds to Be Wary Of

Global funds

Global funds invest overseas and in the U.S. It's hard enough for a manager to be good at investing in the U.S. *or* abroad, without trying to do both well. Besides, as I mentioned in Chapter 13, global funds can make it hard to tell what percentage of your total assets are invested overseas.

Balanced funds, flexible funds and asset-allocation funds

These types of funds decide what percentage of your assets to put into stocks and bonds. You don't need that when you're doing it yourself.

Two exceptions to the rule, **Fidelity Asset Manager** (800–544–8888) and **Fidelity Asset Manager Growth**, are discussed on page 45.

Other exceptions include **Berwyn Income, Greenspring** and **T. Rowe Price Capital**

Appreciation (described on pages 216 through 225). They provide superior low-risk returns by buying high-yielding securities.

Funds of funds

Funds of funds, which are funds that invest only in other funds, typically tack on an extra layer of fees, and don't seem to be able to pick funds well enough to justify their costs. Other funds of funds are run by a single fund company. While this latter type doesn't usually charge additional fees, generally the fund company's offerings are not broad enough to give a fund of funds good choices.

Two exceptions here, **T. Rowe Price Spectrum Growth** and **T. Rowe Price Spectrum Income**, are discussed on page 44. Vanguard also offers funds of funds with no additional expenses and decent choices.

five and ten years. Turnover is a tiny 7%, and expenses are just 0.38% (though there's a 1% redemption fee for selling shares held less than a year).

THREE-YEAR RETURN:	33.14%
FIVE-YEAR RETURN:	28.20%
TEN-YEAR RETURN:	22.77%
ANNUAL EXPENSE RATIO:	0.38%
ANNUAL PORTFOLIO TURNOVER:	7%
VOLATILITY:	3
SAME MANAGER SINCE:	1984
TOTAL ASSETS:	$5.3 billion
MEDIAN MARKET VALUE:	$16 billion
MINIMUM INITIAL INVESTMENT:	$3,000, $1,000
PHONE NUMBER:	800–635–1511
WEB SITE:	www.vanguard.com

Key Points

- *Most sector funds are extremely risky and should be avoided, except perhaps in small doses as part of a well-diversified portfolio.*
- *Funds that invest in real estate investment trusts, however, are often a good source of income for conservative investors.*
- *Sector funds aren't the only funds to be wary of.*

Doing Good and Doing Well

The promise and perils of socially responsible investing; some funds perform well

O YOU FEEL UNCOMFORTABLE INVESTING IN TOBACCO companies? In companies that may exploit child labor in developing countries? How about companies that produce sex- and violence-laden movies and television programs? Most people can identify certain stocks that they might not feel comfortable investing in. And if they were buying individual stocks they might well avoid them. But it's a different story when you're investing in mutual funds.

Most mutual fund managers say their sole obligation is to earn shareholders the highest returns they legally can—regardless of the practices of the companies they invest in. "As a reformed smoker, I've always had qualms about investing in tobacco companies," says David Schafer, manager of Strong Schafer Value. "But people don't pay me to invest based on my ethical feelings." By the same token, many corporate officials say their duty is to seek the maximum returns they can for shareholders—regardless of any ethical concerns these corporate chieftains may have.

For more than 25 years, small bands of "socially responsible" investment professionals have tried to provide mutual fund options for ethically concerned fund investors. However, they have run up against two major problems:

● **It's impossible to come up with just one set of criteria** that will satisfy everyone's ethical concerns.

●**The performance** of many socially responsible funds has been mediocre.

In the 1970s, during and after the Vietnam War, many socially responsible funds refused to buy shares in firms that produced military weapons. But many investors, particularly after the war ended, had no objections to investing in companies that helped ensure the nation's defense. Nowadays, "liberal" socially responsible funds generally avoid alcohol, tobacco and gambling stocks, as well as arms manufacturers and nuclear-power plants. Many also try to invest in companies that help improve the environment. Others seek out corporations that treat workers well, while still others will invest only in companies that treat homosexuals equally. A few concern themselves with animal rights. Many liberal funds, however, will invest in companies that produce sex and violence in movies and on television.

In the 1990s, a whole new set of socially responsible funds has grown up. Many of these funds describe themselves as promoting "conservative" or "Christian" values. In direct opposition to their liberal counterparts, these funds often won't invest in a company that provides an atmosphere conducive to homosexual employees and their partners. They usually won't invest in companies that promote sex and violence in the media. Companies that provide insurance coverage for abortions may also be off limits. Like the liberal funds, though, the conservative funds often disagree on which companies should be shunned.

Not Great Investments

TODAY, THERE ARE DOZENS OF SOCIALLY RESPONSIBLE FUNDS, and investors shouldn't have much trouble finding a fund that matches at least some of their beliefs. The problem is finding socially responsible funds that produce good returns. While no one is sure why these funds have underwhelming records, two theories have been advanced.

The first is that by limiting the universe of stocks you invest in, you're bound to reduce your investment results. Two studies from outside social-investing circles compared socially screened portfolios with Standard and Poor's 500-stock index and found that investors sacrifice about one percentage point a year in total return.

The other theory is that people who devote their careers to managing socially responsible funds tend to have a lot of interest in advancing social causes—and not nearly so much in ferreting out first-rate stocks.

Whatever the reason, many experts suggest that investors avoid socially responsible funds. "What I tell people is if you are really socially conscious, make all the money you can legally, and give more of your profits to help advance those goals," says John Markese, president of the American Association of Individual Investors.

Some advocates of socially responsible investing dispute the notion that socially responsible funds underperform the average fund. Others point out that losing one percentage point is not a big deal if it frees you to invest in ways you believe, and to avoid investing in companies that work against your beliefs. Many consider it a small cost for exerting their moral or ethical influence in the marketplace. "We're willing to give up some growth, some return, in exchange for knowing that we are pleasing our Lord with what we do with our money," says Virginia Bunton, a broker with Prudential Securities, who looks for stocks for clients "interested in putting their money where their fundamentalist Christian principles are."

Top Performers

HOWEVER, IT MAY BE POSSIBLE TO HAVE YOUR CAKE AND EAT it, too. Increasingly, as socially responsible investing becomes more sophisticated, officials of many of these funds are subcontracting the actual work of picking stocks to professional money managers. The money managers get a list of stocks that they may not invest in. It's too early to tell whether this approach will yield better results, but it holds promise. And, some socially responsible fund managers are simply getting better at their jobs. "Clearly, these funds need to get better at financial analysis," says Parnassus fund's Jerome Dodson, himself one of the more successful managers of such a fund.

For whatever reason, among the socially responsible funds are several that deserve kudos for their performance. When choosing which funds to highlight, my emphasis was on total return. All the funds described below delivered above-average returns the past three or five years and haven't changed managers recently.

AQUINAS EQUITY GROWTH AND AQUINAS EQUITY INCOME

These funds take a unique approach to social responsibility. Equity Income owns tobacco makers Philip Morris and RJR Nabisco. Only after a fund's manager has put a stock in the portfolio does president Frank Rauscher look for social blemishes. Then the fund begins lobbying the company to make social changes. "We haven't had anybody show us that exclusionary investing has changed anything," he says. Besides, he adds, "our investors want financial return, so we pick stocks for financial return."

Aquinas actively promotes the investment guidelines of the National Conference of Catholic Bishops, which include opposition to contraceptive drugs. The funds cooperate with the Interfaith Center of Corporate Responsibility, another work-from-within advocacy group. Rauscher sees no ethical conflict in Equity Income's owning Philip Morris and RJR Nabisco shares. "We are a Catholic-values fund," he says. "Tobacco is not an issue of Catholic values."

The funds hire investment firms. Equity Growth displays a preference for fast-growing medium-size and large companies. Equity Income's largest holdings are Mellon Bank, IBM and Bankers Trust.

INVESTMENT STYLE:	Equity Growth: medium-size company growth (Equity Income: large-company value)
EQUITY GROWTH:	large-company value
THREE-YEAR RETURN:	29.6% (27.46%)
FIVE-YEAR RETURN:	NA (NA)
TEN-YEAR RETURN:	NA (NA)
ANNUAL EXPENSE RATIO:	1.5% (1.4%)
ANNUAL PORTFOLIO TURNOVER:	112% (32%)
VOLATILITY:	6 (3)
SAME MANAGER SINCE:	1994 (1994)
TOTAL ASSETS:	$37.4 million ($71.5 million)
MEDIAN MARKET VALUE:	$4 billion ($10 billion)
MINIMUM INITIAL INVESTMENT:	$500, $500 for IRAs ($500, $500)

PHONE NUMBER: 800–423–6369
WEB SITE: www.aquinas.com

DOMINI SOCIAL EQUITY

This passively managed no-load fund invests in the Domini 400 Social index, which was devised in 1990 by Amy Domini, a principal in a Cambridge, Mass., firm that does social research on corporations. She began with stocks in Standard & Poor's 500-stock index and applied a range of social criteria to screen out unacceptable companies. The index eliminates companies that derive more than 2% of their sales from military weapons or that are involved in tobacco, alcohol or gambling. It also excises utilities that own nuclear generating stations and companies with poor records on the environment, employee relations, product quality, safety or sales practices.

To the 250 or so S&P 500 stocks that survive the screening, Domini added "good" companies not in the S&P index to bring the number to 400, with a nod toward sector diversification and smaller corporations that meet her criteria. What you get is a fund tilted toward large companies experiencing earnings growth. It closely tracks the S&P 500.

An alternative

A newer index fund, which delivered better results than Domini during both 1996 and 1997, is Citizens Index ($2,500 minimum investment; 800–223–7010; www.citizensfunds.com), which uses similar criteria.

INVESTMENT STYLE:	Domini: large-company blend of growth and value (Citizens: large-company growth)
THREE-YEAR RETURN:	32.61% (33.40%)
FIVE-YEAR RETURN:	21.26% (NA)
TEN-YEAR RETURN:	NA (NA)
ANNUAL EXPENSE RATIO:	0.98% (1.59%)
ANNUAL PORTFOLIO TURNOVER:	5% (19%)
VOLATILITY:	6 (7)
SAME MANAGER SINCE:	1991 (1995)
TOTAL ASSETS:	$397.5 million ($309 million)
MEDIAN MARKET VALUE:	$41.3 billion ($25.3 billion)

MINIMUM INITIAL INVESTMENT: $1,000, $250 ($2,500, $250)
PHONE NUMBER: 800–762–6814
WEB SITE: www.domini.com

DREYFUS THIRD CENTURY

For years, this fund's results were unimpressive. Then in 1994 Dreyfus hired NCM Capital Management, of Durham, N.C., to pick stocks. Third Century delivered total returns of 35.8% in 1995, 24.3% in 1996 and 29.4% in 1997—in each instance, well above the average for long-term-growth funds. Third Century avoids tobacco, liquor, gambling and defense stocks.

INVESTMENT STYLE: large-company growth
THREE-YEAR RETURN: 32.55%
FIVE-YEAR RETURN: 19.15%
TEN-YEAR RETURN: 16.53%
ANNUAL EXPENSE RATIO: 1.03%
ANNUAL PORTFOLIO TURNOVER: 67%
VOLATILITY: 7
SAME MANAGER SINCE: 1994
TOTAL ASSETS: $899.7 million
MEDIAN MARKET VALUE: $20.3 billion
MINIMUM INITIAL INVESTMENT: $2,500, $750
PHONE NUMBER: 800–373–9387
WEB SITE: www.dreyfus.com

PARNASSUS

The on-the-job education of manager Jerome Dodson has been a recurring theme. Dodson produced bottom-of-the-barrel results in four of his first five years. Then, in 1990, he adopted new methods and sent Parnassus on a four-year romp. Among long-term-growth funds it finished in the top 10% in 1992 and 1994, in the top 20% in 1991 and in the top 30% in 1993. But Parnassus had a poor 1995 and 1996, before rebounding in 1997. Dodson's style is to buy small companies at bargain prices when they are out of investor favor. His concentrated portfolio of only 35 stocks is heavily weighted toward out-of-favor technology issues.

The fund may not invest in companies involved in alcohol, gambling, tobacco, weapons production or nuclear power. It has a 3.5% sales charge.

INVESTMENT STYLE:	small-company value
THREE-YEAR RETURN:	13.77%
FIVE-YEAR RETURN:	14.25%
TEN-YEAR RETURN:	14.68%
ANNUAL EXPENSE RATIO:	1.11%
ANNUAL PORTFOLIO TURNOVER:	69%
VOLATILITY:	9
SAME MANAGER SINCE:	1984
TOTAL ASSETS:	$368.2 million
MEDIAN MARKET VALUE:	$1.5 billion
MINIMUM INITIAL INVESTMENT:	$2,000, $500
PHONE NUMBER:	800–999–3505
WEB SITE:	www.parnassus.com

OTHER OPPORTUNITIES

There are also several fund families that don't advertise it, but they avoid certain kinds of companies. For instance, Templeton funds shun tobacco, alcohol and gambling stocks and Pioneer funds also avoid tobacco and alcohol stocks.

Key Points

• *Investors can find socially responsible funds to suit their criteria.*
• *Overall performance has been mediocre, and many experts counsel against using these funds.*
• *But some funds have produced good returns.*

PART FIVE

For Advanced Investors: Two More Ways to Profit

E ven the most knowledgeable investors will discover some new investment ideas in this section. If you're a newcomer who finds some of the concepts a little hard to follow, keep reading: The information is well worth the effort. This section describes a little-known method to protect more of your truly long-term money from the tax man, through the use of tax-managed funds, and also explains why comparing ordinary funds' "tax efficiency" is of little or no value. It also details how to reap profits from one of the most obscure and complex type of mutual fund, closed-end funds. Many bargains can be found among these funds.

Funds for Tax-Shy Investors

Tax-efficient funds work sometimes—but not always

IDELITY MAGELLAN HAD A FAMOUSLY BAD YEAR IN 1996, returning just 11.7% for investors—about half the return of Standard & Poor's 500-stock index. But shareholders were hit with more bad news at the end of the year: Magellan distributed 15.5% of its assets to shareholders in taxable capital gains and dividends. So the dismal returns that year didn't prevent a migraine for investors in taxable accounts: They had to pay income taxes on more than they earned from the fund—in effect, paying taxes on money they would never see. Investors can be forgiven for scratching their heads and asking: Isn't there a better way?

Money paid to the tax man isn't around to grow for you. Even though almost two-thirds of fund investments are *not* in tax-deferred retirement accounts, "it's amazing how few mutual funds have a focus on taxes," says Jeffrey Coons, a co-manager of Manning & Napier Tax-Managed fund. "That's because in the mutual fund world you're trying to beat a benchmark." Most funds are so focused on performance that they overlook taxes.

But, how about you, the fund investor? Should you pay more attention to the taxable gains generated by your funds? Yes, if—and only if—you're investing for the really long haul. With 20 years or more to go, you probably should, at least with some of your money. It could make an enormous difference in your future lifestyle.

While actively managed funds try to beat an index such as the S&P 500, tax-managed funds generally are designed merely to mirror an index (although there are some tax-managed funds that are actively managed). But they are index funds with a twist. Using accounting techniques and trading strategies, they seek to distribute little or no capital gains. This means you'll pay little or no capital-gains taxes until you sell. Note that Roth IRAs offer even more tax benefits. No taxes will be assessed on dividends or capital gains after you put money into such accounts. But Roths are limited to $2,000 per person per year. (For more on IRAs, see Chapter 5, "Investing for (and in) Retirement.")

In tax-managed funds, the money saved in taxes each year compounds in much the same way it would in an IRA, 401(k) or other tax-deferred retirement-savings plan. Over two or three or even five years, the tax advantage is negligible. But over 20 or 30 years, tax-managed funds are likely to deliver better after-tax returns than all but a handful of actively managed, large-company funds.

Impossible to Match

I TALKED ABOUT THE ADVANTAGES OF INDEX FUNDS IN CHAPTER 4. Once tax advantages are grafted atop an S&P index fund, the resulting tax-managed index funds become well-nigh impossible for actively managed funds to match in taxable accounts over long periods. To understand why, let's take another look at index funds.

Over the ten years ending in 1992, Vanguard's Index 500 fund outperformed 78% of actively managed funds. After taxes, however, the S&P index fund did even better, besting 85% of actively managed funds. The Vanguard Index 500 fund distributes about 0.5% or less of its net asset value in capital gains in an average year. And a tax-managed fund can be expected to distribute nothing—or virtually nothing—in taxable capital gains. "The arithmetic shows that when you defer the taxes over a long period of time, what you end up with after taxes in retirement is considerably higher," says Duncan Pitcairn, who manages trusts and estates in the Philadelphia area.

WHAT SHOULD YOU DO?

Is it a good idea, then, to put *all* your long-term taxable investments in tax-managed funds? Not necessarily. As I pointed out in

Chapter 4, fund managers who specialize in stocks of small companies and foreign stocks have done a better job against their benchmarks than managers of large-company U.S. stocks have done against the S&P 500. Moreover, indexes of smaller stocks and foreign stocks tend to add and lose stocks more frequently than the S&P does. That means the funds that track those indexes incur more taxable capital gains, and tax-managed funds that follow those indexes likewise have a tougher time avoiding capital gains.

An ideal strategy might be to select actively managed funds that invest in small-company stocks and foreign stocks for your tax-deferred retirement savings plans and Roth IRAs, and to invest more for retirement in a large-company, tax-managed fund outside your retirement accounts.

Looking at the Numbers

L ET'S CONSIDER TWO INVESTORS. JOHN SMITH INVESTS $10,000 in an actively managed stock fund. George Jones invests the same amount in a tax-managed fund. Let's assume that each will sell shares in order to pay the taxes incurred annually on their fund income (so the government's take isn't around to compound), and that after five years, both have earned an annualized 10% before taxes. After taxes, Tax-Managed Jones has made a scant 1.5%, or $220, more than Actively Managed Smith. At the end of ten years, Jones is ahead of Smith after taxes by 4%, or $847—still not enough to get too excited about. "Unless you have at least a ten-year time horizon, it's ludicrous to spend your time worrying about taxes," says Sue West, an investment strategist with SEI Investments, which markets four tax-managed funds through financial planners and brokers. But after 20 years, Tax-Managed Jones has earned 10.8%, or $4,996, more than Actively Managed Smith. That's real money.

Moreover, our example assumes that Actively Managed Smith held the same mutual fund he initially purchased for the full 20 years. To stay just that 10.8% behind Jones, he would have had to pick a single mutual fund that would match (or exceed) the S&P over the 20-year-period—a selection task that would take near-psychic powers. Even the best funds can lose their touch over such a long period.

How $10,000 Grows: Tax-Managed Versus Actively Managed

THIS TABLE COMPARES the after-tax performance of a $10,000 investment in a tax-managed fund—which pays out no capital-gains distributions—with that of a fund that realizes and pays out 50% of its capital gains each year. For each fund, we assume an annual return of 10%: 7% from appreciation and 3% from dividends. Other assumptions are detailed on page 265.

	5 YEARS	10 YEARS	20 YEARS	30 YEARS
Tax-managed fund	$14,743	$22,094	$51,150	$120,950
Non-tax-managed fund	14,523	21,247	46,154	101,348
Tax-managed advantage ($)	220	847	4,996	19,602
Tax-managed advantage (%)	1.5%	4.0%	10.8%	19.3%

SOURCE: VANGUARD

In the real world, the average investor holds a fund only about five years. If Actively Managed Smith swapped funds every five years, after 20 years he would trail Tax-Managed Jones by 15%, or $6,658 (assuming Jones holds tight to his fund for the entire 20 years). Why the bigger spread? Because on each switch, Smith would realize—and have to pay tax on—all the gains that had not been paid out in annual distributions. That would leave less to reinvest. The table above shows how two investors would do after taxes—one who chooses actively managed funds and exchanges them every five years, and the other who buys and holds a tax-managed fund for the entire period. As you can see, the longer your holding period, the greater the advantage of the tax-managed fund.

All these examples, assume that you sell your funds at the end of the period. In actuality, when you retire you'll want to spend all your retirement-plan savings first, and only then begin to dip into your tax-managed fund. That's because if you don't need all the money, your heirs won't have to pay capital-gains taxes on any unrealized gains in mutual funds (or other property, for that matter) in your estate.

The assumptions
For our two investors, Smith and Jones, we've made a number of assumptions.

First, we assume that their funds will return 10% annually—slightly less than what large-company stocks have averaged since 1926—7% from price appreciation of the stocks in their funds and the other 3% from stock dividends.

Second, we assume that about half of the capital gains in the actively managed funds are realized and paid out each year—which is about how the average fund operates. Of the gain that is paid out, we assume half is short-term (from securities owned by the fund for one year or less), which is taxed as ordinary income, and that the other half is from securities held more than one year, which therefore may enjoy a gentler capital-gains tax treatment. Our calculations assume that none of the gain in the tax-managed fund is realized or taxed until the shares are sold at the end of each period.

Finally, we assume that Smith and Jones are both in the 28% federal tax bracket; if they were in a higher bracket, the advantage of the tax-managed fund would be larger.

What's the Secret?

HOW CAN A FUND OPERATE WITHOUT PAYING OUT ANY taxable capital gains? In part, this involves an accounting method that any fund—tax-managed or otherwise—may employ: identifying to the IRS exactly which shares it sells each time it sells shares. That means selling shares first that were bought at a higher price and holding on to shares that were bought at a lower price as long as possible. This technique reduces taxable distributions to shareholders (for details, see page 105 of Chapter 9, "Paying Uncle Sam"). Some fund companies—including T. Rowe Price, SteinRoe, Strong and Vanguard—do this routinely, but most companies don't bother, and that's a shame because their practices cut into returns.

The other key is selling losers. Geri Hom, who runs four tax-managed index funds at Charles Schwab, makes sure to sell losers—particularly if, in order to keep in line with her index, she has been forced to take gains on other stocks in her portfolio because of corporate mergers and other changes in an index's composition. Thirty-one days after dumping a loser, Hom can buy it back and still book the tax loss. At times, that means the fund may deviate slightly from the index it's tracking, but the differences are usually minute.

One of Hom's satisfied shareholders is Charles Schwab, founder of the discount brokerage. He has between $2 million and $3 million invested in the *Schwab 1000* fund, which contains the 1,000 largest companies in the U.S. In six years, it has never paid a capital gain, and Schwab says, "I don't believe it ever will."

Likewise, Gus Sauter's Vanguard tax-managed funds, which started operations in 1994, have never made any capital-gains distributions. Some skeptics argue that if the market fell and investors begin pulling out of Sauter's funds en masse, he would be forced to sell stocks—and end up with capital gains. But Sauter—and Schwab—counter that if the market declined, their funds would have more losses to take. "There's no reason we can't go on forever without realizing gains," Sauter says.

If you're concerned that a mass exodus from a tax-managed fund might stick you with unwanted capital-gains distributions, you might consider SPDRs, index securities that trade like stocks on the American Stock Exchange. Pronounced "spiders," their official names are *Standard & Poor's 500 Depositary Receipts* (ticker symbol SPY), which tracks the S&P 500, and *Standard & Poor's Midcap 400 Depositary Receipts* (MDY), which tracks the mid-cap index. You have to pay a broker to buy and sell SPDRs, but there is probably less risk of mass liquidations of SPDRs because they are sold to other investors (much like the closed-end funds described in the following chapter), rather than redeemed like open-end mutual funds.

There's always an old-fashioned way to invest tax-efficiently: Buy blue-chip stocks and hold them a very long time. Legendary investor Warren Buffett almost never sells a stock, no matter how richly priced it becomes.

But there's an important advantage to buying a tax-managed index fund. Index funds tend to slowly increase the weightings of growing companies and industries while decreasing—and eventually eliminating—declining ones. That enables investors to keep up with change. For instance, a blue-chip portfolio put together 30 years ago likely would have given a lot of emphasis to steelmakers and textile manufacturers and little or none to computer-chip makers and software developers.

Tax-Efficient Funds: Not!

MOST OF THE ADVICE you'll see about avoiding taxes in stock funds is devoted to funds' short-term tax efficiency, rather than to holding tax-managed index funds for the very long term. Some business publications and fund-rating services regularly report on how tax-efficient individual funds have been—and encourage investors to heed these rankings. Most investors will do well to ignore this advice. Here's why:

Investing in tax-efficient funds makes only a tiny difference unless a fund is very tax-efficient over many years.
Take two funds. One is extremely inefficient and realizes all its taxable gains every year; the second is fairly efficient, relative to other actively managed funds and realizes its gains only every three years. At the end of three years, the tax-efficient fund has netted shareholders in the 28% tax bracket less than six-tenths of one percentage points more than the inefficient one. For a tax-efficient fund to produce any significant benefit, it must delay realization of capital gains for a decade or more—not just a couple of years. Virtually no actively managed funds operate like that.

Few investors hold actively managed funds long enough.
"Every time you sell a fund you make it completely tax-inefficient," notes Susan Belden, co-editor of *No-Load Fund Analyst*.

It's surprisingly difficult to predict which actively managed funds will be tax-efficient in the future.
A study by *Morningstar Inc.* found that funds ranked in the top third for tax efficiency for the three years from 1991 through 1993 had little better than a 40% chance of remaining in the top third in the subsequent three years. A fund may have a history of not realizing taxable gains, whether by design or accident, but then may get a new manager who sells a big chunk of the portfolio, handing investors a huge taxable distribution. The best predictor of poor tax-efficiency, Belden says, is that a fund invests in high-yielding stocks.

Finally, low turnover does not equal tax efficiency.
Pennsylvania Mutual, for instance, which turns over only about 10% to 15% of its portfolio annually, hasn't been tax-efficient, while momentum-style funds like PBHG Emerging Growth—which have roughly 100% turnover ratios every year—have been very tax-efficient. The reason is simple: Funds such as PBHG Emerging Growth hold their winning stocks a long time, but they jettison their losers with alacrity. Value-oriented Pennsylvania Mutual, by contrast, often sells winners and holds losers.

Alternative to Variable Annuities

T HE ABSENCE OF CAPITAL GAINS IN TAX-MANAGED FUNDS MAKES them a good alternative to variable annuities for retirement savings. As discussed on page 72, variable annuities are sold with a tissue-thin layer of life insurance, which qualifies them for preferential tax treatment. They look and feel much like IRAs: Investors typically have a choice of funds in which to invest. But variable annuities are more costly to invest in than mutual funds. And, in an emergency, you can't get at the cash in a variable annuity nearly as easily as you can sell a tax-managed fund.

Glenn Daily, a fee-only insurance consultant in New York City, says that under many circumstances an investor would do better in a tax-managed Vanguard fund than in that company's low-cost variable annuities. Tax-managed funds are better particularly if you plan to leave part of the money to your heirs. A person who inherits your annuity will owe tax just as you would: Earnings will be taxed in his or her top bracket. The lucky soul who gets a tax-managed fund will get it income-tax-free.

The Top Choices

T AX-MANAGED FUNDS ARE RELATIVELY NEW, BUT MORE companies are offering them as investor interest grows. For instance, *T. Rowe Price Tax Efficient Balanced,* launched in 1997, contains municipal bonds and low-dividend stocks. And *Fidelity* planned to open an actively managed tax-managed fund in late 1998. Here are thumbnail descriptions of some of the most attractive tax-managed funds:

SCHWAB 1000, INTERNATIONAL INDEX, CAPITAL TRUST S&P 500 INDEX *AND* CAPITAL TRUST SMALL-CAP INDEX

(800–266–5623; $1,000 minimum initial investment; 0.5% redemption fee in Schwab 1000 and the small-cap fund, and 0.75% redemption fee in all three funds for shares held less than six months)

With portfolio turnover of just 2% and expenses of 0.46%, the Schwab 1000 fund has done a good job tracking the 1,000 largest U.S. stocks since its inception in 1991. The S&P 500 fund has expenses of 0.35% annually. The international fund holds 350 of the largest foreign stocks and has expenses of 0.58%. The small-cap fund holds the second-largest 1,000 U.S. stocks. It has expenses of 0.49%, and had annual turnover in 1996 of 24%—but, like all the Schwab funds, it still has managed to keep from paying out capital gains. (Another share class of each Schwab fund is available with $50,000 minimums and lower expenses).

USAA GROWTH & TAX STRATEGY
(800–531–8722; $3,000 minimum investment)
Created in 1989, this is not an index fund, but rather an extremely low-risk mix of high-grade muni bonds and under-valued stocks. The fund is just a little more than half as volatile as the S&P, and has lagged badly in bull markets—returning just 11% in 1996, for instance. It pays out more in taxable gains than its competitors. Still, it could be a good choice for a retiree who wants security, income—and the possibility of passing on the principal to heirs.

VANGUARD TAX-MANAGED GROWTH AND INCOME, CAPITAL APPRECIATION *AND* BALANCED
(800–635–1511; $10,000 minimum investment; 2% redemption fee on shares held less than one year, 1% redemption fee on shares held less than five years)
Growth and Income mirrors the S&P 500. Capital Appreciation invests in large-company stocks that pay little or no dividends, and seeks to track the Russell 1000 index. (Some studies show, however, that stocks that don't pay dividends tend to underperform their dividend-paying peers, a potential pitfall.) Balanced invests 50% to 55% in municipal bonds, and the remainder identically to Capital Appreciation. Vanguard's low costs (expenses on all these funds are 0.2%) makes them hard to beat.

Key Points
- *Tax-managed funds offer after-tax returns that few, if any, actively managed funds can beat—if you're investing for at least ten years, and preferably 20 or 30 years.*
- *Tax-managed funds make the most sense when investing in stocks of large U.S. companies.*
- *Comparing the "tax efficiency" of actively managed funds is folly; there's only a tiny difference in after-tax performance of funds. Plus, it's extremely difficult to identify funds that will be tax-efficient.*

269

Funds on Sale

Closed-end funds offer bargains for knowledgeable investors

OULD YOU STOOP TO PICK UP A $20 BILL ON THE sidewalk? Of course you would. Well, when they are selling at a discount, closed-end funds are a little like found money. That's because the stocks or bonds in the fund are worth more than the fund is selling for. The catch is that it's not always possible to extract the full value from a closed-end fund. Nevertheless, closed-end funds offer tantalizing opportunities, albeit sometimes with high risk. They are a good way for sophisticated investors to add a little spice to their fund investments.

Closed-end funds are different from other mutual funds in some fundamental respects. Ordinary mutual funds, sometimes called "open-end" funds, always stand ready to buy shares back from investors at the underlying value of the stocks or bonds the fund holds (usually referred to as the fund's net asset value) and to issue new shares to investors. But closed-end funds typically issue shares only once: at inception. After that, if a shareholder wants to dispose of his shares in a closed-end fund, he must find another investor willing to buy them.

Wall Street often takes things to extremes—and closed-end funds are no exception. Either it's euphoric and insists that you pay far more than a closed-end fund is worth, or it's mired into despair and all but gives the fund away. Closed-end funds have gone through periods of being loved, followed by periods of being shunned, since they were first introduced in the U.S. in the early 1900s. As a result, these funds often sell at huge premiums or discounts to their net asset value.

Savvy investors can profit from these mood swings. Blindly

buying all closed-end funds with a 25% or larger discount each year between 1981 and 1994 would have netted an annualized 21.2% return, according to a study by *Mutual Fund Forecaster* newsletter. Purchasing all closed-end funds with a 10% or larger discount would have returned an annualized 18.5% over that same period, and buying all of them with any discount would have returned an annualized 16.4%. By contrast, the average open-end fund returned an annualized 12.2% over the same years.

You might do even better, if you consider not only a closed-end fund's discount, but also how that discount compares with the fund's own average discount in past years. Funds that usually trade at small discounts or premiums can occasionally be snapped up at big discounts.

The Cash-Flow Advantage

CLOSED-END FUNDS HAVE OTHER ATTRACTIONS BESIDES THEIR discounts. Because of closed-end funds' structures, their managers don't have to worry about cash flows from investors. Waves of money cascading into open-end stock funds may force managers to buy more stocks when they'd rather not, because the stocks they specialize in appear overpriced. And in a market plunge, large numbers of investors bailing out of open-end funds may force managers to sell stocks when they'd rather be buying them. Closed-end funds don't have to play that game. That shows up on the bottom line—at least of funds that specialize in infrequently traded securities.

Take Templeton Emerging Markets, a closed-end fund piloted by Mark Mobius. As good as Mobius's open-end Templeton Developing Markets has been, the closed-end fund outperformed the open-end fund on a net asset value basis (net asset value refers to performance of the securities the fund owns, as opposed to the market price of the fund) by an annual average of 5.9 percentage points over the five years ending April 30, 1998. Why? In part, because Templeton Emerging Markets wasn't forced to sell stocks when emerging markets were out of favor with investors, nor to buy stocks when emerging markets were wildly popular.

Similarly, Charles Royce's closed-end version of Royce Micro-Cap beat his open-end version every year from 1994 to

1997 on a net asset value basis, despite employing identical investment methods.

So even if you aren't attracted by the discounts of closed-end funds, they can often be a good way to invest in thinly traded corners of the markets—such as biotechnology stocks, stocks of emerging markets, and stocks of a single foreign country or region. (See Chapter 16 for a refresher on the problems of buying and selling small stocks that don't trade much.)

Before You Venture In

JUST BECAUSE A FUND IS SELLING AT A DISCOUNT DOESN'T MEAN its discount won't widen further. Conversely, you should *never* buy a closed-end fund that's *not* selling at a discount. If you stick to funds selling at discounts that meet the criteria you apply to open-end funds (turn back to Chapter 15 for a review if you'd like), you should do well.

Beware, however, of this trap: Don't ever buy a closed-end fund when it first goes public. This is the time brokers are most likely to promote these funds, sometimes claiming that the funds sell without commissions. Uh huh. In fact, hidden commissions can run as high as 6%. What, in fact, happens is that for every dollar you invest, only 94 cents or so goes to the fund. The result is that the share price, by definition, trades immediately at a premium to the fund's net asset value.

Even if you aren't attracted by the discounts, closed-end funds can often be a good way to invest in thinly traded corners of the markets.

In general, you'll want to invest in funds with good long-term records, proven managers and low expenses. While you can find decent broad-based U.S. stock funds among closed-end funds—such as General American Investors, Salomon Brothers and Tri-Continental—closed-end funds are often best used to gain access to those obscure corners of the markets I mentioned a few paragraphs ago. Think of them as icing on your portfolio's cake, not the main course.

WHERE TO BEGIN

Of all mutual funds, closed-end funds have the most wrinkles. They are, in one sense, funds and, in another sense, stocks. All the funds listed in this chapter trade on the New York Stock

Exchange unless indicated. You'll need a broker to buy and sell them. Unless you're willing to devote some time to understanding them, steer clear of them.

The numbers provided in this chapter are accurate up to the end of April 1998. Discounts can change rapidly. For up-to-date weekly discounts and premiums, check Sunday's *New York Times,* the weekly *Barron's* or Monday's *Wall Street Journal.*

Of all mutual funds, closed-end funds have the most wrinkles. They are, in one sense, funds and, in another sense, stocks.

Some funds will also give you daily discount numbers over the phone; call and ask. Incidentally, don't expect the level of assistance from closed-end funds that you get with an ordinary open-end fund. After all, these funds raise most of their money at inception; after that, they sometimes don't seem to care much about their shareholders.

At this writing, one of the biggest difficulties with closed-end funds is that they are so out of favor it's hard to find good, much less inexpensive, sources of information about them.

Among the best sources are:

Morningstar Principia for Closed-End Funds ($195 quarterly, $395 monthly, $95 once; 800–735–0700; www.morningstar.net), software (IBM only) that gives a one-page look at most closed-end funds and allows you to search for funds meeting your criteria.

The Investor's Guide to Closed-End Funds (monthly; $365 per year; 800–854–3863; in Florida, 305–271–1900), a newsletter that covers 20 to 40 funds representing a variety of objectives.

Closed-End Country Fund Report ($225 annually; 202–783–7051), a newsletter that examines and makes recommendations from among single-country and regional funds.

Closed-End Fund Digest ($199 annually; 805–884–1150), a newsletter that offers analysis and commentary, as well as model portfolios of closed-end funds.

The Thomas J. Hertzfeld Encyclopedia of Closed-End Funds ($125 plus $10 shipping; 305–271–1900), a book that provides an introduction to closed-end funds, as well as detailed information on more than 480 funds.

Investors who have a full-service broker also can get help. Many brokerages have analysts whose full-time job is to track closed-end funds.

Closed-End Stock Funds

LOOK FOR SOLID STOCK FUNDS SELLING AT HISTORICALLY HIGH discounts. You'll typically find these in out-of-favor sectors. When the sector comes back into favor, you'll often get the double whammy of a higher net asset value *and* a smaller discount—or even a premium. That's usually the time to unload these funds and move on to another unloved sector. (*Note:* All the stock funds listed below are quite risky because they invest in very small stocks and in emerging markets.)

Here are some funds worth considering:

HAMBRECHT & QUIST HEALTHCARE INVESTORS AND HAMBRECHT & QUIST LIFE SCIENCES

(ticker symbols HQH, HQL; call 800–327–6679 for a shareholder report or visit their Web site at www.hamquist.com)

These two funds are run virtually identically. They have returned an annualized 25.5% and 21.9% on net asset value over the past three years. Their discounts are both around 18%, and each charges annual expenses of about 1.6%. Both are run by Alan Carr, who has been searching for values in biotechnology for decades.

These are feast-or-famine funds. In 1995, for instance, when biotech was hot, HQL returned 64.7% on net asset value. In 1994, though, it lost 23%. In 1991, HQH gained a breathtaking 93.6% on NAV, and its discount evaporated. That meant the fund's *market* return was 142.9%. At one point, the fund sold at more than a 10% premium. HQH and HQL are high-risk vehicles, made riskier by the fact that Carr invests a substantial percentage of assets in private companies—companies not yet traded publicly on stock markets. Such companies are often tiny, and their stock can be extremely difficult to sell.

When the sector comes back into favor, it's usually time to unload and move on.

While this pair of funds has lagged blue-chip health-care stocks the past several years, should biotech take off again, these funds are likely to lead the charge.

MORGAN STANLEY EMERGING MARKETS

(MSF; 800–221–6726)

This fund buys stocks in fast-growing emerging markets. This is an aggressive fund that has done well when emerging markets are hot and poorly when they are cold. For instance, the fund rose 97.1% on net asset value in 1993—nearly 25 percentage points more than the average open-end emerging-markets fund—but lost 16% in 1995—12 percentage points more than its peers. The fund has returned an annualized 11.9% on net asset value over the past five years, and recently sold at a 17% discount. Expenses are 1.87%, about what most funds charge in this rarefied sector. As with biotech, you can expect a bumpy ride in emerging markets. The closed-end format is particularly favorable here.

MORGAN STANLEY RUSSIA AND NEW EUROPE
(RNE; 800–221–6726)
This fund, which began operations in September 1996 and recently sold at an 8% discount, provides a concentrated bet on nascent capitalism in the former Soviet Union and other old Eastern block countries, such as Poland and Hungary. This kind of fund deserves only a fraction of your most aggressive money; the risks and volatility are enormous here. Russia in 1996 and 1997 had the best-performing stock market in the world. In the first half of 1998, though, Russia's stock market was among the world's worst.

ROYCE MICRO-CAP
(OTCM; 800–221–4268; www.roycefunds.com)
Royce Micro-Cap invests in the tiniest of U.S. stocks. The average market value of its holdings is a mere $192 million. Charles Royce, who has been investing in stocks of small companies for more than 25 years, maintains that these micro-caps offer the same unexplored values that mere small stocks offered when he began his career. The fund sells at a 10% discount, and has returned 24.4% on net asset value over the last three years.

TEMPLETON EMERGING MARKETS
(EMF; 800–526–0801; www.franklin-templeton.com)
This fund has returned an annualized 23.4% on net asset value over the past ten years, thanks to the globe-trotting value orientation of ace manager Mark Mobius. All other things being equal, this fund is probably a better one than the Morgan Stanley fund, but it usually sells at a premium to its net asset value. Watch for

a buying opportunity if it slips to a discount.

Two other Mobius-run funds give you a sliver of the world economy, but a sliver Mobius knows better than he knows other emerging markets. Mobius has used Asia as his base for more than 25 years. Both *Templeton China World* (TCH) and *Templeton Dragon Fund* (TDF) invest almost exclusively in China—another extremely volatile area of the world that offers both enormous peril and vast opportunity. (Lately the region has provided far more peril than opportunity.) Both funds sell at discounts of about 15%, and both should take off like rockets if China prospers.

Closed-End Bond Funds

BOND FUNDS OFFER SOME OF THE SWEETEST VALUES AMONG closed-end funds, yet few investors consider them. Closed-end bond funds tend to trade based on their yields. In other words, if a fund's portfolio has a high yield (usually because it owns low-quality, "junk" bonds), short-sighted investors often bid up the price of the fund until it sells at a premium to its underlying net asset value. (Remember, when bond prices go up, their yields go down.) These funds do not represent good value.

On the other hand, high-quality funds whose portfolios have low yields will often languish, neglected by investors, and sell at big discounts to their net asset values. For the most part, these funds pay higher yields than high-quality open-end bond funds. These are the bond funds worth taking a closer look at. Here's how to do it:

Look at the fund's expense ratio. Don't buy a bond fund that's charging much more than 1% in annual expenses. The lower the expenses, the better.

Check to see if a fund can maintain its dividends. Call the fund and ask for an annual report. Make sure the fund's "income per share" after expenses exceeds its rate of "dividend payouts." Otherwise, the fund may be paying out more in dividends than it is earning, often a recipe for future problems.

Learn what's in the fund. Take a look at the annual report to see what type of bonds the fund holds. If you want a high-quality-bond fund, for instance, stick with funds that hold corporate and government bonds of at least single-A credit quality.

Make sure a fund's bonds aren't about to be redeemed. Managers of municipal funds usually don't trade much. Ask a fund not only what its weighted average maturity is (see page 234), but also what its "weighted maturity to call" is. This number tells you how long it will be before the bonds' issuers may redeem the bonds— the longer, the better. If bonds are redeemed early (called), the fund will have to buy new bonds, often with lower yields.

Find out whether a fund can use leverage. Many closed-end bond funds use leverage (borrowed money) to buy more bonds. They do this by borrowing short-term money and investing it in long-term bonds. This usually works out okay, but the more leverage a fund employs, the more volatile it will be when interest rates move up and down. Investors who are risk-averse should avoid such funds.

For truly long-term investors, the real beauty of closed-end bond funds is that it doesn't matter much if the discount never goes away. That's because you are paid your dividend yield based on the fund's net asset value—not on its (generally lower) market price. So even if the market price of a fund falls, you can continue to collect a healthy income.

THE FUNDS
Here are several funds to consider:

Excelsior Income
(EIS; 800–257–2356)
This mutual fund holds high-quality (AA or better) corporate bonds with a weighted average maturity of about 8 years. The expense ratio is fairly high at 1.08% annually, but the fund employs no leverage. At this writing, the fund sells at a 13% discount and yields 6.9%.

MFS Intermediate Income
(MIN; 800–225–2606; www.mfs.com)
Another unleveraged fund, MFS Intermediate Income yields 8% and sells at a 13% discount. It holds AAA bonds with a weighted average maturity of 6 years.

MFS Charter Income
(MCR; 800–225–2606; www.mfs.com)
Similarly, MFS Charter has a yield of 8%, sells at a 6.6% discount

and holds single-A bonds with a weighted average maturity of about 8 years.

InterCapital Quality Municipal Securities
(IQM; 800–869–6397)
InterCapital Quality Municipal Securities sells at about a 10% discount and provides a tax-free yield of 6%. Even if you're in only the 28% federal tax bracket, that's equivalent to an 8.3% yield on a taxable investment. The tax-equivalent yield is computed by dividing the tax-exempt yield (6%) by 1 minus your tax bracket (1 – .28 = .72), which equals 8.3%. (See page 242 for details on computing tax-equivalent yields.) Expenses are 0.83%, and the fund holds bonds with a long, 20-year weighted average maturity. Average credit quality is AA. This fund borrows the equivalent of 40% of its assets to invest in more long-term bonds—so this is a high-risk fund (it lost 17.3% on NAV in 1994). Nevertheless, the yield is higher than you can find on nearly any open-end muni funds, even "junk" funds.

MuniInsured
(MIF; American Stock Exchange; 800–543–6217)
MuniInsured sells at a 10% discount and yields 5.4%. This fund charges 0.79%, and it doesn't employ leverage, reducing its risk. Its average bond is rated AAA, and its weighted average maturity is 21 years.

From Closed-End to Open-End

ONCE YOU OWN A CLOSED-END FUND, ONE OF THE BEST things that can happen is for your fund to convert into an open-end fund. That means you can get all your money out at net asset value as opposed to the discount to net asset value that you bought it for. Funds are sometimes pressured by large shareholders to convert to open-end status if they sell at persistently large discounts. The one problem with conversions is that if the fund invests in thinly traded securities, it may not be able to do as good a job of investing as it did. So after a fund becomes open-end, you may want to sell it.

Rights Offerings: When They're Wrong

RIGHTS OFFERINGS ARE THE ENEMY OF CLOSED-END investors. They are a way for funds to raise more money from shareholders. That's fine if you want to accumulate additional shares. But if you have all the shares you want, thank you, a rights offering can be like having a gun to your head. If you participate, you end up investing more in the fund than you wanted to. If you don't participate, the value of your holdings will decline.

Ask a fund how often it has held rights offerings. If it has held a lot of them, you'll do better to look elsewhere.

Why do rights offerings hurt investors? Suppose you own 100 shares of a closed-end fund and the fund has 100,000 shares outstanding. Now, suppose the fund proffers a two-for-one rights offering (in other words, allows you to buy one additional share for each two shares you own—usually at a slight discount to the market price). If you exercise your rights, you'll now own 150 shares of the fund, which will now contain 150,000 shares—assuming all shareholders exercise their rights. So, you've invested 50% more money, yet still own the same percentage of the fund's now-enlarged portfolio that you did previously. If you don't exercise your rights, however, things are even worse: You are left owning 100 shares of a 150,000-share fund—so the value of your shares is now much lower.

Some funds issue transferable rights; in other words, rights that can be sold to other investors. You'll usually still end up a little in the hole on these, but if you don't want to buy more shares of a fund, selling your rights is a way to recoup much of your losses. If your rights aren't transferable, it's usually best to take your medicine and buy more shares.

In general, though, the best option is to try to avoid funds that hold numerous rights offerings. Ask a fund how often it has held rights offerings. If it has held a lot of them, you'll do better to look elsewhere. Or buy a small holding in the fund, knowing you may get the "opportunity" to buy more shares in the future.

One caveat: Some funds, including the Royce funds, hold frequent rights offerings, but they are tiny: for instance, giving you the right to buy one share for each 20 you already own. These are a fine way to slowly increase your holdings. The offerings that most investors don't like give you the "right" to buy one share for each two or three shares you already own.

Key Points

- *Closed-end funds offer bargains for investors who take the time to understand them.*
- *Closed-end funds are the most complicated of all funds. They behave partly like a fund and partly like a stock.*
- *These funds offer a great way to invest in markets where trading is light. They also offer extra income for investors.*

The DiBenedettos: Novices No More

P AUL AND NANCY DIBENEDETTO HAVEN'T APPEARED much in the book since Part Two. Yet a lot has changed for them since I first knocked on their front door just before Christmas 1996. On October 12, 1997, Nancy gave birth to their second son, Andrew. As a result, the DiBenedettos are already salting even more money away for college—a move made easier since Nancy got a promotion at work, too. Instead of a recreation therapist at the National Rehabilitation Hospital, she's now a quality improvement specialist, working, among other things, to prepare the hospital for visits by hospital accrediting organizations. Paul Jr., now 4, and Andrew are thriving in day care. Paul has begun his own book project. He has teamed up with the parent of a disabled child to write an educational book for parents and children about students with learning disabilities.

The DiBenedettos' investing plans are on track, too, helped by the soaring stock market of 1997 and early 1998. Paul is adding more each month to his 403(b) plan through his employer, the Arlington County, Va., school system. Nancy's retirement plan at work is funded entirely by her employer. The DiBenedettos chose the retirement and college portfolios laid out in Part Two of the book, except for Paul's 403(b) plan, which he has invested in USAA funds—one of the few no-sales-charge options available to him. Another $14,000 is waiting in a money-market fund to help pay the down payment on a house, but the couple were still having trouble selling their condo, even though it was priced at a bit less than they paid for it.

Why did they delay investing until I visited? "The biggest barrier for us was procrastination," Paul says. Adds Nancy, "We were a plain and simple couple in terms of not investing a lot and trusting in the good old savings account. Taking that first leap into finally investing in something was definitely difficult." Indeed, the first step in investing is usually the hardest. Nancy's father, a retired Navy admiral, loves stocks. But she says the couple has discovered that funds are more their speed. "We don't have the time to find the stocks and track them. Instead, we trust in the funds to do it for us." While Nancy admits to still being a little intimidated by the numbers in the business section of the newspaper, Paul says he reads the fund listings and the business news more often than he used to. "Owning funds gives you more of a feeling of personal interest. It gives you more of an ownership." I hope it will do that for you, too—and help you make your financial dreams come true.

INDEX

NEW HANOVER COUNTY PUBLIC LIB.

3 4200 00498 5533

DISCARDED
from
New Hanover County Public Library

11/98

NEW HANOVER COUNTY PUBLIC LIBRARY
201 Chestnut Street
Wilmington, N.C. 28401

GAYLORD S